THE THRESHER DISASTER

By the same author

THE THRESHER DISASTER

The Most Tragic Dive
In Submarine History

John Bentley

NEW ENGLISH LIBRARY
TIMES MIRROR

Credits

Photos 1–15, 18–26, 27–35: Official Photographer, U.S. Navy

16, 17: Official Photograph, Courtesy Ingall's Shipbuilding Division, Pascagoula, Mississippi, who built the USS *Dace*; U.S. Navy

26A: Courtesy of the Woods Hole Oceanographic Institution

Charts 37, 38: "Bathymetric data from the search for the USS Thresher," by R. J. Hurley, charts (Fig. 2 and Fig. 8), were first printed in *International Hydrographic Review,* Vol. XLI, No. 2, July 1964.

Map 39: Courtesy the American Society of Naval Engineers, Inc., *The Naval Engineers Journal,* August 1965.

Excerpts from "Search for the Thresher" copyright©1964 by Norman Polmar from THE UNDERWATER SOCIETY OF AMERICA. Reprinted by permission of Chilton Book Company.

Excerpts from "Navy Held Thresher Facts 18 Months" by Luther J. Carter, article appeared in Jan. 10, 1965 issue of the Washington *Post*, Copyright © 1965 by The Washington Post Company. Reprinted with permission.

First published in the United States of America
by Doubleday and Company Inc, New York in 1974.

First published in Great Britain by New English Library,
Barnard's Inn, Holborn, London EC1N 2JR in 1975

Printed in Great Britain by
Thomson Litho Ltd, East Kilbride, Scotland.
Bound by Hunter and Foulis, Edinburgh.

4500 25896

"In persons grafted with a serious trust, negligence is a crime."
William Shakespeare

Inboard Profile

USS Jack SSN–605, identical to USS Thresher SSN–593 except that engine-room is 10 ft. longer to accommodate large turbine. Two contra-rotating propellors driven by a shaft within a sleeve-like shaft utilize a 10 per cent power increase. Aft of Sonar sphere, Thresher was divided into five compartments.

A SONAR SPHERE: sonar transducers normally flooded in sea water.

B FORWARD COMPT: *Upper level,* Main Ballast Tanks 1 & 2. Escape Hatch.
2nd level, Forward Crew's Quarters (3-man bunks) & Emergency UQC.
3rd level, Electronic Spare Parts Stowage; Sonar Equipment Room; Diesel Generator Room.
Lower level, Forward Trim Tank; Main Ballast Tanks 1 & 2; Collection Tank.

C MIDSHIP COMPT: *Upper level,* Ship's Control Center (C.O.'s post at time of disaster), where ship's attitude, depth, surface or submerge controls are located. Also, periscope, fire control equipment & main UQC. Electronic Equipment Station (basically a Sonar Information Center); Radio Room (ship's external communications equipment) & Fan Room.
2nd level, Crew's Washroom; WRSK No. 2 (Wardroom-Stateroom of Lyman, Henry & McCoole) WRSR No. 4 (three other officers); Executive Officer's Stateroom (Garner); Commanding Officer's Stateroom (Harvey); Officer's Wardroom; Dry Provisions Store Room.
3rd level, Crew's Quarters (10-man Bunk Room); Torpedo Room (storage & torpedo tubes); Air Regeneration Room.

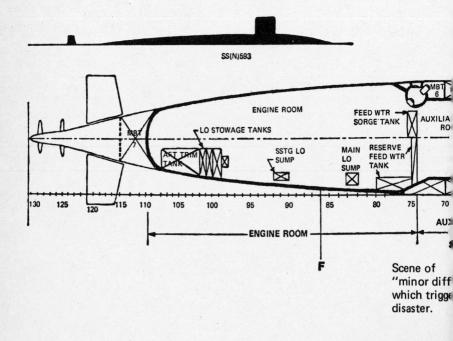

SS(N)593

ENGINE ROOM

MBT 6

FEED WTR SORGE TANK

AUXILIA RO

LO STOWAGE TANKS

MBT

AFT TRIM TANK

SSTG LO SUMP

MAIN LO SUMP

RESERVE FEED WTR TANK

| 130 | 125 | 120 | 115 | 110 | 105 | 100 | 95 | 90 | 85 | 80 | 75 | 70 |

ENGINE ROOM

AUX

F

Scene of "minor diff which trigge disaster.

Lower level, Sanitary Tank No. 1; Pump Room (Trim, Drain or Bilge pumps; various cooling system pumps); Battery Compt (ship's emergency battery for light & propulsion); Auxiliary Tanks (filled with sea water to maintain neutral buoyancy); Diesel fuel oil tank.

D REACTOR COMPT: *Upper level*, Reactor Tunnel, heavily shielded, for access to Auxiliary Machinery Room. *2nd level*, Reactor; auxiliary components & steam generators; normal fuel oil Tank No. 2 inside shielding. (Possible contributing factor to explosion following implosion).

E AUXILIARY MACHINERY ROOM: *Upper level,* Main Ballast Tanks 4, 5 & 6. Rear Escape Hatch.

2nd level, Ship's main electrical panels & bussing.
3rd level, Pumps & complex auxiliary sea water system, (probably where "minor difficulty" occurred).

F ENGINE ROOM: Thresher's largest compt, housing ship's turbines; main condenser; SSTG (Ship's Service Turbine Generator); feed water systems pumping condensed water back to steam generator; main sea water cooling system. *Upper level,* Engineering Control Panels (Reactor Control, Steam, Feed Water & Electrical Control Panels). McCoole's position.
Lower level, Reserve Feed Water Tank; Main Lube Oil Sump; SSTG Oil Sump; Lube Oil Stowage Tanks; After Trim Tank; Main Ballast Tank No. 7.

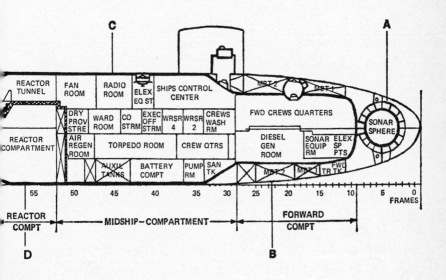

CONTENTS

THE LAST 24 HOURS
April 9, 1963

During the early hours of Tuesday morning, April 9, 1963, weather reports held the promise of a bright day with moderate seas. The wind rippled the darkened waters of the Piscataqua River, however, still carrying the chill bite of winter.

Lying quietly at her berth alongside Pier 11 in Portsmouth Naval Shipyard, New Hampshire, the long, sleek shadow of USS *Thresher* (SSN-593) gave no hint of the activity going on inside her 278-foot hull. But aboard it was a different story. The interior of the Navy's newest, fastest, deepest-diving, and most lethal nuclear attack submarine was ablaze with lights. The constant clatter of footsteps echoed along her seemingly endless passageways or clanged up and down the rungs of her steel ladders. Everyone was busy with some chore, either finding their way around or helping to get the ship ready for her first shakedown cruise after a nine-month overhaul, much of that time in dry dock.

Thresher was way overcrowded. Besides her regular complement of 12 officers and 96 enlisted men, she carried 21 "observers." These included three officers and 13 civilian employees of Portsmouth Naval Shipyard, one officer from the staff of the Deputy Commander, Submarine Force, Atlantic Fleet, and four civilian contractor representatives. Finding bunks for all these guests was no mean job. Since, however, the skids in *Thresher*'s Torpedo Room were not in use (she carried no weapons), this compartment down on the third level (see Profile), which spanned the width of the ship, had been turned into sleeping quarters by bolting bunks to the skids. These had to be secured because of the "large angles" (sharp turns and dives during maneuvers). Some 30 of these bunks were made up in the Torpedo Room, which gives a good idea of the size of this compartment.

But no one cared. To a man, the ship's company was interested in seeing *Thresher* put through her paces during the next 48 hours. By Thursday, April 11, she would be back at Pier 11, with most of the thousand items on her Sea Trial Agenda checked off as satisfactory or requiring nominal attention. So everyone hoped.

It was now 0615 and *Thresher*'s Engineer Officer, Lieutenant Commander John Lyman, reported to the captain.

"Reactor critical, sir."

"Very good," Lieutenant Commander Harvey replied. "Commence heating up the primary loop." This essentially means that, once the reactor is critical and capable of putting out sustained heat, you can start heating the water in the primary system at a fixed rate. It is vital not to exceed heat-up curves on the metals in the reactor, since too rapid heat-up could cause cracking of the envelope.

The next hour passed quickly as late arrivals came down the brow (gangplank), but the full loading of supplies, which normally consumes hundreds of man-hours, would not take place until *Thresher*'s return from her brief shakedown cruise. Besides food for at least a month, she would then take on such items as transistors, hydrogen, acetylene, freon, carbon dioxide (for the ship's Coke machine), alcohol, soap, two dozen grades of oil and grease, film, paper, typewriters and cleaning rags. At least she would take on a great deal *more* of all these things than the minimum now aboard. There would also be a wide range of medical supplies from cough syrup to hypodermics and pain-killing drugs.

At 0715, Lyman requested permission to shift the internal load to the SSTG's (Ship's Service Turbo-Generators). This meant that the reactor had by then generated a full head of "clean" steam, ready for immediate use.

"Very good. Shift loads to SSTG," Wes Harvey, *Thresher*'s new commanding officer, said. Regardless of his rank he was known to the crew as "the captain."

Lyman, in the Maneuvering Room, aft, confirmed the order. "Shift loads to SSTG. Maneuvering Room, aye." To avoid confusion an order from the captain is repeated in exactly the same terms, even when the original request was also in those words. There are exceptions, and this is where the inevitable "aye" comes in. This means, "I understand." "Aye aye" is used where the order is not repeated and means, "I understand and will carry it out."

Thresher had two SSTG's, miniature steam turbines that drove generators powerful enough to take care of all electrical needs on board, from operating an automatic can opener to supplying current for the air-conditioning plant, several hundred light bulbs, and even the stereo system that piped soft music throughout the ship.

Within minutes, the cables providing outside power to *Thresher* were disconnected from their sockets and hauled ashore.

"Station the maneuvering watch," Harvey ordered as he climbed up the interior of *Thresher*'s sail to take his place on the bridge. These were members of the ship's crew whose sole duty would be to make sure no mishaps occurred while *Thresher* maneuvered to conform to the Piscataqua Canal and headed for the open sea. Lieutenant John Smarz, the Diving Officer, was temporarily in charge of this party. Even a seasoned pilot can make a mistake, and so can the skipper of one of those fussy little tugs that hover alongside a departing submarine.

On the waterfront, during the early dawn, spotlights from the dockside installations etched out the forlorn silhouettes of little knots of people—mostly next-of-kin of the ship's company—who had come to wish them well. But by far the biggest audience as *Thresher*'s mooring lines were cast off an hour later, and she began easing away from Pier 11, consisted of dockworkers and sailors. There were sailors lining the decks of other submarines, and yet more sailors cheering and waving from the barge that, for nine long months, had served as *Thresher*'s shipyard barracks and workshops.

Aboard SSN-593, the formality of putting out to sea was a precise ritual, as punctiliously observed for a two-day run as for a journey around the oceans of the globe.

Chief Petty Officer Robert E. Johnson, chief of the boat, was in charge of the many "observers" from the shipyard, both civilian and Navy, who had been assigned to *Thresher* for her sea trials. He made sure all these people were in the right places and were comfortable. He also answered innumerable queries.

Astern, on the rounded deck, the ensign was hauled down. Almost immediately, the American flag broke out aft of *Thresher*'s tall, knife-edged sail. Soon, the shipyard, with its numerous piers, cranes, and other installations, began to fall back. The tugs turned away, carrying with them the pilot, and the Maneuvering Watch was secured—that is, called off special duty and returned to their various assignments for that Watch. The churning propeller of the big black submarine set up a creamy wake, and those aboard began to feel the ship's agile surges and pitches. Only in the deep would she run rock-steady and so swiftly as to outpace any ship at sea, even a destroyer.

At 0800 (the start of the Blue Watch) the crew was mustered on station. The roll call disclosed no absentees, but in the light of what was to happen it is hard to conceive of any disciplinary action being taken against anyone who might not have made it.

Unlike ballistic missile submarines (SSBN's), whose Blue and Gold crews relieve each other at monthly intervals, each with its own commanding officer, *Thresher* had only one crew, but its tours of duty were normally of shorter duration.

Now, as *Thresher* steamed south for a while, then turned abruptly on a northeasterly course, testing her navigation and communications systems, some of the ship's company were putting out to sea for the first time. For many of the civilian observers it was not a very comfortable situation. While the big sub headed for her rendezvous point with USS *Skylark*, detailed to escort her, the constantly changing surface of the writhing sea, with its glistening swells and dips, brought to mind an intertwining of angry pythons. There were few white-caps—just this restless, undulating motion that caused the ship to pitch and roll incessantly. As a result, a number of stomachs unused to this sensation felt somewhat queasy, but their owners tried hard to cope by swallowing frequently and thinking of other things. There was certainly no shortage of things to think about.

At 0949, the two vessels made contact approximately 42° 56′ north and 70° 26′ west, in the operational area east of Boston, as had been ordered. *Thresher*, the Navy's most deadly "killer" sub then in commission, was a unit of Submarine Development Group (SUB-DEVGRU) #2 and was operating under the orders of Vice Admiral Elton W. Grenfell, Commander Submarine Force, Atlantic Fleet, Norfolk, Virginia.

Just then she had less than 24 hours of survival left.

Skylark (ASR-20), assigned to act as *Thresher*'s escort for the two-day trial, was a drab-gray, 205-foot submarine rescue ship, already a bit long in the tooth. Her skipper was Lieutenant Commander Stanley Hecker, who had received by mail a copy of the Sea

Trial Agenda promulgated by *Thresher*, Notice 9080 of April 2. Still the only communications equipment common to both vessels was an underwater telephone (UQC) and pulse-code radio (CW) system. The only knowledge they shared, besides the Sea Trial Agenda, was that *Thresher*'s captain had been designated tactical commander of both ships for the duration of the exercise. *Skylark*'s personnel did not even know how deep *Thresher* could go.

Each vessel had an operational code name. *Thresher* was designated War Club and *Skylark* became Dipper Sierra. However, to avoid confusion, these code names are used only in the chapter which records the submarine escort's actual log of the UQC conversation during *Thresher*'s tragic last dive.

Consonant with Military Sea Transportation vessels of her type, *Skylark* was equipped with a McCann rescue chamber dating back about 25 years. It was made up of two compartments and could operate at a depth of 850 feet. This was comfortably deeper than the 600-foot floor of the Continental Shelf along the Atlantic seaboard. But once beyond that point, if *Thresher* elected to dive in very deep water and ran into trouble, there was nothing in this world *Skylark* could do to help her beyond relaying messages to Radio New London (DBL) or the sprawling Portsmouth Naval Shipyard.

Thresher did so elect, although with one notable exception—Machinist's Mate 2nd Class George J. Kiesecker —no one aboard had the slightest premonition of the awesome disaster that was about to engulf *Thresher* the following morning. Kiesecker, a genial, open-faced man, quick to flash a smile that displayed fine teeth, was certainly not a morbid or introspective individual. Quite the contrary. He was an easy mixer and an excellent dancer who also played the piano and organ commendably well. Nor could his courage in any way be questioned. He was a veteran World War II submariner who had served with distinction on the diesel boats *Sea Dragon, Salmon,* and *Diodon,* and had earned his combat insignia for taking part in various patrols. Testifying to this was an impressive array of ribbons besides the Navy's Good Conduct Medal.

Yet, for days before *Thresher* sailed on her last trip, George, who was also a nuclear reactor operator, made no bones about his uneasiness. *"Thresher's* a coffin," he reportedly told his wife Lily. "I don't want to go on it. I'm scared to death." As Kiesecker saw it, the work on *Thresher* had been hurried so much that he didn't think her ready for sea. "There was too much trouble from the beginning," he maintained. "I know what I'm talking about. I've been working twelve hours a day, seven days a week, helping to get her in shape." So strong was Kiesecker's foreboding that he added wistfully, "I have a feeling this will be our last trip, honey. Before this week is over you'll be a wealthy widow!"

Certainly none of the 17 observers aboard *Thresher* had his mind on anything but the way her enormously complex machinery and equipment were performing. These men, some of whom were highly qualified technicians of long experience, included 55-year-old Henry Charles Moreau, leadingman air conditioning at the Portsmouth Yard, where he had been employed for 23 years. They all looked a bit incongruous in their vari-colored hard hats and khaki work clothes. The hat color indicated which shop they belonged to. Blue, for example, meant the Machine Shop, green was for the electricians, and so on. The regular crew, however, scarcely gave them a second glance as they swarmed over the ship, checking new equipment they had installed or old machinery repaired. Everyone from the captain on down knew they stood ready to help if any part of their specialized equipment should go wrong or fail to meet specifications. Most of the 17 carried clipboards with mimeographed sheets indicating things still to be done, or else making interim progress reports.

At 1200 (noon) Tuesday, April 9, *Thresher*'s assistant navigator, Lieutenant Merrill F. Collier, reported the ship's position to the captain. She was then about 30 miles southeast of Portsmouth.

Harvey immediately announced over the 1-MC (the ship's public address system), "Rig ship for dive! Rig ship for dive!"

Thresher's decks were already awash to keep her riding steady, but this was going to be the first real dive after her lengthy overhaul, so it had to be a shallow, careful one, well inside salvageable waters and precisely in accordance with the book.

Standing next to Harvey in the Control Center were 32-year-old Lieutenant Commander Pat Mehaffy Garner, the Executive Officer, and Quartermaster Chief Gunter, popularly known as Jackie. Garner was a slender-built man of average height, clean cut, deceptively alert and endowed with typically Irish good looks. He was noted, however, for never allowing his inner feelings to surface. While tension built up around him —this was, after all, *Thresher*'s first dive in a very long time—Garner remained as usual inscrutable, unruffled, and carefree. Besides being blessed with the ideal poker face, the XO had many other valuable attributes. With four and one half years on the nuclear submarine *Skate* behind him (he had taken part in all three of her arctic trips under pack ice) Garner knew his job thoroughly. It was common knowledge that he had been promoted a full year ahead of his contemporaries and had also been nominated by the New London Chamber of Commerce as one of the 10 outstanding young men in the nation. In fact, he was one of the only two officers aboard, besides the captain, qualified for command of submarines.

Among the enlisted men, Quartermaster Gunter was an extremely competent chief petty officer who had served under Commander Axene, *Thresher*'s first skipper, and earned himself a letter of commendation. From a perfectionist like Axene, that was saying something. Added to which, Gunter's roguish smile inspired considerable confidence.

"Secure bridge and lay below," Harvey told the OOD (Officer of the Deck), who was at that moment on the bridge. The captain spoke over the 7-MC, the ship's station-to-station control communication system.

"Aye aye, sir," came from John Smarz.

Within seconds, personnel on the bridge came scuttling down the iron ladder in the sail. The hatch slammed shut with a hard clang and was quickly "dogged."

"Topside secured, sir."

"Pressurize the boat." This order was given to Lieutenant Smarz, who had reassumed his duties as Diving Officer.

A minute later, due to a release of compressed air, there was a slight rise in atmospheric pressure aboard *Thresher,* normally kept at 14 psi, the same as on land. No one felt any discomfort, but any important leak undetected until then would quickly betray itself. None did.

"Ship is rigged for dive and ready to submerge, sir," came from John Lyman, Engineer Officer, probably the busiest man on the ship, even with the help of Mike Di Nola, Main Propulsion Assistant.

"Very good. Sound diving alarm," ordered the captain.

The startling noise that reverberated throughout the ship was like that of a hand-operated klaxon in a 1925 car, only about fifty times louder.

"AH-OO-GAH! AH-OO-GAH!"

"Make your depth sixty feet," the captain told John Smarz.

"Sixty feet. Aye aye, sir."

The Planesman eased forward on his wheel-like joy stick, and the big planes in *Thresher*'s stern and sail moved in unison, but the ship was slow to respond. A good sign.

The captain, who now had the Conn, told John Smarz, "Make turns for twelve knots." (Increase speed.)

Smarz passed the order to the Talker in the Control Center, who in turn relayed it to the Maneuvering Room Talker, from whom the Engineer Officer picked it up. Each talker in the various compartments of the ship wore a headset and a push-button mike connecting him with every other talker during a dive.

The turbine increased speed as more high-pressure steam passed through its blades. Still the depth gauge moved slowly. "Driving" the sub under without additional help would take too long.

"Flood auxiliary tanks," Harvey ordered.

These tanks are used to trim the ship—that is, give her either neutral buoyancy, a condition where she displaces exactly the same amount of water as she weighs, or a small margin of negative buoyancy. In that condition, bereft of power, she would slowly sink, but under power, provided her diving planes were used, descent would be much more rapid. Conversely, given power, the sub could quickly surface, even if trimmed for negative buoyancy.

It came back to Lieutenant Smarz that, only the previous evening, while *Thresher* was still moored at Pier 11, shipyard people had been putting in some hard-pressed overtime, correcting problems with the stern and sail planes. They would not synchronize properly, and this was a condition no amount of ballast tank trimming could put right. Eventually, they had solved the problem, which stemmed from a defective pilot valve in the hydraulic system.

There was a gushing sound as the vents opened to admit water, which expelled the air contained in the auxiliary tanks. Then *Thresher* started to go down and her decks canted a little. The workmen, seemingly, had done a satisfactory job of repair.

When 60 feet came up on the depth gauge, the Planesman leveled out. *Thresher*'s radio mast was still above surface, permitting radio contact to be maintained with the outside world.

After an hour of this, which was ample time for any serious leaks to show up, the big black steel shark blew tanks and returned to the surface.

In the Communications Section of the Control Center, Radioman 1st Class Joseph A. Walski, only 24 years old and looking much younger, handed some notes to the Communications Officer, Lieutenant Junior Grade Ronald C. Babcock.

"Communications systems checked out with harbor control [Portsmouth], sir. No discrepancies." This meant that Walski had fully tested the ship's radio equipment.

"Very good," Babcock said, nodding, and passed the information on to the captain.

Harvey now took the ship down to 400 feet, using the main ballast tanks, and minor leaks may have squirted thin streams of water into some of the compartments due to packing glands or valve operating mechanisms, but none of this was serious. The problem was either corrected on the spot or else noted as one of the lesser glitches that would require attention when *Thresher* returned to port. Nothing urgent, at all events.

Thresher blew tanks and surfaced without incident and all that day continued her trials in the Boston Operational Area.

Over the 1-MC word now came from Harvey. "This is the Captain speaking. All hands secure loose gear and prepare for heavy rolls during surface full speed trials."

Some 20 minutes later, the XO came into the captain's cabin.

"Captain," he said in his relaxed tone of voice, "I just took a stroll through the ship and everything looked secure."

"Very good." Harvey cut short a brief rest and returned to the Control Center. Over the 7-MC he passed the order to the Maneuvering Room. "All ahead, full!"

As *Thresher* quickly responded and was soon cleaving through the water at 35 knots and beyond, a small shudder ran through the hull. But the whole evolution to maximum speed was incredibly smooth compared with the speed runs of the old diesel boats. Trimmed so that only her sail rose above water, the ship ran steady and true with an ease that gladdened the hearts of all aboard.

Next came the "Crash Back" test. With the ship still at maximum speed, the captain suddenly passed the order, "All back, emergency!" The Helmsman immediately turned the handle on the engine telegraph, transmitting the order to the Maneuvering Room. In response, the Propulsion-Panel operator spun open the "stern turbine" throttle. As two gigantic forces suddenly opposed one another and the hull took the full strain in opposite directions, the ship vibrated violently. *Thresher*'s impetus was still driving her forward, while the propeller backed madly to bring her great mass to a halt. She came to a stop within prescribed limits, then the giant blades got enough of a grip to start the ship reversing. A huge cascade of foam erupted from astern, but there was no apparent damage to the hull or interior.

Thresher then calibrated her sonar and radar at various speeds, but the Sonar Officer, Lieutenant Junior Grade Frank J. Malinsky, one of the crew's four lieutenants who did not yet have a division assignment but was capable of overseeing all kinds of jobs, looked less than happy.

Outside the Officers' Wardroom he ran into Pat Garner as they were both going in to grab a quick cup of coffee.

"How's it going, Frank?" the Executive Officer asked, by-passing the Navy rule against the use of first names on duty.

"Would you believe, XO"—Malinsky made a gesture of disappointment—"the active sonar just went out again. That's the second time today. I knew our calibration tests were a little sour this morning. But to have this happen during sea trials, of all times!"

"Don't worry about it, Frank." Garner sounded as carefree as ever. "You've got all night and plenty of good help. I saw your note on the discrepancy list. Probably a matter of tuning."

"We'll get it licked, I'm sure." Malinsky ran a weary finger over his thick black eyebrows. "Ellwood Forni [*Thresher*'s Chief Sonarman and a graduate from the Navy's Fleet Sonar School at Key West, Florida] is on the job."

"They don't come any better."

"I know, but this is new and highly advanced equipment. I hope we can meet the Navy specs before we get back from this trip."

On the Wardroom table there was still a stack of pamphlets describing the ship's tests. This was *Thresher*'s Sea Trial Agenda, dated April 2, 1963.

Malinsky who already had a copy, sighed as he stirred his coffee. He was in his early twenties, a Bachelor of Science and a serious, dedicated young man. This was his first assignment on submarine duty. Naturally, he wanted to make good.

Finally the captain ordered a series of "large angles" —tight radius turns to port and starboard that put maximum stress on the hydraulic system operating the great rudder as well as the diving planes. Considering this was about the last item the Yard men had worked on, right at the end of *Thresher*'s PSA (Post Shakedown Availability), the observers on board, though they got thrown around a bit, watched the proceedings with great interest.

Late on the afternoon of April 9, 1963, *Skylark* received an untimed communication from SSN-593, requesting a change of rendezvous the following morning. The original meeting place had been ordered for 1100 at 41° 42′ north and 62° 27′ west.

After a brief session with the Executive Officer, Harvey sent out a radio message to his escort ship, pinpointing a new rendezvous on the 10th, approximately 20 miles east of the original one. The new co-ordinates were 41° 46′ north and 65° 03′ west, and the time for the rendezvous was changed to 1200 zulu hours.

As dusk began blanketing a restless sea, the two ships parted and proceeded independently. Over the 1-MC, Harvey informed his crew, "This is the Captain speaking. The surface portion of our sea trials is over. We have few discrepancies. We're now on our way to the deep diving area and should be there at about 0700."

Thresher now traveled part of the time submerged and the rest surfaced. She steered "various courses at various speeds and depths," including some full-power runs, but, to enable those of the ship's complement who were off duty to get some sleep, she proceeded for several hours at shallow depth, where the hull was subjected to hardly any motion. Almost certainly she went no deeper than 400 feet. The over-all picture remained very good, and no part of the ship gave any indication of what was to happen next morning.

There was no movie show that night, but softly piped music was available throughout the ship for those who found a little time to relax. John Lyman, unfortunately, was not one of them. As the ship's Engineer Officer, his many duties included co-ordinating the efforts of electricians, enginemen, electronics technicians, sonarmen—in fact all the different engineering rates on the ship were primarily his responsibility. For example, he kept a sharp ear open for reports on the temperature of the propeller-shaft bearings. Any sudden rise might indicate trouble serious enough to compel the captain to abort the cruise. No such thing happened, but this was the reason why Lyman did not have any Watch. He was continuously on duty, spending much of his time in the Maneuvering Room and snatching a few winks of sleep when he could.

Nobody bothered to write any letters, of course, but many observers scribbled down their impressions and some of the enlisted men got involved in the usual game of chess or card session in the spacious Crew's Quarters, forward. In the Officers' Wardroom, as elsewhere, the clean smell of the beautifully waxed linoleum deck deferred to the appetizing odor of steaks on the broil as officers and civilians came off the various Watches. All they had to do was raid the freezer, select a succulent T-bone, porterhouse, or sirloin, and cook it to exactly their liking. As usual, when it came to food, jovial, burly Lieutenant Commander Mike Di Nola, who weighed 200 pounds and was an outstanding cook by avocation, took care not to miss his turn. Mike, who was Main Propulsion Assistant aboard *Thresher,* had served more than two years under her first commanding officer. Besides Garner, he was the only other officer qualified for submarine command.

As the hours of darkness wore on and the new Dog Watch came on at 2400 (midnight), to be succeeded four hours later by the Swing Watch, so the check marks on the mimeographed forms carried by the officer and civilians aboard became more numerous. *Thresher*'s progress also was being continuously noted in the Quartermaster's Log. The thoughts that crossed the mind of George Kiesecker, as he lay in his bunk, trying to get some much-needed sleep, will never be known. Hopefully, some of his fears were allayed. Everything appeared to be going well.

The one remaining obstacle was that deep dive scheduled for the next morning.

THE LAST DIVE
April 10, 1963

At 0745 next morning, 15 minutes before the Blue
Watch took over from the Swing Watch, *Thresher* was
steaming about 10 knots at periscope depth. Her skipper,
Lieutenant Commander Wes Harvey, although he had
snatched no more than a few hours' sleep during the
night, was alert as ever while headed for the rendezvous
with *Skylark*. In fact he was already thinking about the
many things that would have to be done that day, starting with the Sea Trial Agenda's most important item, a
deep dive to test depth.

There was no reason to defer this exercise any longer. *Thresher* had done everything asked of her since the previous morning. The only uncertain quantity was how the reducer valves in the main ballast tanks would respond when compressed air rushed into them at high pressure to expel sea water from test depth. These valves were designed to reduce the pressure of the blow from the compressed air flasks, but at the same time to increase its length in terms of actual duration.

Harvey, a serious-minded man of 34, very technically inclined and a stickler for detail just as the book told it, was aware of this problem. He also knew that regaining the surface with a full head of steam was more important than total deballasting. This was just the opposite of the principle obtaining on diesel subs, but the problem was that *Thresher* had what Admiral Rickover had termed a small blow capacity, far from adequate for the job. On top of that, she had never yet tried to deballast at test depth, but had relied solely on her tremendous power and on going down with her trim giving an absolute minimum amount of negative buoyancy. Commander Axene, her first captain, had been very leary of this weakness, preferring to "drive" the ship under, watching the trim closely, and bringing her back up on power.

Although *Thresher* was Harvey's first nuclear submarine command, his long experience aboard ships of this type fully qualified him for the job. He could look back on seven years' service as a submariner with "nukes," first as Reactor Control Officer during the 100,000-mile submerged cruise of *Nautilus* (SSN-571), which had crossed the pole on two historic occasions; then as Engineer Officer of *Tullibee* (SSN-597) and

Executive Officer *Sea Dragon* (SSN-584). On the latter ship, he had participated in the north polar rendezvous with *Skate* (SSN-578) a year earlier.

Today, Wednesday, April 10, 1963, he planned to spend about six hours submerged, and this much *Skylark* already knew. An hour earlier, *Thresher* had picked up *Skylark* 10 miles away on her sonar scope (the active portion of the sonar suit had been repaired during the night) and followed up with a radio check.

Just then, Harvey had his eye glued to the periscope sight while he scanned the horizon, looking for visual identification. As he moved the periscope slowly around on its quadrant, the sea appeared empty and much calmer, with only a moderate swell. Visibility was excellent, about 10 miles. The wind blew seven knots from the north-northeast, to *Thresher*'s port quarter. Cloud ceiling was about 3,000 feet.

Suddenly, the captain caught the drab gray silhouette of the escort ship squarely in his sights. Obedient to the motion of the swell, she would wallow for a moment in the depths of a huge, slow-moving trough, then reappear much higher as the motion of the sea carried her to a new peak. She was near enough, however, so that the large, white-painted number 20 could clearly be seen on her bow.

"There she is," Harvey told the Quartermaster, who was standing by in the Control Center, close to the UQC phone which dangled from a thin cable. Over the 7-MC, Harvey spoke to the sonar operator. "Sonar Con, go active. Range to the target. Bearing 147."

"Aye aye, sir."

Sonar then sent out a ping on that bearing and picked

up the echo, giving him the exact range. Back came the answer.

"Con, Sonar. Bearing 147. Range 3,400 yards."

"Very good," Harvey acknowledged. He turned to the Quartermaster of the Watch, Jackie Gunter. "Pass that information to *Skylark*."

"Aye aye, sir." Gunter immediately reached for the mike. "Dipper Sierra, this is War Club. We hold you 147 degrees true at 3,400 yards. Over."

The reply was clearly understandable, even if the voice could not be identified. "Dipper Sierra to War Club. Roger and out."

A navigational check by Lieutenant Merrill F. Collier, Assistant Navigating Officer, based on the rendezvous co-ordinates, showed that the two ships would meet pretty much as intended. *Skylark*'s exact position was 41° 45' north, 65° 00' west. This was only about one minute north latitude and three minutes west longitude from rendezvous. Allowing for the distance separating the two ships, it could be called dead-on, although *Thresher*'s SINS equipment (Ship's Inertial Navigation System) was so accurate when in use that it could guide her to within 50 feet of a given point.

The captain nodded, satisfied.

Two minutes later, at 0747, he ordered over the 1-MC, "Rig for deep submergence. Rig for deep submergence!"

This meant that every nonessential aperture in the hull must at once be closed against sea water and double-checked by an officer for correct functioning and freedom from leaks. There was no need for the shattering blast of the diving alarm, since *Thresher* was already under, but the BCP (Ballast Control Panel) operator,

Chief Hospital Corpsman Andrew Gallant, a chief petty officer, had by then indicated to the Conning Officer, Mike Di Nola, that he had a "straight board." This meant that the ship's hull was tight, with all openings closed. A series of pale green bars on the board indicated when each valve or hatch was in a closed position.

Looking over Gallant's shoulder was Chief Electrician's Mate Leonard "Len" H. Hewitt, with kindred experience in three diesel and one nuclear submarine, USS *Skipjack* (SSN-585) before transfer to *Thresher,* back in February 1961. Dark-haired, neatly groomed, and gifted with a pleasant, knowing smile, 29-year-old Len Hewitt was a prime solver of electrical problems.

The panel monitored the hull openings for normal submergence, all the way from the main ballast tank vent valves, eight inches in diameter, to auxiliary tank flood and drain valves of only half that size.

Thresher was now committed to her last and tragic adventure.

It was 0749 when Harvey ordered the Diving Officer to start the ship down to test depth. John Smarz passed the order directly to the planesman.

"Make your depth 400 feet, five-degree down angle."

His order was repeated, "Four hundred feet. Five-degree down angle. Aye, sir."

Seated at their stations before the Diving Panel were two seamen, John P. Inglis and Pervis Robinson. Inglis manned the sail planes; Pervis the stern ones, which could also operate independently. They began pushing forward on their plane controls, only pulling back to level off when the depth gauge indicated that the order was carried out. Meantime, the Helmsman, another seaman, named Peter DiBella, maintained the ship's course.

A lot would be asked of *Thresher* during the next couple of hours, but there was no reason to suppose her performance would be less than excellent.

"Dipper Sierra, this is War Club," Gunter informed the escort ship. "Starting deep dive."

"Roger," came the answer.

To get some feeling for what happened aboard *Thresher* during the next 90 minutes, and particularly during her last agonizing moments, which took about four minutes (says Lieutenant Commander Ray McCoole, whose personal recollections of the tragedy appear in later chapters), you need to project yourself into what was then the Navy's most advanced and complex attack sub. You need to identify with what went on. All around you, every spare inch was crammed with machinery of one kind or another. I've said elsewhere that *Thresher*'s interior was far roomier than that of any other contemporary nuclear submarine, but no matter where you might be sitting or standing, you could hardly stretch out an arm without touching some rack of equipment, some projecting paneled surface that neatly housed a bewildering array of pipes, electrical harnesses, valves, levers, and switches. It was, in fact, this highly decorative concealment impeding access to vital components that bothered Captain Dean Axene, *Thresher*'s previous skipper, more than anything else.

With few exceptions, none of the ship's longitudinal corridors was more than three feet wide, no ceiling more than a foot above your head. Often, a tall man would need to stoop to avoid bumping his noggin, but it's surprising how quickly one adjusts to problems of this kind. Still, thanks to the herculean efforts of the crew, *Thresher* was once again spotlessly clean after her seem-

ingly endless stint in dry dock. Then there was her pleasing brown and white décor, with figured linoleum to
match, and the cool, odorless filtered air that went a
long way toward dissipating any feeling of claustrophobia. Except in the galleys and machinery spaces, and
despite cigarette smoke, the air was far cleaner than in
the average apartment or house, let alone a deserted
stretch of highway. In fact, the ship's company was operating under ideal shirt-sleeve conditions, despite the
intense cold just the other side of *Thresher*'s steel plates.
Protecting them was a layer of special insulating cork
lining the ship's hull.

The safe limits of atmospheric pollution provide for
perhaps 15 to 20 parts per mille of carbon monoxide
and less than one per cent carbon dioxide. The oxygen
content in the air was constantly kept at 21 per cent; the
interior temperature of the ship was 72°F., with relative
humidity 50 per cent. *Thresher*'s air-revitalization machine, which automatically pumped oxygen into the atmosphere as required, had been installed and was in
good order. So was the chemical air "scrubber," a sodium
carbonate compound used to remove exhaled carbon
dioxide. What was missing was the equipment designed
to extract oxygen from sea water. This still stood on the
pier, awaiting *Thresher*'s return. The air conditioning,
however, functioned reasonably well and in any case was
being monitored by the shipyard personnel aboard. It
also was possible by fairly accurate guesswork to make
up for the oxygen consumed by the crew. A man uses
nine-tenths of a cubic foot of oxygen per hour for normal
labor, so an abundance of clean fresh air is a priority,
but reserve oxygen tanks could quickly be bled as needed.

Backtracking a few minutes, by 0745, six minutes before the end of the Swing Watch, just about every seat in the Wardroom was taken by men more interested in bacon and eggs and hot coffee than in the clipboards so many of them carried. Those coming on duty after a somewhat restless night were hurrying to get served so that they might make way for the detail that had been on since 0400 and, despite the strain imposed by their many duties, looked forward to breakfast before getting some shut-eye.

Quartermaster Gunter had just finished talking to the escort ship by underwater phone. What he had told them was, "My future reference to my depth will be Test Depth." This message made little sense and was, in fact, just a slip of the tongue. What it meant was, "Future depths will be in reference to my Test Depth." For example, "Test Depth minus 600 feet" would mean that *Thresher* was some 400 feet beneath the waves. This was so as not to reveal information over an open line such as UQC. Two minutes earlier, in fact, Gunter had informed *Skylark* (Dipper Sierra), "We are now at 400 feet and checking for leaks," but that was the maximum depth to which the Navy would own.

The procedure was thorough. Every compartment was scrutinized by an enlisted man technician for the minutest intake of water and double-checked by an officer. The watertight doors between compartments were slammed shut in case of emergency, and ready to be dogged (locked). So far there had been no leaks apart from the usual seven gallons of sea water an hour *Thresher* could easily live with by working her pumps, and which were well inside safety limits. Such leaks can come from glands on the propeller shaft, from a badly packed periscope, or from literally a thousand joints and fittings which remain tight until the ship contracts at the enormous pressures and very low temperatures of the deep. Even the sea-water pumps themselves might be leaking slightly.

Jackie Gunter kept an accurate and detailed log of everything that happened aboard *Thresher*. It contained far more information than the regular deck log signed off by the Officer of the Watch, but in less than 70 minutes it would be lost forever, carrying with it vital details of the doomed submarine's last moments.

After crossing the Reactor Tunnel aft of the Fan Room, a narrow gangway over the heavily shielded Reactor Compartment, and gripping the handrail to steady himself, anyone with business there would step down into the Auxiliary Machinery Room, which was aft of *Thresher*'s midpoint (see Profile). From there on to the stern the ship was painted a spotless, clinical white with highlights in gleaming stainless steel. This décor, combined with the fact that the afterpart of the ship had only two decks instead of the usual four elsewhere, contrived to give the Auxiliary Machinery space an almost "concert hall" feeling of spaciousness, even though the upper compartment was only 15 feet long and about 20 feet wide. Here, too, for the first time, the dry, indefinable smell of steam mingled with faintly acrid whiffs of hot lubricant and even hotter metal.

An electric bulkhead clock with a red sweep-second hand was pointing to 0810 and *Thresher* had by then lost perhaps another 100 feet but was proceeding cautiously. She was close to one-half her test depth, however, and this time it was the Executive Officer, Pat Garner, who gave *Skylark* the news from the Control Center. Guardedly, he said, "Am proceeding [toward] one-half set distance," and got a "Roger, out," in reply.

It didn't take long to develop an acute sensitivity to the least change of the deck from a horizontal position, so it was obvious that if the Planesmen had received orders to increase depth, they were going about it with extreme care. Although the Auxiliary Machinery Room was separated from the Engine Room proper only by the feed water surge tank, the muted sound of the big turbine was very deceptive. Its perfect balance, helped by a resilient mounting—one of many features designed to make *Thresher* the quietest submarine afloat—restrained the noise of the whirling blades to a soft, booming whistle. At all events, the speed indicator over the Officers' Wardroom door, just a few moments earlier, held a steady 10 knots. This was only about a quarter of the ship's maximum underwater speed, so the power plant was just loafing along.

Despite the hive of activity aboard *Thresher,* things were strangely subdued. An occasional groan from the hull plates or a squeak from a protesting rivet might cut across the spoken word, sharply interrupting the speaker, as the outside sea pressure probed relentlessly for a weak spot; but these sounds were more of an obbligato to the low-keyed voices of the Watch, giving and confirming orders. The vessel's tear-shaped hull, moving at that depth through water as calm as a millpond, gave no hint of rolling or pitching.

Suddenly, at 0835, Wes Harvey made up his mind. *Thresher* was close to 600 feet down and the last compartment had reported back on her watertight integrity. It was now time to start the really deep dive off the Continental Shelf.

"Proceed to test depth," the captain ordered the Diving Officer.

"Test depth, aye aye, sir," Smarz acknowledged.

In turn, standing behind the Planesmen, he passed the order on directly, giving the angle of dive. The Control Center deck began to cant down another 15 degrees, quite a "large angle" precarious to those not seated.

Back in the Engine Room, eagle-eyed Donald Wise, Chief Machinist's Mate, was at John Lyman's side. He was then acting Chief of the Watch.

Confirming the captain's decision, QM Jackie Gunter transmitted on UQC to *Skylark*, "Proceeding to test depth."

To Lieutenant Commander Lyman, Engineer Officer, the captain said, "Make turns for five knots." (Reduce speed to five knots.)

"Five knots. Aye aye, sir," Lyman acknowledged.

Steam pressure decreased and the smooth hum of the turbine dropped to a mere whisper. With the checking-over phase, every hundred feet, now completed, it was going to be a very slow, careful dive to that fabled 1,000-foot mark known as Test Depth. The entire crew of the Blue Watch and most of the observers aboard were now keenly on the alert, listening or gazing about them.

Seven minutes later came *Skylark*'s reply. It was difficult to identify the speaker's voice, but his "Roger, out," sounded matter-of-fact. Certainly there was not yet need to switch from the UQC to CW (Morse code), which carried much further, but only in dot-dash pulse-code. Seemingly, the delay had occurred while the escort ship plotted the relative positions of the two vessels.

At 0842 plus a few seconds, Harvey, who now had the Conn, passed word directly to DiBella, the Helmsman, whose position was only a few feet away.

"Make your course two-seven-zero."

"Two-seven-zero. Aye aye, sir."

Heading due north, *Thresher* had been steering a very wide circle which, when completed, would give her descent a corkscrew effect. Due north, due east, due south, and now due west. It needed only one more quadrant to complete the circle.

Gunter again grabbed the underwater phone and informed *Skylark,* 850 feet above, "Corpin two-seven-zero."

Under average conditions, the UQC's voice range was limited to perhaps 10,000 yards for effective communication, and its gurgling echo could easily distort a word like "course." For that reason, the Navy decided on "corpin" as a substitute.

A minute later, *Thresher* now on course "zero-zero-zero" started the last quarter of the circle, moving toward due north. She was then sliding over the edge of the Continental Shelf, past a very steep cliff with a sheer drop of well over a mile. From now on, no rescue gear known to man could help her if she got into trouble. She must rely entirely on her own resources to regain the surface. The freezing blackness of a hostile, implacable sea was waiting to grab her like some giant, evil octopus. Despite her 278-foot length and 4,500-ton displacement (submerged), *Thresher* suddenly became very small in these surroundings. No more than a tiny speck in the ocean. It was not a comforting thought, but most of the ship's company avoided dwelling on it. She was responding to every command with the precision of clockwork.

Seventeen minutes later (0900) *Thresher* had reached a depth where more than 480 pounds was pressing on every square inch of her structure. Still no apparent problems.

For the last time, Gunter informed *Skylark*, "Proceeding to test depth." SSN-593 had just about made it. Her reactor was generating full heat. The turbine idled as sweetly as ever in response to the high-pressure steam passing through its whirling blades.

There was no cause for worry.

THE FINAL 15 MINUTES
April 10, 1963

At 0902, with all the breakfast dishes cleared in the Officers' Wardroom and the Crew's Mess, and the commissaryman supervising preparations for the noon meal, the downward tilt of *Thresher's* deck increased noticeably. In fact, it was sufficient to make anyone who happened to be standing brace his legs and hold onto the nearest fixed object.

The ship was again steering "corpin zero-nine-zero," as she informed *Skylark*, and was beginning her second wide downward circle. Since the depth gauge was now only a couple of hundred feet above test depth, this was going to be a shallow circle, but the term "shallow" could be called a relative one. Anything over 10° of tilt makes it advisable to sit down unless it is absolutely necessary to move from one station to another aboard the sub.

Eight minutes elapsed before Skylark responded to *Thresher's* last message, and then the voice that came through with a "Say again?" sounded far from clear to Quartermaster Gunter.

The underwater telephone transmission from *Thresher* might be deteriorating as she slid deeper beneath the waves. Perhaps it was passing through thermal layers where a sharp temperature drop made it harder for sound to penetrate.

Those who from habit or necessity happened to glance at the electric clocks dotted over the ship would have been thunderstruck had they even remotely guessed that *Thresher's* remaining span of life was less than 15 minutes.

Back in the Control Section of the Engine Room, the Engineer Officer, John Lyman, and the Assistant Reactor Control and "E" Division officer, Jim Henry, a lieutenant junior grade who was taking McCoole's place and also acting as Engineer of the Watch, were looking over the shoulders of the engineering plant operators. But for the accident to his wife, Barbara, this was where Lieutenant McCoole would have been standing. In this busy spot were located the steam, electric, and reactor control and feed water sections. Each was represented by a panel and monitored by a specialist enlisted man. To get some idea of how busy these four men were, one had only to count eight different meters on the steam panel, 64 on the electric panel, 31 on the reactor panel and 24 on the feed water panel.

Soft-spoken Lieutenant Commander Mike Di Nola, the main Propulsion Assistant, wasn't wasting a moment either. He was wandering around the engineering spaces, checking his personnel at their stations. Di Nola was first assistant to the Engineer Officer, responsible for all the main propulsion equipment, such as the turbine, reduction gear, propeller shaft, and all accessory equipment connected with these main components.

Two minutes later, Jackie Gunter may well have picked up the phone to repeat *Thresher*'s course to *Skylark*, but at precisely that moment the surface vessel came through to ask for a "Gertrude Check", which meant "Re-establishing communications, please." The UQC is a one-way line, and whoever speaks first blots out the other voice.

In the Control Center, Pat Garner, the Executive Officer, his face inscrutable as ever, stole a quick look at the depth gauge. It was very close to test depth (generally assumed to be about 1,000 feet), and now the squeaks and groans of the hull's outer structure were more frequent. This was as deep as *Thresher* had ever been and perhaps a little deeper.

Suddenly, the men in the Control Section of the Engine Room heard a sharp metallic "bang!" coming from the adjacent compartment—the Auxiliary Machinery Space. It was followed almost at once by an ominous hissing sound that quickly rose in pitch like the pressure relief valve of a steam locomotive.

Although John Lyman was six foot two, he probably reacted quicker than anyone. In a couple of strides he shot out of the Maneuvering Room, turned forward and swung through a watertight door into the next compartment—the Auxiliary Machinery Space (see Profile). There, a hatch gave access to the lower level by means of a steel ladder. As Lyman scrambled down the rungs he found himself in a dense, salty mist that obscured everything. Instinct and training told him all he wanted to know. Probably a packing gland had let go somewhere along that segment of the salt water system. He did not want to dwell on anything worse than that. At this time the leak was still a small one and the enormous incoming pressure was atomizing the water into an opaque fog that even tasted salty. With only that pervasive hiss as a guide, it was impossible to locate the exact source of the trouble. One thing, however, was obvious to John. The underside of the 5SA panel, which housed the ship's main electrical connections and was located just above his head, had no bottom shield and was therefore being sprayed by mist so opaque that it at once condensed into sea water. Since the reactor received its electrical source from this panel, it was essential to isolate the leak as quickly as possible. Another thing that bothered Lyman was how long the defective gland (if that was the problem) would hold out. He grabbed the sound-powered handset phone nearest to him (the 7-MC system) and passed the word to the Maneuvering Room and Control Center.

"Control, this is engineer. We have a salt water leak in the auxiliary machinery space, lower level. The main electrical connections are getting saturated with salt water. Request an all-stop bell." This meant the stoppage of the main turbine. Lyman quickly added, "Maneuvering Room, shut the main sea water valves."

Harvey at once responded, "Maneuvering. This is the Captain. All stop!"

Back went the reply to the Control Center. "All stop. Aye!"

Answering John Lyman next, the Maneuvering Room confirmed, "Main sea water valves are shut."

Now it was Harvey's voice again. "Maneuvering. Give me a report as soon as you can."

Lyman was able to reply immediately, "The compartment is saturated with a dense fog, but the leak is subsiding."

The important thing was to isolate the defective component as quickly as possible, so as to be able to reopen the sea water valves which supplied cooling water to the main turbine condensers. Meantime, more trouble developed. The electrical plant control operator, Ray Denny, Electrician's Mate 1st Class, reported to Jim Henry who was standing behind him, "Full [electrical] ground on the port main bus. Loads shifted to starboard bus."

This meant the salt water had caused a short circuit in the 5SA electrical panel and tripped the breakers (fuses) open. Within a split second, the Reactor Operator, Raymond Foti, Electronics Technician 1st Class, informed Jim Henry, who was also standing close to him, "Reactor scram!"

Henry picked up the 1-MC and passed the word to the whole ship. "Reactor scram! Reactor scram! Secure all unnecessary electrical loads!"

What had happened was that the automatic bus (fuse) transfer switch that shifted over the electrical loads, including the power supply to the reactor, had operated too slowly. The reactor safety circuitry had sensed a loss of power quicker than the switch-over from port to starboard bus. The main turbine had already stopped. The propeller blades were now at a standstill. As could be seen from the reactor panel, nuclear fission had ceased. *Thresher* was continuing forward only on her momentum.

To add to all this, the turbo-generators, starved of steam, also came to a stop. Since they supplied electrical power to the whole ship, it was plunged in darkness until the emergency batteries took over. As a precautionary measure, the air-conditioning system had already been switched off to save the batteries. These had never been known to hold a charge at more than 80 per cent of their capacity. They needed nursing. Another of the many procedural steps taken when the reactor "scrammed" had been to shut the main steam stop valves. Mike Di Nola had taken care of this. It would give protection against drawing heat from the reactor too quickly, damaging its envelope and putting it out of action for good.

Everyone in the Engineering Divisions was aware that a nuclear sub relies mainly on power to extricate itself from an emergency situation, unlike diesel boats, which depend primarily on deballasting to regain the surface. All this had happened in a matter of seconds, but now Lyman rushed back into the Maneuvering Room, grabbed the 7-MC microphone, and reported, "Captain. This is the Engineer. The leak has been isolated. It was a silver-brazed joint in the auxiliary sea water system gauge line. Request permission to withdraw rods to critically." This meant to again start up the reactor.

"Permission granted," at once came back from the captain. This operation did not mean that new heat would be generated right away, but that the reactor would again come to critical with a sustained nuclear reaction. The minimum time required would be about seven minutes. At that point it would be possible to start drawing steam in limited quantities.

The ship already had an up-angle and was now operating on her EPM (Electrical Propulsion Motor). However, the slow-turning propeller supplied nothing like enough power to drive *Thresher* back toward the surface.

In the Control Center, as soon as the Engineer requested that the turbine be stopped, the captain had ordered the ship to assume an up-angle so as to decrease depth. For the upward surge he was banking on a roller-coaster effect. His order was, "Full rise on both planes. Give as much up-angle as you can. Make your depth 500 feet."

Thresher answered her planes, but this only put the ship into a stall, after which she began to wallow and mush downward, stern first.

On the Upper Deck, all eyes were watching the three gauges upon which the immediate future depended. And it was not a good picture. Speed had dropped to zero, even though the ship was sinking by the stern with increasing momentum. Submarine speed indicators do not function in reverse. The ship now had a 30° up-angle while the depth gauge was steadily moving toward the red band that would indicate crush depth. There was nothing to stop it, except as Harvey knew, about a 300-foot "safety margin" built into the ship.

Soon after, when John Smarz, the Diving Officer, reported to the captain, "Full rise on both planes. Unable to control depth!" tension began to mount throughout the sub. Although the ship's company was scattered over many compartments, the potential danger of the situation was not lost on them.

Smarz now turned to the Ballast Control Panel (BCP) operated and ordered, "Pump from the auxiliaries into the sea!" (Eject water ballast from the auxiliary trim tanks.) This was an attempt to restore some neutral buoyancy to the ship, which kept getting heavier due to the tremendous pressures on her as she went deeper.

The BCP operator's voice betrayed anxiety and his reply was scarcely reassuring, "I *have* been pumping from the auxiliary tanks into the sea since commencing the dive, sir." The truth was that *Thresher*'s auxiliary trim pumps were nowhere near adequate for the job and simply could not compensate for the continually increasing weight of the ship as she went deeper.

Despite his remoteness from the source of the trouble, much farther aft and several decks below, Harvey had by then a pretty good idea of what was going on. He knew that *Thresher* was wallowing and had begun slipping back. If something wasn't done at once, her motion would become uncontrollable. He grabbed the overhead UQC mike and sent *Skylark* the message, "Experiencing minor difficulty. Have positive up-angle. Attempting to blow..."

It was then almost 0913 and *Thresher* had slipped past her test depth toward terrible danger. Just as were Lyman, Di Nola and Smarz, the captain was well aware of what might be facing them. The "minor difficulty" was only a hairline away from potential disaster. A large fire hose delivers water at 50 pounds per square inch, and at only 400 feet, a quarter-inch gauge line could deliver an equally powerful stream of water. *Thresher* was far below that depth—below twice that depth—and right then the enormous sea pressure not only was squeezing her pressure hull in a viselike grip of monstrous strength, but at the same time was trying to rip the defective pipe flanges apart. At any moment the rupture might burst into a flood, piling danger on danger.

Harvey could quote from the technical manual with his eyes shut. Three things became vital if you got into trouble in the deep. In their textbook order they were, "Power, up-angle and deballasting." Deprived of the first, and with the second producing no results, he hesitated no longer.

"Blow all main ballast tanks! Blow safety! Blow negative!" he ordered Smarz.

"Aye, aye, sir."

The main ballast tanks are used for normal surfacing and submerging. The safety tanks are held in reserve for emergencies. The auxiliary tank serves to trim the ship to neutral buoyancy, where she weighs exactly as much as the water she displaces. Now, all three were being blown simultaneously. Harvey's words were scarcely out than a tremendous hiss pervaded the whole ship, rising to a deafening crescendo as it blotted out internal communications. The compressed air banks, storing air at a pressure of 4,000 pounds per square inch, sent their contents ramming into the ballast tanks with a force seven times greater than the pressure of the sea water. If anything could do it, this could. Or so it should have done. But *Thresher*'s deballasting system, at maximum blow, could only expel about one-seventh of the water she displaced, and she had never before tried deballasting at test depth. Given adequate power from the big turbine, even so she might have risen back to a safe level.

The Planesman kept his control column firmly pulled back, as would a pilot trying to gain altitude. He was almost willing the ship to rise. Momentarily, some of the tenseness eased out of 129 faces as the depth gauge ceased its perilous rate of descent and came to a standstill. The deck angle leveled off a little, and everyone realized they had been holding their breath. Now, surely, the gauge hand would reverse its motion as *Thresher* began her climb back up to safety. But the hope was short lived. Within moments the ship started down again towards depths that were waiting to destroy her. Deprived of 18,000 hp from her mighty turbine, she was helpless on weak electrical power that could barely generate three knots.

The situation had now become critical, although most of those aboard were sustained by a desperate hope that everything would turn out all right. With the air conditioning and ventilation blowers stopped through lack of electrical power, the temperature inside the ship rose rapidly, bringing out many odors that normally did not intrude. Blending in the warm, stuffy air were the acrid smells of human perspiration, hot lubricating oils, and steam pipe lagging. Down in the engineering spaces, men worked frantically to build up enough steam pressure for use in the main turbine, using the existing heat reserves.

Lieutenant John Smarz turned to the captain. "Unable to control depth with EPM and all tanks blown, sir!" He shook his head. "As you can see, we're sinking fast ..."

There was now only one card to play, and the captain knew it. Since *Thresher* would reach and probably exceed crush depth long before the seven minutes needed to bring the reactor back to critical, Harvey decided to utilize the last available reserve of steam. This was actually residual heat stored in the reactor system and steam generators. It was called the "heat sink," and, providing enough pressure could be built up, it would start the turbine going again.

"Answer bells on the main turbine!" came from the captain.

"Answer bells on the main turbine, aye, sir," Lyman replied. "But the reactor is not yet at critical."

"Understand," Harvey insisted. "But I need propulsion immediately." By this time the captain meant that he was aware of the possibility of a damaged reactor envelope, due to an overrapid cool-down as the last of the primary system coolant was converted into steam with nothing to replace it. But he assumed full responsibility for this emergency measure.

In the Maneuvering Room, John Lyman ordered the main steam stops opened. Jim Henry, standing by him, objected, "But we'll be exceeding the cool-down rate, John!" (Luckily there was no depth gauge in that compartment to tell the men of the desperate situation they now faced.)

"I know that!" Lyman nodded tersely, shifting from one foot to the other. "But it's the captain's orders."

Engineman 2nd Class Richard Brann, at the Steam Control Section Panel, instantly obeyed the order. Along with leading Electronics Technician Raymond Foti, Brann had been a special duty trainee of McCoole's for eight months while *Thresher* lay in dry dock. And like Foti, he knew his job thoroughly. But it was now too late. *Thresher*, already far below crush depth and sinking ever faster, had exhausted her last hope. As the hands of the clock moved inexorably toward 0917, the Navy's most advanced attack submarine, built at a cost of $45 million, had a life expectancy of about a minute.

Up in Control, *Skylark*'s insistent "K...K...?" (meaning "Over...Over...?") was coming in almost continuously, but Harvey had no new information to give. With bitter irony, during those last moments, reassurance came through from Lieutenant Commander Hecker, riding *Skylark*, far above:

"No contacts in the area..."

By this he meant there were no ships anywhere near and there was therefore no danger of collision in the event that *Thresher* suddenly bobbed up to the surface with great force.

Even now, Harvey refused to give up hope. If the pressure hull could only hold out a little longer—just long enough so that the turbine would restart, the resultant forward motion, or "planing along," would prevent her from sinking further.

But already reports began coming in from various compartments that leaks were developing at an uncontrollable rate. One by one the sea water systems were giving way. The Torpedo Room, Engine Room and the Auxiliary Machinery Space were in serious trouble.

For the last time, Harvey grabbed the UQC microphone.

"We're exceeding test depth..." he began, unaware that his transmission to *Skylark* was so garbled it could hardly be understood.

The clock's minute hand touched 0917, and whatever else Thresher's gallant skipper intended to say, he never completed his message. A monstrous sound racked the ship as the pressure hull gave way somewhere in the region of the Engine Room. Instantly, a 1,500-ton battering ram of sea water hurtled into the crippled sub, annihilating everything and everyone in its path. This sent the atmospheric pressure rocketing up from a normal 14 pounds per square inch to at least 800 psi. The resultant implosion triggered a total disaster, and if by some freak of chance all human life aboard was not extinguished, its span endured only a few seconds longer.

Experiments have determined that lethal nitrogen narcosis will catch up with a diver when the air pressure he breathes rises to about 88 psi, which represents a depth of only 200 feet. Even those on *Thresher*'s Upper Level where the ship's Control Center was located, must have lost their hearing immediately and their ability to think or give orders a moment later. The inrushing torrent sent escaping high pressure bubbles soaring upward and outward, collapsing anything and everything within the submarine's pressure hull which contained air. Cans of food, bottles of liquid, circulating water pipes—anything of that nature was ruptured and smashed into indescribable junk. Within a second or two, thousands of skillfully fashioned but puny man-made parts disintegrated into twisted scrap.

How swiftly the final curtain came down on this appalling tragedy is anyone's guess, since *Thresher* had a very stout pressure hull, and—despite many errors— was built as strongly as the state of the art then permitted. The ship's broken, half-buried remains give no clear indication of the implosive force that sent her plummeting to the sea bed, more than 6000 feet below; but a fair estimate would be the equivalent of a ton of dynamite. What was left of the interior boggles the imagination.

For those of the crew who were still alive milliseconds before total oblivion, the effect must have been as violent as a head-on collision between two runaway freight trains.

At all events, examination of *Thresher*'s seabed wreckage appears to uphold the view that an explosion followed the implosion and this logically occurred in the Diesel Generator Room (see Profile) on the lower deck. It was here that the large diesel oil storage tanks were located, and this normally ignites at about 460 psi. It would be an error to assume, however, that the fuel "dieseled" or exploded simply because it was exposed to double its normal flash point. Various other factors (such as air mixture, nozzle pressure, etc.,) need to be taken into account, and there would be no way of determining these at such a critical moment. Sufficient that there almost certainly was an explosion in that compartment.

As to what happened next, the field of conjecture is open to any number of grimly fanciful theories. What did *not* happen was anything like the harrowing sketch that occupied a full page in a topical issue of *Life* magazine. This showed two men vainly struggling to free themselves from pinning debris in *Thresher*'s half-flooded Torpedo Room, while jets of water threatened to engulf them. The caption read (with blatant disregard for surviving relatives and families), "Water popped open the seams of the torpedo room under a staggering pressure that could collapse the hull. Two men are shown struggling with the flood that quickly gained ground."

This gruesome flight of fancy may have been inspired by uninformed stories of what occasionally happened to pre-War diesel boats. In a modern nuclear submarine imploding at perhaps twice her test depth, it doesn't make a grain of sense. And in any case, as we have seen, *Thresher's* Torpedo Room contained little besides bunk beds hastily rigged to accommodate the large over-flow of "observers" aboard.

One possibility, however, stands out, which no one (except the Navy) has been able to refute.

The force of the explosion may have blown *Thresher*'s forward compartment clear of the ship. Loosely known as the "electronics space," it included besides the Forward Crew's Quarters, the Electronics Spare Parts Stowage, Diesel-Electric Generator, Forward Trim and Main Ballast Tanks, the Collection Tank and the Sonar Sphere, normally flooded in sea water.

By one of those freaks of chance that defy the laws of probability, it is possible that someone might have "dogged" the watertight door, trapping a very few men in that general area. Separated from the main hull at or beyond crush depth, this compartment still might not have collapsed, and in that event would have remained for a while in a state of limbo, resting perhaps on a cold water layer, of which there were many in the vicinity.

This point deserves mention because of persistent re-ports from one of the submarines ordered to the scene to help in the search for *Thresher*. These reports indicated that this sister ship of the lost sub was unsuccessful in making sonar contact with *Thresher*, but never men-tioned (let alone placed on record) the fact that she may, over a brief but unstated period, have picked up the garbled sound of human voices on her UQC. It was impossible (hearsay) to unscramble these sounds or make any sense out of them, except perhaps a desperate sense of urgency. Since *Thresher* did have an underwater telephone in her forward section, this lends substance to the possibility that a small handful of survivors might have escaped instant death at the time she plunged to the ocean floor, nearly three miles below her.

In those days—and we are speaking of a decade ago—even advanced nuclear submarines did not carry "little black boxes" containing retrievable tape recorders such as are found in all modern air liners. Had listeners aboard the searching sub been able to record these sounds, which seemingly were as incoherent as a tape played backward, much might have been learned—or possibly nothing. A cryptographic machine and a computer would, between them, almost certainly have solved the mystery.

Nowadays, tape recorders are part of the equipment of every submarine—another lesson probably learned from the *Thresher* disaster.

To ignore the possibility that the sea did not instantly engulf everyone aboard would be as unrealistic as the Navy's attempt to "classify" the entire proceedings relating to the loss of *Thresher*.

The general area of wreckage (described in a later chapter by Lieutenant Commander Keach as "looking like a large automobile junkyard") proved highly productive. Underwater cameras photographed torn-up parts of the sonar equipment that had been located in the bow of the ship, and even a section of the bow itself. However, the main debris was scattered over at least 140,000 square yards—a vast territory of ocean bed. There is nothing, therefore (in the public domain) either to disprove or support the assumption that *Thresher*'s forward compartment may have been severed by the diesel-effect explosion which immediately followed the implosion (sudden flooding and interior collapse).

Yet, if only in the light of logic, one was left with an uneasy feeling. Contributing to this nagging doubt was a curiously interesting statement which appeared in an article jointly written by two eminent oceanographic and marine scientists, Drs. F. N. Spiess (Marine Physical Laboratory, Scripps Institution of Oceanography) and A. E. Maxwell (Geophysics Branch, Office of Naval Research). Dr. Arthur E. Maxwell, Senior Oceanographer, was Chairman of the Scientific Committee appointed to Task Group 89.7, which led the *Thresher* search. He was (as will be seen later) awarded the Superior Civilian Achievement Award for his outstanding contribution to this difficult job. The article, titled "Search for the *Thresher*," which appeared in *Science*, Vol. 145, No. 3060 of 1964, concluded with this paragraph:

"Specifically, the location and remains of the pressure hull and reactor [of *Thresher*] are of considerable interest, particularly in view of the variety of *credible hypotheses* as to their behaviour that have been proposed (put forward). These range from a hypothesis of complete burial in the sediment due to the high sinking speed, to one of *possible temporary surfacing of a portion* [of *Thresher*], *resulting from a diesel-engine like explosion following rapid flooding from one end* [author's italics]."

Interesting, to say the least.

Estimates of the speed at which *Thresher* (or major parts of the ship) hit the bottom, vary—depending on her angle of dive—between 15 and 114 knots. Photomosaics, matched against the sub's original blueprints, have identified much of the wreckage but not all of it by any means. And certainly not all of it as a continuous entity. The reactor compartment, for example, is assumed to be buried deep in the silt.

It is true that neither an assumption nor even a probability should be taken as fact. He is blind indeed who fails to recognise this. But by the same token it is hard to explain away the vocal scramble which reportedly (though unofficially, of course) may have been overheard by a searching submarine on her UQC.

PLACED IN COMMISSION
August 3, 1961

When a new ship is "placed in commission" with the U. S. Navy, be it a surface vessel or a submarine, the traditional ceremony is always rather an emotional event. And, depending upon the ship, it can also be an occasion of great importance—a turning point for testing out operationally various new concepts in design or construction, or some momentous advance in the ancient but enduring art of shipbuilding.

Such an event was the commissioning of USS *Thresher* (SSN-593), which was the forerunner of a new class of attack submarine, so advanced in performance, so superior in equipment as to put her a decade ahead of any other killer sub in the world.

Early in May 1960, only two months before she was launched, *Thresher* went on the Master Urgency List. For a ship of this type—bigger, heavier, faster, deeper diving, quieter, far better armed and equipped with navigation worthy of trans-lunar rocketry, it was a very significant order. What it meant was that the U. S. Navy and the Department of Defense wanted *Thresher* commissioned and ready to join the submarine fleet as quickly as possible. To this end, no effort was to be spared. *Thresher* was suddenly given top priority in manpower, raw materials, and the means of fashioning those raw materials into intricate machinery, as well as putting it all together.

This was how Rear Admiral Robert L. Moore, Jr., Acting Chief, Bureau of Ships, expressed it in a letter to the Portsmouth Naval Shipyard dated May 4, 1960:

"It is essential that construction of *Thresher* (SSN-593) be accomplished with all practicable speed, this being a deep-submersible submarine of new design, incorporating the latest developments in propulsion plant and equipment. As you know, *Thresher* is now on the Master Urgency List and priorities for all urgently required components for *Thresher* have been approved by the Secretary of Defense. Therefore, the future construction rate will depend almost entirely upon the efforts of the Portsmouth Naval Shipyard employees, who have demonstrated their skill and resourcefulness on many occasions in the past. In urging early completion of *Thresher* construction, however, I do not wish to minimize the importance of the timely completion of . . . other submarine work now in progress at Portsmouth.

"I am confident that all of you at Portsmouth appreciate the importance of the submarine construction program to our country's security. I urge you to do everything in your power to expedite this vital program."

From the time *Thresher*'s keel was laid, May 28, 1958, to the day of her launching, July 9, 1960, only 28 months elapsed, and this, considering the tremendous task she represented and the fact that she had then no special priorities, was not exactly slow going.

But as soon as she was placed on the Master Urgency List, things really got into high gear. For example, it took less than a year from *Thresher*'s launch to her commissioning, and that period encompassed some of the most difficult assembly and completion work on the ship, including her builder's sea trials. During that time, all kinds of complex equipment which is installed on the upper decks but is too large to be lowered through any of the regular hatches goes in through a "hard patch." That is, at a convenient place, a large circular hole is cut out of the ship's pressure hull, through which, for example, some of the bulkier complex electronic consoles can be slipped with relative ease. Excepting the turbine and reactor anything must be able to go through that hole. The patch is then welded back on again, exactly in the same position. There must be absolutely no deviation from the contour of the hull—no break or "bump" which will upset its hydrodynamic qualities. Every inch of that hard patch must be as smooth as though it had never been removed, and the weld itself must have tremendous strength and absolute integrity. That is, it must be at least as strong, all the way round, as the surfaces it is bonding back together.

Even as these things go, *Thresher*'s commissioning at Berth 6A, Portsmouth Naval Shipyard, New Hampshire, was an impressive occasion, attended by many dignitaries who were accommodated as closely as possible on piers adjacent to *Thresher*. It took place during the bright and sunny afternoon of August 3, 1961, fanned by just enough breeze to make things pleasant. Everyone, from the commissioning speaker through the ship's first commander and the commissioning crew, wearing dazzling whites, presented an immaculate appearance.

Thresher, since her launching, not only had inherited the name of a tough breed of shark equipped by nature to seek out and kill, but she was, interestingly enough, the second submarine of that name commissioned by the U. S. Navy. The first *Thresher* (SS-200) a diesel boat launched March 27, 1940, at Groton, Connecticut, was already in Hawaiian waters December 7, 1941, and at once began active participation in the struggle against Japanese shipping. During World War II, the original *Thresher* had successfully completed 15 war patrols and sunk 17 enemy vessels for a total of 66,172 tons. Her War service earned her the Navy Unit Commendation with 15 battle stars. She was finally retired from active service and decommissioned in 1946 at the Portsmouth Naval Shipyard.

The new *Thresher* (the one hundred twenty-seventh submarine built at Portsmouth) had much to live up to but also had far superior equipment, from her nuclear power unit on up. Her device (see plate) was both graceful and apt, while her motto, *"Vis Tacita,"* could hardly have been better chosen. Meaning—Silent Strength. The Thresher shark apparently is easy to recognize because its tail is longer than the combined length of its head and body, while the first dorsal fin does not extend backward to the pelvic fin. The Thresher derives its name from the supposed habit of using its tail to beat the water in a compact school of fish, stunning some and eating the injured ones. Perhaps the most ironical and tragic part of the Thresher shark's description is that it is harmless to man.

SSN-593, first of her class, could also lay claim to another "first" at her launch, which sent her sliding into the water bow first. Such a thing had not been done in the U. S. Navy for at least 40 years and certainly never with any submarine, but in this case it was dictated by circumstances. These took into account *Thresher*'s difference in distribution of buoyancy and the depth of the water at the end of the building ways.

After an Invocation by Commander Carl G. Petersen, USN, the Navy Protestant Chaplain (who 20 months later was to be the participant in Memorial addresses deploring the loss of this splendid ship and her crew), the program got underway.

There followed some remarks and an introduction of distinguished guests by Rear Admiral Charles J. Palmer, USN, Commander of Portsmouth Naval Shipyard. The choice of this particular flag officer, while logical and according to protocol, could hardly have been less fortunate. He recently had succeeded Captain H. P. Rumble as commander of the yard, and he apparently suffered from glaucoma.

"*Thresher* is another Portsmouth first," the Admiral reminded his audience. "She is the prototype of a new class of unusually deep diving and silent submarines. We in the Naval Shipyard are very proud of her. I am sure that the many other activities of the Navy Department and the private technical and industrial firms who have worked with us in her building share in this pride.

"We are very happy, too, that this product of our hands and minds is to be in the capable hands of such an outstanding crew as you see assembled here aboard ship."

Next came Vice Admiral Elton W. Grenfell, then Commander Submarine Force U. S. Atlantic Fleet. It was his responsibility to introduce the commissioning speaker, Vice Admiral Harold T. Deutermann, USN, then Chief of Staff and Aide, Supreme Allied Commander, Atlantic. Deutermann, a clean-shaven, distinguished-looking gentleman of mature years, with graying temples, bushy eyebrows, and a rich gold cordon around his left shoulder, was not a difficult officer to eulogize. The career that had led to the position he then held was indeed an outstanding one. During World War II, he had stood out first as a destroyer commanding officer, and then as a destroyer division commander. Among the numerous medals and citations awarded him for his campaigns were the Silver Star, the Bronze Star and the Legion of Merit. During the Korean conflict, Admiral Deutermann had been Assistant Director of Fleet Operations. His first assignment to NATO had come in January 1960, eight months earlier, as NATO's Commander Striking Atlantic Fleet.

There was in effect not much anyone could say about *Thresher* that had not already been said or written with a liberal interlarding of hopes and superlatives, but Admiral Deutermann acquitted himself very well with a controlled but contagious enthusiasm. Speaking into a battery of microphones thoughtfully provided by WHEB for the amplification of its radio broadcast, he said:

"Today, as we commission *Thresher* and make her officially a part of the Atlantic Fleet, we reach a point in submarine development long awaited by our Navy. *Thresher* is not just another nuclear submarine. She is not just one more SSN to add to the too few that are already members of our fleets. She is not just another ship. *Thresher* is totally different," Deutermann reminded his audience. He went on in part, ". . . In *Thresher* we see gathered for the first time the marvelous energy of nuclear power; the evolutionary development of submarine hull forms. We see the inclusion of a sonar system so sensitive and powerful that the ocean around her for greater distances than ever becomes her territory.

"We see a weapons system so advanced in concept and design that no other submarine in the world today can equal her range and fire-power for antisubmarine weapons . . . A submarine designed to cruise at deeper depths than ever before, and to operate in those depths more quietly and efficiently than heretofore possible.

"The sea is a vast geographic fact of life. In its agelessness it transcends all wars, all weapons and weapons systems, and in turn all strategic concepts. It cannot and it will not be ignored by the contestants of any war in the future.

"We note the impressive and fantastic scientific advances made in seagoing weapons in the last decade, and nowhere have we a better example of this progress than the ship commissioned here today . . . We are fortunate indeed that at this time in our Navy's list of varied capabilities appears the new *Thresher*.

"The most advanced nuclear attack submarine in the world, capable of sustained and effective use, if the need arises, against submarine forces of aggressor nations, wherever they may appear.

"Your challenge [this was addressed to the ship's company] as you enter the realm of the new and the untried, is tremendous. Equally great is your opportunity to contribute in very large measure to the new tactics and new capabilities of our Navy today. I know you would not have it otherwise.

"And with my intimate daily association and work with the Naval Forces of our NATO alliance, I can offer you a genuinely warm welcome to our team, with the added appeal to bring more of your kind . . ."

There were other comments in the same vein, but one of Admiral Deutermann's remarks, if only because of its historical context, is worth recording. He pointed out that he was happy to visit historic Portsmouth, where, on another August day, over half a century earlier, negotiations had begun to end a foreign war. He was referring, of course, to the peace treaty between Russia and Japan, signed at Portsmouth in 1905 with President Theodore Roosevelt participating.

Deutermann, obviously sincere and dedicated, received a prolonged round of applause.

It now fell to Palmer to introduce the Commandant of the First Naval District, Rear Admiral Carl F. Espe, who was not a difficult man to praise either. He had held this post since May 1958, and during World War II had served as Commander Destroyer Squadron 46 and Destroyer Division 91. The rows of ribbons on his left breast told much of their own story. He held among other distinctions the Legion of Merit with two gold stars; the second star for exceptionally meritorious service in the Planning Department of the Chief of Staff of the

Commander-in-Chief, U. S. Pacific Fleet. Since the War he had been assigned to Naval Intelligence and the Naval War College, as well as having command of Destroyer Flotilla One, Amphibious Groups Three and One, and the Amphibious Force, Pacific Fleet.

Admiral Espe performed *Thresher*'s actual commissioning ceremony at 1435, in accordance with CNO (Chief of Naval Operations) letter OP 431J1, dated April 27, 1961. Espe avoided any address which at that point might be construed as a speech and did not strictly follow Navy protocol.

The National Anthem followed, impressively played by the Boston Naval Base Band, its brass instruments agleam, after which the Ensign, Jack, and Commissioning Pennants were hoisted.

Next, Commander Dean L. Axene, *Thresher*'s first skipper, fresh from the Naval Reactors Branch, U. S. Atomic Energy Commission, Washington, D.C., read out his orders appointing him to the command of the ship. He then set the Watch. Vice Admiral Deutermann thereupon broke his personal flag aboard *Thresher* at 1439. Little did anyone know that of the 12 officers who were part of the commissioning crew, only three would remain when she made her last dive. Of her original 17 chief petty officers, only eight would be aboard at the end. Of the original 74 enlisted men who were the bulk of *Thresher*'s complement the day she was commissioned (a total which was later increased to 96), only 31 would still be with her on the day she went down.

Commander Dean L. Axene, the ship's commanding officer whose name frequently appears in this book, and who survived the fatal dive against his own strong objections to being transferred, could scarcely have been a better man for the job. His entire naval career was tailored for this responsible task, and he had exactly the right temperament. He got to know *Thresher* so well, in fact, that he could almost anticipate how she was going to react to any given situation. His experience as a submariner fitted him pre-eminently for the assignment. After graduation from the U. S. Naval Submarine School in December 1944, he was ordered to the diesel boat USS *Parche* (SS-384) and completed two successful war patrols in Japanese Empire waters. On his second patrol he was awarded the Bronze Star Medal with Combat "V." In 1946, Axene began postgraduate instruction at the Massachusetts Institute of Technology.

Following a two-year course in electronics he commissioned USS *Tiru* (SS-416), later converted to a Guppy III Class sub. In June 1950, young Axene was detached from *Tiru* and assigned staff duty until his transfer to USS *Sea Robin* (SS-407), another Guppy, as Executive Officer.

Commander Axene's next position was that of Prospective Executive Officer aboard USS *Nautilus* (SSN-571), the first nuclear-powered submarine destined to fame for her daring round-the-world and under-the-ice trips. *Nautilus* was commissioned September 30, 1954, and Axene served with her for nearly a year. He was then again detached to assume command of USS *Croaker* (SSK-246), a Gato Class diesel sub, remaining with her until February 1957, when he was ordered to submarine school as Director, Nuclear Department.

At the time of her commissioning, he was the perfect captain for USS *Thresher,* bringing with him an outstanding backlog of experience in submarines of widely varying types, plus a thorough indoctrination in controlled atomic energy. Looking back now, despite her superb lines, enormous power and almost unlimited attack potential, *Thresher* carried with her the seeds of a terrible lurking danger which Axene was able to master by keeping an eye on everything, every moment she was afloat, and never allowing the ship to take over. It is difficult to explain otherwise *Thresher*'s almost constant need for overhauls and checkups, for repairing and refitting. Inherently, her great strength in some areas was counterpoised by a brittle weakness in others.

But to return to the commissioning, that momentous afternoon of August 3, 1961, proceedings moved toward their close with the order and impressive precision of a perfectly rehearsed ceremony.

Vice Admiral Harold T. Deutermann, USN, now hauled down his flag, and Commander Axene proceeded with some appropriate remarks while he presided over a number of important ceremonial presentations.

Commemorative plaques were presented to *Thresher* by Robert E. Whalen, Chairman of the Military Affairs Committee, Greater Portsmouth Chamber of Commerce, and by Louis R. Watson, Commander Squalus Chapter, Submarine Veterans of World War II.

A Benediction followed, by Lieutenant Commander John P. Fay, Chaplain Corps, USN, and finally it was the turn of Mrs. Mary Warder, wife of Rear Admiral Frederick B. Warder, Commandant of the Eighth Naval District, New Orleans, Louisiana, both of whom were among the dignitaries attending the commissioning. As sponsor, Mrs. Warder had broken the traditional bottle of champagne over *Thresher*'s stern at the time of her launch, 13 months earlier. She had then spoken those momentous words, "In the name of the United States I christen thee *Thresher,*" while the trigger releasing the ship and starting it down the ways had been pulled by Elroy Moulton, Foreman Shopfitter, Shop 11, and the band struck up "Anchors Aweigh."

Mrs. Warder now presented Commander Axene with a fine painting of a New England scene as her gift to the men of the 593.

Unfortunately, the one man whose tremendous determination and herculean toil had turned the dream of controlled nuclear power into a practical reality without which there could have been no *Thresher,* was unable to attend. He sent, instead, a Congratulatory Message which was duly read out by the Commandant, First Naval District.

"Congratulations to all hands in the *Thresher* on your commissioning. Your continued hard work will extend the outstanding performance you achieved throughout the *Thresher* sea trials. All of us in Naval Reactors wish you good sailing."

It was signed: "H. G. Rickover, Vice Admiral."

Already, Admiral Rickover had locked horns with the Portsmouth Naval Shipyard during the construction of *Thresher*'s nuclear reactor piping system. Displeased with the silver-brazing technique used, and lacking confidence in its integrity under heavy stress, he had ordered all the reactor coolant piping unlagged and done over again using welded flanges.

With Rear Admiral Charles J. Palmer, commander of the Yard, this decision had gone over like a lead balloon. But Rickover was, of course, absolutely right.

ANATOMY OF A KILLER SUB

What is a "Killer Sub?"

Generally speaking, it's a refined and far deadlier version of the original nuclear powered "attack" class submarine pioneered by the U. S. Navy, or more specifically by Rear Admiral Hyman G. Rickover, head of the Naval Reactors Branch in the Bureau of Ships.

The U.S. had at least 14 attack submarines powered by controlled nuclear fission, steaming along the high seas before *Thresher* was commissioned. Prototype of these was *Nautilus* (1954), famous for linking the Pacific with the Atlantic by steaming directly under the ice pack at the North Pole. In fact, when *Nautilus* flashed her famous message in clear, "Underway by nuclear power!" she beat the Soviet Union to the punch by five years.

This type of ship, however, while a giant step forward over the most advanced diesel sub, was designed to seek out and destroy enemy *surface* vessels.

Meantime, the Navy's first half-dozen ballistic missile or "Polaris" type subs had also gone on station, acting as a powerful deterrent to nuclear attack by land-based missiles against the vast industrial complex of the North American Continent.

Predictably, since the Russians knew how to split the atom, they would soon learn about controlled nuclear fission and follow in the wake of the U. S. Navy with atom-powered, missile-firing submarines of their own. Here too, our long-term naval strategy anticipated the U.S.S.R.'s next move. As a result, the Submarine Desk at BuShips got the job of designing an entirely new type of attack sub, configured and equipped specifically with ASW (Anti-Submarine Warfare) in mind. Its task would be to seek out and destroy enemy *submarines*, rather than surface vessels.

Thus was *Thresher* conceived as the forerunner of a new type (ASW/Attack) submarine, known also as the SSN 593/594 Class. The criteria to which *Thresher* was designed were highly exacting. She must be able to dive deeper and steam faster submerged than any other nuclear submarine ever built. She must be far quieter than existing undersea vessels to avoid detection and increase the element of surprise in attack. At the same time she must carry listening equipment that would enable her to hear better and farther when submerged, pinpointing enemy targets with deadly accuracy. Further, her navigation must be so reliable and accurate as to make it a mathematical certainty of going where her skipper intended.

Let's review these characteristics: deep diving, speed, silence, underwater detection ability, and unerring navigation. And of course a weapons system that would do the job at one stroke.

An impressive list, yet one by no means beyond the technology of the day—and we are speaking of more than a decade ago.

When the Kremlin's naval architects heard about *Thresher*, it's a safe bet that the order went out, "Back to the drawing board!" .

A Fact Sheet was put out by Portsmouth Naval Shipyard on July 28, 1961, when *Thresher* had already completed her builder's trials and a week before she was commissioned. As an example of dull, repetitious and ungrammatical prose, seemingly aimed at fourth-grade intellects, it does a good job. It is also inaccurate, misleading, or ambiguous and deals in statements and opinions rather than facts. True, some of the facts which were detrimental to *Thresher* could hardly go into a handout extolling with fuzzy superlatives the virtues of a Navy product costing $45 million. As we shall see, however, many pertinent facts that are omitted would have been of interest to the public without revealing so-called "classified" material. Said the Fact Sheet:

1. "SS(N) 593 (*Thresher*) is the lead ship of the Navy's newest class of nuclear attack submarines. She is similar to the other recent submarines with the *Albacore* teardrop-shape hull, a Westinghouse S5W reactor plant and a single propeller driven by a geared

turbine. However, she represents a tremendous advance over all other submarines in the areas of performance, depth quieting and sonar. *Thresher,* in becoming our country's best ASW defense, will be a true submarine, independent of the surface with unmatched submerged maneuverability and speed. In order to achieve the quietest position, the sonar (underwater listening devices) have been moved to the bow of the submarine, and the torpedo tubes to the midships area. Conventional and advanced weapons are fired therefrom at a 10-degree angle to the hull.

2. "An entire new sonar suit has been designed for *Thresher,* enabling her to hear enemy ships and submarines at far greater range than has ever been possible before. Her active sonar will allow her to "ping" on other ships and submarines at great ranges. *Thresher* has over 1000 transducers and hydrophones installed along the length of the ship. The majority are concentrated in the quiet forward area, making her our most effective underwater listening post. Raytheon Manufacturing Company is the prime contractor for the majority of this sonar, but special portions are furnished by Edo Corporation, Sperry Company, Bell Laboratories and others.

3. "Noise in a submarine has two effects. The first is radiation into the ocean which allows the submarine to be detected by others. The second is noise interference with the submarine's own listening devices. In order to make this sonar equipment effective, tremendous quieting measures have had to be made in *Thresher*. Refinements and developments of machinery have been made specially for *Thresher* to reduce the noise output of all equipments installed in this submarine. Great pains

have been taken to smooth the hull and optimize its shape to reduce the hydrodynamic noise to a minimum. *Thresher* will be by far the quietest nuclear submarine afloat or submerged. Naval activities, notably Portsmouth Naval Shipyard, have led the development of quiet machinery but private industry has picked up the ball and made great strides in machinery equipment design and construction to silence the Silent Service. A few of the many groups involved in these efforts are General Electric, Westinghouse, Louis Allis, Electro Dynamic Division of the General Dynamics Corporation, Ingersoll-Rand, Allis Chalmers, Cutler-Hammer, Aurora Pump Division of the New York Air Brake and DeLaval Steam Turbine Company.

4. "Another significant advancement of *Thresher* is the ability to cruise the oceans at far greater depths than any other submarine. Problems in welding and forming of heavy structural members in development of piping systems and hull fittings for deep submergence have been encountered and successfully solved. A vast program was set up to test each and every item required to operate this submarine at these unprecedented depths. Again the Navy and private industry worked in cooperation to develop and test thoroughly hundreds of items required. Never before has such an extensive development program been necessary for a naval ship and never before have such extensive tests been undertaken to give complete assurance that the submarine is safe.

5. "Another area of development has been in the increasing of habitability and operability of submarines. Great efforts have been expended on increasing the habitability standards to make the crew's life as pleasant as possible. Operating stations have been worked out in

great detail to assure simple and safe operation with a minimum of personnel and operator fatigue. One particular area is in the weapons handling and firing system. Weapons are loaded into the torpedo tubes and fired in "push button" fashion in *Thresher* with a minimum of personnel. Special equipment for air revitalization will allow *Thresher* to operate completely independent of the atmosphere for long periods of time.

6. "General Characteristics.

LENGTH	278-ft. 6-in.
BEAM	31-ft. 8-in.
DISPLACEMENT SURFACED	3,732 tons
DISPLACEMENT SUBMERGED	4,311 tons
ENDURANCE FOR STORES AND FOOD	90 days
OPERATING DEPTH	Deepest in the world
SPEED	Over 20 knots
ARMAMENT	Four 21-in. diameter torpedo tubes amidships with semi-automatic loading and firing equipment
COMPLEMENT	Eight officers Seventy-five enlisted men

"There are presently 13 submarines in the SS(N) 593 Class being built. Other shipbuilders are the New York Shipbuilding Corporation, Camden, New Jersey; Ingalls Shipbuilding Corporation, Pascagoula, Mississippi, and Mare Island Shipyard, California and Electric Boat Division of General Dynamics Corporation,

Groton, Connecticut. Many *Thresher* concepts are incorporated in our entire shipbuilding program. *Thresher* is the world's most advanced nuclear powered submarine and was designed and built by the Portsmouth Naval Shipyard."

Here are some of the facts that were either left out, misrepresented or confused.

1. *Thresher* had nothing in common with *Albacore*, *except* a teardrop or "modified spindle" hull pioneered by this diesel sub. *Albacore* (SS-569) was a Phase IV one-off test vehicle, commissioned May 1953, more than seven years before *Thresher*. Superior hydrodynamic characteristics enabled *Albacore* to travel underwater much faster than any earlier submarine. This spurred the construction of three more High Speed Attack diesel subs of which *Barbel* (SS-580), commissioned 1959, was the forerunner. *Barbel* introduced the concept of a centralized location (control and attack center) for vital equipment operation, which was adopted in all later combat submarines.

That same year, *Skipjack* (SSN-585), lead ship of a nuclear powered class of six High Speed Attack submarines bearing her name, also was commissioned. *Skipjack* featured the teardrop hull with a length-to-beam ratio of 7.8 to 1. This vastly improved her submerged performance. It was the *Skipjack* Class nuclear subs which used the Westinghouse S5W reactor plant carried over into *Thresher*. Not *Albacore*.

Snook (SSN-592), last of this class to be commissioned (October 23, 1961), three months after *Thresher*, shared with that ill-fated vessel "the vulnerability of her sea water system." These were the words of her first skipper, Commander Axene.

What happened to *Thresher* during builder's trials should have been ample warning to look more closely into the complex maze of piping common to both vessels. This warning apparently was ignored, and *Snook* had some hectic moments. A silver-brazed joint in a five-inch line let go while she was submerged. The cause was first attributed to the use of stainless steel instead of Monel, a tremendously tough, corrosion-resistant nickel-copper alloy. But the joint itself turned out to be faulty. Although results could have been disastrous, more trouble followed. Three grease lines passing through the after engine room bulkhead were carried away during a dive. The problem again was poor workmanship, yet even this was not the end. A one-and-a-quarter-inch nipple in the HPAC (High Pressure Air Compressor) cooling water discharge pulled out of a pipe boss at test depth. With a sea pressure of 440 pounds bearing on every square inch of the ship, the reader can imagine what might have happened but for the crew's prompt action and the fact that *Snook*'s reactor did not "scram," or shut down.

2. An entirely new sonar suit was not "designed for *Thresher*." It was *Tullibee* (SSN-597) commissioned November 9, 1960, nine months earlier, which had the most advanced sonar suit at that time, with the 15-foot-diameter sphere located in the bow of the ship. *Thresher* inherited this BQQ-2 sonar from *Tullibee*. Had the former survived, further improvement to her sonar was planned. A Digital Multi-Beam Steering modification (DIMUS) did in fact go into *Permit* (SSN-594), the next ship in line. This equipment provided automatic capability for tracking several targets, and other refinements.

Thresher did not have "over 1000 transducers and hydrophones installed along the length of the ship." While transducers and hydrophones belong to the same sonar suit, they are different components with different locations. To lump them together without explanation is misleading.

A sonar suit consists of two parts—"passive" and "active." The passive part uses hydrophones (underwater microphones) mounted along both sides of the ship with the greater number forward. The active part relies on transducers located inside the sonar sphere, which in *Thresher*'s case was in the bow.

The function of *passive* sonar is to listen intently to underwater noises. Water is an excellent sound conductor, and the deep sea is anything but a silent place. There is something continually going on. Porpoises talk to each other. Sharks disport themselves. Distant echoes are picked up, or the propeller noise of a surface vessel (or another submarine) comes through so clearly that the operator can tell at what rpm the propeller is turning.

The hydrophones are connected to an electronic circuit which compensates for the frequency differences of incoming sound waves. This is the heart of the sonar suit. It also takes into account temperature changes, currents and variations in salinity (the amount of salt in sea water at any given point).

Active sonar relies on transducers. A transducer is a sound-seeking device. It converts electrical energy into acoustic energy and sends out sound impulses or "pings." When a "ping" encounters an underwater object, it is reflected or bounced back to its source. A recorder translates on paper how long it took for the "ping" to return. From this time interval the distance of the object is worked out accurately and at once.

Without its sonar suit, a submarine would be "deaf" and defenseless. Sonar is therefore very much a part of the anatomy of a killer sub.

3. "Tremendous quieting measures" were not intended to make *Thresher*'s sonar equipment effective. Rather were they made so that the sonar of enemy submarines would become *less* effective. A ship's noises can interfere with its own listening, but that is far less important than the risk of those noises being picked up by enemy sonar. The quieting measures applied to *Thresher* involved careful studies relating to the *source* of underwater noise. The sound waves of a ship come mainly from cavitation of its propeller. Cavitation is the result of bubbles produced by the whirling propeller blades. Since water cannot follow a rapidly moving blade, local pressure drops to or even below vapor pressure of the surrounding liquid. This is what creates bubbles, but it is their immediate collapse that produces violent destructive-type sounds, easily picked up by a hydrophone.

Studies in propeller configuration—the number, shape and size of the blades—have done much to reduce cavitation and its associated noises.

Engine vibration is the next most prolific source of underwater sound, especially with a steam turbine of great power (over 18,000 shaft horsepower) such as *Thresher* had. Then there were two small turbines driving generators which supplied current to the entire ship. There was also the diesel unit used for charging the auxiliary batteries through a generator. Further sources of unwanted sound would be the emergency electric motor in case of reactor failure, the engine drive shaft, the reduction gear to the propeller, the large reactor coolant pumps and various other pumps circulating sea water in and out of the ship.

As a result of these studies, every moving piece of equipment aboard *Thresher*, large or small, was flexibly mounted to absorb vibration. Everything from the main turbine on down. This made a world of difference in noise reduction.

The numerous hull noises which can betray the presence of a submarine and nullify the advantage of stealth, also came in for close attention. *Thresher*'s teardrop hull, in many places almost perfectly round and smooth from bow to stern, gave her considerable extra speed and at the same time minimized the sound of her passage through water. Her small sail, which could accommodate only one periscope, also helped reduce drag and turbulence.

4. "Problems in welding and forming of heavy structural members in development of piping systems and hull fittings for deep submergence" had not been "successfully solved," even after *Thresher*'s commissioning. Let alone before that time. Therefore her "ability to cruise the oceans at far greater depths than any other submarine" was an illusion based on a dangerous element of wishful thinking.

The pressure hull of the ill-fated submarine was made of HY-80 steel with a yield strength estimated at 80,000 pounds per square inch. It was a big advance over previously used high-tensile steels with a little over half that strength, but this figure, taken out of context (disregarding the shape of the hull), is meaningless. Yield strength is primarily tensile strength or resistance to pull or bending. It is not the same thing as *compression* strength, which would be far less in a long, welded teardrop-shaped hull of circular section like that of *Thresher*. Sea pressure (compression force) increases by 44 pounds per square inch for every 100 feet of depth. Because of its almost perfect spherical shape, the gondola of the Bathyscaphe easily withstood a *compression* force of over 14,000 psi (approximately 32,000 feet), but *Thresher* imploded far above that depth—probably at around 1,800 feet, under a compression force of some 800 psi. Possibly, had she not already been leaking badly, she would have gone a little deeper before collapsing and imploding. However, the welded transition joints and variable taper of *Thresher*'s elongated hull (see Profile), would be called upon to withstand enormous stresses when subjected to twisting and bending forces while the ship moved at high speed through the deep. That is in addition to the tremendous pressure of the sea water. These cumulative stresses are often so great that they distort a submarine's hull to a measurable extent. For the purpose of monitoring the extent of this distortion, strain gauges are located at various points of the ship's pattern.

In *Thresher* (and she was not alone), the danger areas created by transition joints stemmed from the welding. Theoretically, a perfect weld is as strong as the parts it binds together, but in those days the Navy was having serious weld problems with steel as hard as HY-80. One reason was that the steel had to be kept thin enough to conform with the over-all weight specifications of the ship. Any vessel which weighs more than the water it displaces has no reserve buoyancy. In a submarine this is a critical factor. The ship must weigh a lot less than the water it displaces. Otherwise it could never be trimmed to varying degrees of buoyancy by means of ballast tanks. *Thresher,* for example, weighed 579 tons less than the water she displaced. This was her reserve buoyancy.

Every engineering problem involves a compromise. To regain the strength lost by thinning out *Thresher*'s hull section, the steel had to be toughened. As a result it became more brittle. That was where the trouble arose. After welding, toughened HY-80 steel showed a tendency to develop cracks. To ensure against this risk, thousands of X rays had to be taken. These are called radiographs. Unfortunately even the Navy's own shipyards didn't always conform with this requirement. Or else the radiographs were mislaid by an antiquated filing system.

The heavy structural members supporting *Thresher*'s riveted outer skin were no doubt adequate, and this gave the ship two "fringe benefits." The usual giveaway creaks and groans of riveted plates when a submarine is diving deep were far less frequent in *Thresher*. And her added strength meant the ability to better withstand the shock tests which would come during the postcommissioning shakedown cruise.

However, piping systems and hull fittings gave *Thresher* a lot of trouble. Months *before* the Navy's Fact Sheet of July 28, 1961, was written, *Thresher* had already suffered two piping failures. Both occurred during her builder's trials. In the first incident, a quarter-inch salt water vent line failed due to defective silver brazing while under full power, allowing water to spray back into the ship. This was exactly the same problem that was to occur in *Snook* (SSN-592) three months later. Original suspected cause: the use of stainless steel piping instead of Monel. Final diagnosis: silver brazing failure.

The second incident was even worse. That time a one-inch trim system priming line let go at test depth. The silver brazing joint gave way because someone had forgotten the insert ring between two pipe flanges. That these failures were not publicized was understandable. But identical failures in two different subs within three months of each other suggest that the Navy's information pipeline was in need of overhaul.

The rude awakening when *Thresher* went down possibly galvanized the Navy Yard into long-overdue action. *Tinosa* (SSN-506), a sister ship of *Thresher* launched 17 months later and due to go to sea about the time *Thresher* was lost, luckily remained in Portsmouth. The radiographs of her hull welds (required for departure clearance) turned up "missing" and may never have been taken. A new set had to be made, but the delay certainly was justified by this precaution.

5. References to increased "habitability and operability" in *Thresher* are nothing but vague generalities. It is left to Lieutenant Commander Ray McCoole (he was later promoted) to describe elsewhere his extremely favorable impression when first he reported aboard *Thresher*. She offered nearly 10 times as much space per man as did many earlier nuclear submarines. Compared with the doughty *Nautilus,* she was a floating palace. *Thresher's* color-keyed interior, concept of an interior decorator hired for the job, is not even mentioned. Nor are her vastly improved living quarters, both for officers and enlisted men. And what of the smooth, restful bulkhead and ceiling panels which hid unsightly pipelines, electrical harnesses, and associated equipment? Another ingenious novelty was in the crew's spacious quarters, where a different movie was shown every evening. By

tilting back table tops with padded undersides, and swinging them over the rocker-type seats, these became comfortable seat backs offering individual support.

There was more. *Thresher's* well-stocked library, for example, her tiled washrooms with showers, the photographic darkroom, and the elaborate washer-dryer equipment.

Reference to the "push-button" firing of weapons, by dismissing in a sentence what *Thresher* was all about, does the Navy small credit. *Thresher* had the Mk 113 torpedo fire control director, which could handle either SubRoc or anti-submarine torpedoes and put them on target with unerring accuracy. Both were fired through the same 21-inch torpedo tubes located aft of the sail and angled out at 10° from the ship's center line on either side.

SubRoc (contraction for Submarine Rocket) was and still is the most sophisticated "subsurface to subsurface" missile available to the Navy and functions precisely as its name implies. The missile travels a preset distance submerged before angling up into an air trajectory which lifts it clean out of the water and transforms it into a rocket. A solid fuel motor accelerates the rocket to supersonic speed while four jet deflectors, which function both in the water and the airborne part of the trajectory, ensure the missile's stability. When the target area is reached, a nuclear depth bomb separates from the missile and follows a ballistic path which ends with re-entry into the sea. The nuclear charge then sinks to predetermined depth when a sensor detonates it in the vicinity of the target. Anything within the orbit of a SubRoc explosion is totally disintegrated.

To give private industry its due, SubRoc uses

a Raytheon ANBQQ-2 integrated sonar detection system, the Librascope Mk 113 SubRoc fire control system and the Kearfott (SD-510) inertial guidance system.

An attack submarine, or for that matter any undersea vessel, relies heavily on its modern navigation equipment. And since most of the navigating is done in the deep, conventional surface aids such as a sextant or magnetic compass are carried only as a standby. To use a sextant, you need to get a look at the sky, while a magnetic compass does not point true north, but toward the Magnetic Pole, several hundred miles south of the North Pole. Correction is therefore made by using points of reference, but unlike a surface vessel a submarine in a deep dive has no points of reference. It is totally "blind."

Even a passing mention of *Thresher*'s navigational aids would have put some backbone into the Navy's Fact Sheet. But there was none.

Thresher carried no navigational break-through, yet, like other ships of her class, she could find her way to a pinpoint in the ocean with two independent and highly sophisticated pieces of equipment—her gyro-compass and inertial guidance system.

A gyro-compass is a navigational aid which uses a continuously driven gyroscope turning at over 20,000 rpm. It can seek out and accurately determine the direction of true (or geographic) north. It is also immune from magnetic interference and the effects of electrical circuits. When a sub's Navigator of the Day announces the ship's position or heading in "degrees true," this refers to a gyro-compass reading. In modern slang, the ship is "right on."

Thresher's main inertial guidance system (NGA or SINS)—Ship's Inertial Navigation System—was a far more complex piece of equipment which relies on dual computers. It is, in fact, a self-contained "dead reckoning" device and the most valuable aid to submarine navigation. Since speed is seldom constant, variations in the ship's acceleration, negative or positive (as when she goes slower or faster), are integrated into the computers throughout the duration of motion. Reference axes are established by six spinning gyroscopes with offset rotors which cancel out the effect of the earth's rotation. Any deviation from this frame of reference is immediately sensed and fed into the computers, which consolidate and resolve this information into distance and direction of travel relative to a fixed point in space. SINS is invaluable for long-range missile firing or pinpoint rendezvous.

As for the "air revitalization machine" that would allow *Thresher* to "operate completely independently of the atmosphere for long periods of time," that part of the equipment designed to extract oxygen from sea water, simply was not aboard when she left on her last cruise. It was still on the pier, awaiting her return so it could be installed. *Thresher* enjoyed air conditioning but not automatic air revitalization, although this equipment already was well tried in other "nukes" at the time. The principle on which it worked remains the same today. "Used" air, loaded with impurities such as cigarette smoke, multiple odors, carbon dioxide, and so forth, is passed through carbon "scrubbers," then revitalized with the required amount of oxygen (kept in high pressure containers at 3,000 psi or manufactured from sea water). This restores its purity and freshness before recycling.

Using similar equipment, USS *Scorpion* (SSN-589) set a world's record by maintaining a sealed atmosphere for 70 consecutive days. Unfortunately *Scorpion,* a *Skip-jack* class high speed sub commissioned July 29, 1960, 13 months after *Thresher,* also was lost with all hands. On May 21, 1968, some 400 miles southwest of the Azores, while en route from the Mediterranean to Norfolk, Virginia, *Scorpion* disappeared with 99 men aboard. She presumably made her routine 0800 check-in report to the operational commander, ComSubLant on the 21st, but after that nothing more was heard. *Scorpion* was therefore assumed not to have been disabled on the surface but submerged. This triggered another massive search of *Thresher*-like proportions, and five months later her relatively intact hull was located, photographed, and identified by undersea cameras in 10,000 feet of water.

As in *Thresher*'s case, the reason why she foundered (officially) remains a mystery. If she was ever refitted in accordance with the post-*Thresher* submarine safety program, this fact was kept under wraps. While the Navy admitted that *Scorpion* had "several technical problems," it considered these "classified" and released no information beyond reference to a rusty whip (antenna) and a leak in the propeller shaft. The other undisclosed problems allegedly were covered by "backup systems," yet the possibility that *Scorpion* collided with an undersea reef or volcanic sea mount is negligible.

Compared with the number of such obstacles in the eastern and central equatorial Pacific which rise up to more than 3,000 feet from the sea bed, those in the Atlantic are very few. Besides, the depth at which *Scorpion* settled was about nine times greater than her operational depth and three times greater than many of the highest Pacific undersea mounts. At all events, *Scorpion* ranks as the second greatest nuclear submarine disaster in the history of the U. S. Navy, and also the second greatest in loss of life.

6. Aside from at least one glaring inaccuracy which should have been corrected by the Navy before release of its *Thresher* Fact Sheet, some of the "information" appearing under "General Characteristics" is an affront even to a reader with no technical interest. Long before *Thresher* went to sea on her builder's trials, it was common knowledge that the operating or "test" depth for this class of vessel would be at least 1,000 feet. And that would be saying nothing of a 300-foot margin designed into the ship's hull by the builder as a sort of "safety bonus." Many World War II diesel subs were known to have survived a depth of 600 feet with no ill-effects. *Thresher* class deep-diving ships were designed (if not always built) to withstand double that sea water pressure against their hulls. To refer to *Thresher*'s operating depth as "deepest in the world" was therefore nonsense.

A parallel absurdity is found in the Fact Sheet's estimated speed of "over 20 knots." This is like saying that a 100-mph car has a speed of "over 50 mph," or a 600-mph jet can travel at "over 300 mph." One writer got around this charade neatly by stating that *Toro*, an immediate post-War diesel sub, had a surface speed of 20 knots while *Thresher* could move almost twice as fast underwater.

The final error on which this Fact Sheet signs off concerns *Thresher*'s complement. It was not eight officers and 75 enlisted men, but, as we have seen, 12 officers and 96 enlisted men.

THRESHER'S 625 DAYS

August 3—October 15, 1961

The USS *Thresher* (SSN-593) turned out to be something more than the tragic forerunner of a new line of nuclear attack submarines staggering in their complexity. Several other appalling distinctions will forever be associated with her name. She ended up as the worst submarine disaster of all time, claiming far more lives in her last plunge than had ever happened before or has happened since. She had the shortest actual service span of any submarine built in peacetime—certainly any nuclear submarine. And she amortized her basic cost at a daily rate that was absolutely staggering.

Thresher's commissioned life was only 625 days (August 3, 1961, to April 10, 1963), and of this she spent 406 days (nearly 65 per cent of her time) either moored to a pier or resting on keel blocks in dry dock while undergoing repairs and overhauls that lasted from 24 hours to 10 months. That in itself must surely constitute something of a record in inefficiency, poor workmanship and ill-luck.

Another contributory factor could have been faults "built into" the ship because of undue haste. In May 1960, 14 months prior to her actual launch, *Thresher* had the dubious distinction of being placed on the Bureau of Ships' Master Urgency List. This meant that the Department of Defense gave her top priority in labor and raw materials. "Get that ship out as quickly as possible," was the keynote.

At all events, *Thresher* was actively engaged in the sophisticated duties for which she had been designed, during a period of only 211 days. Taking into account only her basic construction cost of $45 million (and this is considered an absolute minimum for a *Permit* Class attack sub), she amortized her purchase price at the rate of $213,270 per day! And that is saying nothing of the cost of repairs and overhauls, supplies and spares, crew's pay, and countless other "incidentals." Nor the tremendous sums spent by the Navy in locating and identifying her broken hull on the sea bed, at a depth at least 10 times greater than that at which contemporary salvage equipment could possibly have brought out anyone alive.

As if that were not enough, *Thresher* was at various

times involved in 24 incidents and one accident during her brief commissioned life span. Included in this total were 11 fires, six of which broke out while she was underway, and five more during her extended periods in dry dock. Among the mishaps which did not involve fires, *Thresher* was rammed by a tug at Port Canaveral, Florida; subjected to shock tests of incredible violence off Key West (thanks to a navigational error), and turned into a blast furnace in Puerto Rico due to the total and simultaneous failure of her entire electrical equipment while her reactor was shut down.

Can *Thresher* be called a "jinxed" ship? In terms of hindsight, it would certainly appear so, yet following the two serious piping failures during her (precommissioning) builder's trials, nothing occurred which specifically pointed a finger at the causes of her catastrophic end. At least to the extent that Commander Dean L. Axene spelled out in a letter to BuShips exactly what it was about *Thresher* that caused him to have serious misgivings about her ultimate safety, he must be called a wonderfully perceptive commanding officer. He did not spare *Thresher* in any way, but through reading her Deck Log you get the distinct feeling that Axene's guard was up every minute of the time. He was keenly aware of the weaknesses in *Thresher*'s salt water piping system during deep dives, and he knew also that the deballasting capabilities of the ship were, at best, a tightrope operation that could not be counted on to extricate her from a flooding situation in the deep. Only power could do that, so Axene was extremely sensitive to the trim of his ship and preferred to "drive her under" with minimum negative buoyancy, hold her submerged with controlled power and bring her back up the same way, rather than depend on the intake or displacement of large quantities of water ballast.

McCoole has spoken of Commander Axene and *Thresher*'s crew as a "close-knit team," and that was a very apt description. Axene, because of his outstanding competence, demanded a lot from his men, both officers and enlisted, but one and all knew that it was not a "Captain Bligh" thing. It was an attempt to thoroughly familiarize them with the quirks and complexities of the U. S. Navy's most advanced killer sub. To that end, Axene kept the ship's company hopping during every moment of each Watch, and where *Thresher* was not being put through some prescribed exercise or maneuver, her skipper came up with an endless succession of drills. For example, there were fire, collision and man-overboard drills; flooding and "major steam leak" drills. There were fire control tracking parties and a simulated reactor "scram," or shut down might suddenly occur without any prior warning—just to test the crew's reaction to this situation and find out how quickly they could "answer bells" (react to Control Room commands) on EPM—Electric Propulsion Mode with the main turbine out of action. Sometimes, Axene would go through this "reactor scram" drill twice running within a very short time, or at least what seemed like it. There were exercises for helmsmen and chartermen. There was training for planesmen and for emergency ventilation of the ship. The sonar men, electrical gangs, enginemen, and torpedomen go through their paces at a word of command. Underwater navigation with Axene was not just a routine function, but an exact science that left absolutely no room for error.

There was a rigorous daily inspection of the ship's

magazines and pyrotechnic lockers. Less frequently, but
at unexpected times, tests were made of the magazine
sprinkler and flooding systems. As a rule, the crew was
mustered at quarters almost immediately the *Thresher*
sailed out of any port, but this roll call might also take
place miles from any shore, right in the middle of a
cruise.

However, the adventure and excitement—the exploring of new depths, the achievement of unheard-of speeds,
the long submerged periods, and the variety of interesting
places visited by *Thresher* during her brief career—in-
evitably bring to mind the nostalgic thought expressed
by Edna St. Vincent Millay: "My candle burns at both
ends; it will not last the night; But, ah, my foes, and,
oh, my friends—it gives a lovely light."

Thresher's Chronology (Appendix 17, Hearings before the Joint Committee, Eighty-eighth Congress) has
all the glamour of a layer of accumulated dust in a forgotten attic. But it was not that way at all.

"August 3–September 24, 1961, assigned to the Submarine Force Atlantic Fleet."

Thresher's Deck Log already has much to say about
that period. She did not get underway for her first real
cruise until August 10, a week after her commissioning,
but during that interval a number of interesting events
took place. For five days after the formal commissioning
ceremony, *Thresher* remained moored at Berth 6A,
Portsmouth Naval Shipyard, yet already things were
beginning to hum. On August 5, Seaman Kenneth C.
Janes of the ship's original company, went AWOL at
0600 and didn't return until 0005 (five minutes after
midnight), August 6. He was the first to disobey orders
aboard *Thresher*, although that day the help of every

officer and crewman was needed to cope with the onrush of 450 visitors which began at 0900 and ended at 1700.

One can imagine the meticulous preparation to shepherd a vast number of curious and well-wishing people through a brand-new submarine, as rapidly (yet as politely) as possible. There was only one way to handle this kind of situation. The tour was carefully guide-roped off through those parts of the ship which the public was permitted to see, and there was no departing from this itinerary. A careful watch was kept to protect *Thresher* from the possible depredations of souvenir hunters, using much the same unobtrusive tactics as store detectives. In addition, every gauge, dial, or panel that could possibly reveal information was covered with a leather apron. And of course, since a crowd this size was bound to include some technically minded gentry, the order was given to answer all queries with vague generalities or total disclaimers. "I'm awfully sorry, sir, but I know nothing about this equipment. I'm stationed in another part of the ship." Or, "*Thresher*'s brand new, sir, and we're all having to learn." If an enlisted man succeeded in convincing a visitor that his level of competence was lower than that of his questioner, all went well. If not, he could always refer the matter to an officer, who in turn smilingly invoked that time-honored cliché, "I'm very sorry, but that's classified information."

Roping off a prescribed route was the easiest way to keep nosy parkers from those parts of the ship which were out of bounds, without giving offense, but even so, there were some funny (and perilous) moments when zealous crewmen attempted to shepherd arthritic or overweight elderly ladies up and down the almost vertical companionways.

All in all, however, *Thresher*'s first open house, which lasted eight hours, was an unqualified success. There were countless "Aah's" and "Ooh's!" at the luxurious appointments and handsome décor of the giant sub, where people usually conditioned to the spartan interiors of U-boats had imagined nothing but steel plates, nuts and bolts and cradled torpedoes.

"You mean you have an ice-cream machine?"

"And color movies?"

And of course there was the joker who never fails to ask the one question calculated to drive Admiral Rickover straight up a tree: "Tell me, with all this atomic power, isn't there the danger of an explosion?"

On August 8, *Thresher* sustained her first casualty. Joseph H. Hoague, Torpedoman's Mate 2nd Class, injured his back in an unscheduled fall when he stepped through the first platform loading hatch, while making a below-decks inspection. Hoague was treated by the Medical Officer, Lieutenant Arthur L. Rehme, and returned to duty. In Naval parlance, the crewman's accident was not due to his "misconduct." Hoague, who was on the original enlisted commissioning crew, later left *Thresher* but returned December 2, 1962, and eventually went down with the ship.

Next day, *Thresher* made her initial commissioned sortie with full crew in "local operational areas." She got underway at noon and was back, moored starboard side to Berth 6A, Portsmouth Naval Shipyard, by 1840. During this brief cruise, which lasted 6 hours 40 minutes, *Thresher* steamed only 57 miles and made two or three shallow dives. She fired dummy signals, four water slugs and a dummy beacon, testing her forward and aft signal ejectors, normally used in case of distress.

Her maximum speed was a modest 10 knots. Her authority was COMSUBLANT Administrative Order 12-61.

Thresher's first of eight full-scale operational trips that made up her tragically short life was an interesting foray. It took her to the warm and languid climes of the Grand Bahama Banks—specifically to the crystal clear waters of the Tongue of the Ocean (TOTO), east of Andros Island.

This body of water has been so named because of the odd configuration of the ocean bed, which, when viewed from north to south, forms the shape of a tongue. Isolated and inaccessible to ordinary shipping, it is 100 nautical miles long and about 15 miles wide. It varies in depth from 3,600 feet in the south to 6,000 feet in the north and can be likened to a gigantic coral bathtub with sudden, immensely steep drops and only one access channel. Here are located three ranges installed by Atlantic Undersea Test and Evaluation Center (AUTEC) contractors, a joint Anglo-American venture of enormous importance to the development and sophistication of undersea warfare elements. Included are submarines, missiles, listening and tracking devices.

The "hardware" end of AUTEC consists of three separate ranges: the Weapons, Acoustics and Sonar Ranges. The Weapons Range, southernmost of the three, provides an instrumented corridor equipped with hydrophones, which make possible the accurate, three-dimensional tracking of any object appearing in this area. Whether a ship or submarine, its location is precisely computed and displayed in real time on a large control board at the AUTEC Data Processing Center. The simultaneous tracking and position display of multiple targets is possible, and even in-air weapons or aircraft are optically tracked by radar.

The Acoustics Range, slightly north of the Weapons Range, was designed to help the U.S. and British Navies acquire valuable data which enables them to build quieter, less easily detected ships—especially submarines. Here is a Tracking Array equipped with hydrophones which accurately measure ship noise such as propellers, hulls and engines. The Tracking Array also has hydrophones which pick up signals sent out by a "pinger" located in the nose of a test submarine. Information as to the exact location of the ship and the direction in which it is moving passes through an Acoustic Data Processor.

The Sonar Range is situated between the Acoustic Range and the eastern shore of Andros Island. Its purpose is to enable ships to check the accuracy of their own sonar suits—their means of determining the distance and position of underwater objects. This is known as sonar calibration and is of tremendous importance to the modern nuclear attack sub.

The "hardware" end of AUTEC, off Andros Island, is 177 miles east of West Palm Beach, where the headquarters of this organization are located (see map). Here the paperwork (or software) is generated.

Because of its stringent requirements, TOTO was not easy to find. It had to meet nine basic prerequisites. Isolation from shipping lines. Low ambient background noises. Deep water close to land. Adequate space for the free operation of ships, submarines, and weapons. Year-round working conditions with minimal sea states (storms, tides, etc.). Stable undersea environment (freedom from violent currents). Proximity to the continent.

Location in a sparsely inhabited area. Finally, controllable access.

It took five years of searching to find the right place before an agreement was reached between the United States and United Kingdom with the concurrence of the Bahamian Government. Six more years (1963–69) were needed to complete the installation of these facilities and make joint use of them.

What better place to test the newest and most lethal attack submarine in the U. S. Navy? The TOTO ranges still needed a vast amount of work, but two immediately available benefits were privacy and seclusion in which to carry out tests.

Thresher departed Portsmouth August 10, 1961, and reached her destination after a leisurely and interesting six-day journey. During that time she racked up a number of "firsts" that offered much promise. She cruised at "over" 20 knots, dived "below" 400 feet, made an active sonar contact and on August 12 remained submerged for 24 hours. Provision was made for her to extract oxygen from sea water at will by means of a fuel cell. So equipped her subsurface cruising capacity would be virtually unlimited. Or it would be limited only by logistics and the psychological ability of the crew to live underwater in close proximity for long periods without becoming overly irritable.

August 15, *Thresher* surfaced in the Tongue of the Ocean and came to a stop while a small boat, the *Lord Kelvin,* drew alongside and transferred two VIP's aboard. They were Vice Admiral E. B. Taylor, COMASFORLANT (Commander Anti-Submarine Forces, Atlantic), who broke his flag in this vessel, and Vice Admiral E. W. Grenfell, Commander Submarine Force,

Atlantic, together with aides. About four hours later, seemingly satisfied, both admirals again boarded the *Lord Kelvin* and departed.

Parenthetically, while extremely poor, Andros Island is a climatic paradise. It has no paved roads, one small store, a bank, and one plush hotel. There are practically no private dwellings outside the base, but the beaches are marvelous, and the big black manta rays lazing close to the surface on the coral reefs resemble great bats when seen from a helicopter.

At that time, Range Support facilities were still a thing of the future, but *Thresher* seemed to have a pretty good time of it, "casing the joint," until August 16, the seventh day of her initial cruise. Then, as she steamed submerged along the Grand Bahama Banks, *Thresher* suffered two incidents in quick succession. First, a leak in the high-pressure air system which took an hour to repair. About 50 minutes later, a high-pressure air line severed in the Torpedo Room, and this too had to be fixed.

Commander Axene put his ship through various sound tests and even secured for "Quiet Condition Three," the most stringent antidetection silencing measures that can be taken in a modern sub. Virtually everything nonessential, or which can transmit any noise into the sea, is switched off, including electric propulsion.

August 19 brought another quota of disruptive events. Seaman Kenneth C. Janes, was convicted by summary court-martial for his unauthorized absence from 0600 on August 5, 1961, to 0005, August 6, and for failing to obey a regulation in violation of Article 86, UCMJ (Uniform Code, Military Justice). Sentence: 21 days' restriction. No shore leave for three weeks. Of all the punishments that can be visited on a submariner for misconduct, loss of shore leave is the one he hates and dreads most. Axene (as will be observed) was more than fair, but he left no one in doubt as to who was the boss aboard *Thresher*.

Three hours later, (1921) a fire broke out in the Wardroom, next to the CO's stateroom on the second level of the midship compartment (see Inboard Profile). The fire was located in No. 1 hot water heater control and was soon isolated and put out. Later that day, *Thresher* resumed her exercise at depths exceeding 400 feet. Even at this early date, there are many Deck Log entries signed by Lieutenant William T. Hussey.

On August 23, *Thresher* left TOTO for Newport, Rhode Island, running submerged for another 24 hours at an increased speed of 20 knots. On August 25, she covered the greatest distance (submerged for 24 hours). She steamed 448 miles (an average of 18.7 mph, or 17 knots). Two days later, *Thresher* made rendezvous with USS *Sea Owl* (SS-405) a diesel sub, and USS *Tullibee* (SSN-597), another nuclear sub. Exercises between the three ships slowed things down a bit, so the return trip to Newport took nine days, but everything went in accordance with Operational Order 15-61. On August 30, *Thresher* took part in sound trials which involved two other nuclear subs—*Skipjack* (SSN-585) and *Scorpion* (SSN-589). *Scorpion* was destined five years later to become the second greatest nuclear submarine disaster after *Thresher*.

On the last day of August 1961, *Thresher* completed her first cruise and moored at Newport, Rhode Island.

Even so, she was plagued by a second casualty at 1216, four hours after mooring. During a torpedo ship-

ping exercise, Raymond C. Mattson, Torpedoman 1st
Class, was struck on the head by a sheet of metal. The
medical officer took some stitches to the wound and returned Mattson to normal duty. He was transferred out
of *Thresher* before her last trip.

Early afternoon, September 1, *Thresher* steamed out
into Narragansett Bay, Area 12B, and practiced firing
a couple of Mark 37 torpedoes. At 2350 that night, however, the crew was mustered at quarters and another
man turned up missing, AWOL. He was Quartermaster
2nd Class George R. Townbee, who had taken the day
off since 0630 that morning. He showed up next morning at 1039, two hours after *Thresher* had docked back
at Rhode Island. Townbee chalked up several AWOL's
—which Commander Axene viewed with strong dis-
favor.

During the entire month of September, *Thresher*
made a series of brief sorties and exercises that took her
in and out of New London, Connecticut, and back to
Narragansett Bay (Operational Areas 23, 26 and 27)
for periods of three and four days at a time. A COM-
SUBREFITRAGRU order sent her on a series of torpedo tube acceptance, torpedo firing and navigation
exercises. She even fired a dummy SubRoc missile and
maneuvered on various courses and at various speeds
and depths, an entry which is repeated countless times
in the Deck Log.

On September 8, the CO "held a Mast" and imposed
"nonjudicial punishment" on George R. Townbee for his
unauthorized absence. He was restricted to the limits
of the ship for 14 days.

Seaman Dudley W. Smokes had gone AWOL for 2
hours 25 minutes on September 5, while *Thresher* was

in the Newport Naval Base. He received the same punishment as Townbee.

September 11, after a two-day rest in New London, *Thresher* headed for Operational Area Tango in Narragansett Bay. At 1423, another fire—a minor one—occurred in the washing machine in the crew's head. It lasted only seven minutes. Two days later, the diesel sub USS *Dogfish* (SS-350) joined in the fun, with *Thresher* acting as target and taking evasive action. *Dogfish* was followed by the nuclear submarine *Skate* (SSN-578) on September 19. Next day, *Thresher* again dived to below 400 feet. Axene, obeying a series of COMSUBDEVGRU orders, didn't let up for a moment. He put *Thresher* and her as yet unseasoned crew through every conceivable maneuver.

There was another Mast, September 23, when Machinist's Mate Roy J. Liverer, was reduced to the next inferior rate for larceny of twenty-three dollars, in violation of Article 21, UCMJ. Axene tempered justice with mercy by suspending the sentence for 60 days.

Next day, *Thresher* ended her second cruise at 1322, when she moored to the starboard side of Berth 6A, Portsmouth Naval Shipyard, Portsmouth, New Hampshire. She was about to undergo a fairly lengthy overhaul, and Commander Axene, mindful of his men's well-being, requested that this period of in-port upkeep be moved from New London, the ship's home port, to Portsmouth, since most of the dependent families were still living there.

In the event, this gave the crew a great many more opportunities of being home with their families than would otherwise have been possible. *Thresher*'s overhaul began September 25, 1961, while she was moored.

Three days later, she went into dry dock No. 2 and remained on keel blocks for a period of 12 days, being refloated October 10. She stayed moored for another five days and did not get underway again until Monday, October 16. Her total period of inactivity was, therefore, 21 days. Even so, George R. Townbee perhaps felt he was a little short on liberty. October 7, since he was supposed to be a member of the duty section (2000–2400) and could not be located, a search of the entire ship was made for him. Lieutenant jg John Smarz reported Townbee as missing. He returned on Sunday, October 8, having again gone AWOL from 2130 Saturday till 0600 Sunday.

The Commanding Officer was less than pleased with this state of affairs, and on Friday, October 13, with *Thresher* back at her mooring, he held another Mast. It was not an auspicious date and this time George R. Townbee, described as a "chronic absentee" in that he had twice gone AWOL (the second time for 8 hours 30 minutes), had the boom lowered on him. He was reduced to the next inferior grade—QM-3.

The very next day, a muster of the crew held at 0745, revealed another absentee. He was Torpedoman's Mate 2nd Class Edmond P. Bither. He was back on board by 2240 the same day, 15 hours 30 minutes later, but the inevitable Mast awaited him.

THRESHER'S 625 DAYS
October 16, 1961—February 2, 1962

One would think that San Juan, Puerto Rico, was an unlikely place to send a nuclear submarine on a cruise. But it doesn't take much digging to find out why COM-SUBDEVGRU-2, Operational Order 17-61, chose this unlikely spot as the destination for *Thresher*'s next trip.

Puerto Rico, though only 113 miles long and 41 wide, is part of the major island group of the West Indies which marks the broken northern boundary between the Caribbean and the Atlantic. San Juan, its capital, is the oldest city under the U.S. flag. Its population at the time of *Thresher*'s visit was nudging 600,000, mostly of Spanish origin, with some admixture of Negro and Arawak Indian. The island's population of over 700 people per square mile is one of the world's densest. When, in 1508, Ponce de León, that dashing and famous explorer, revisited the almost perfectly protected harbor, it was called Villa de Caparra and was located opposite the present site of San Juan. León renamed the harbor Puerto Rico (Rich Port), but gradually the name extended to cover the whole island, while the port became known as San Juan.

The architecture of San Juan is predominantly Spanish—narrow cobbled streets, low terraced houses, baroque styling—but offers visitors everything they could wish. Casino, Yacht Club, horse racing, private country clubs, and night baseball with big league players. Year-round average temperature is 76°F., slightly higher than Florida's so-called "Platinum Coast."

In metropolitan San Juan, living conditions for the upper and middle classes are about equal to those in the United States. That would certainly please the crew of a brand-new nuclear super sub like *Thresher,* and so would the atmosphere of an island paradise. But there was more yet. Oceanographic stuff that of course the U. S. Navy knew by heart. Puerto Rico and the other Greater Antilles are formed by the high parts of what was once a 1,300-mile chain of mountains, whose base and bulk aeons ago sank deep beneath the sea. In fact, the waters adjacent to Puerto Rico are in places staggeringly deep. About 55 miles to the southwest, the Caribbean reaches a depth of more than 17,000 feet. To the northwest, along the direct 1,500-mile route to New York, is the famous Puerto Rico Trench (formerly known as the Bronson Deep). This plunges down to 30,246 feet and must surely come second after the Marianas Trench in the Pacific.

It's a sad coincidence that on a high bluff, guarding the entrance to San Juan's almost landlocked harbor, is Morro Castle, after which was named the passenger liner that caught fire at sea in 1934. Beached at Asbury Park, New Jersey, the *Morro Castle* continued to burn, taking 134 lives.

It was also a sad coincidence that, during her stay in San Juan, *Thresher* became transformed into an oven that nearly cooked her crew alive, although the ship itself suffered little if any damage. But for all those aboard who looked forward to liberty in San Juan as the idyllic end of a beautiful cruise, a rude and painful shock awaited them.

During the two days before she departed for San Juan (October 16 and 17) *Thresher* desported herself in Boston Operational Areas 5 and 7A, conducting sound tests. At 0320 on the morning of Tuesday, October 17, she surfaced and thereafter made a note of weather conditions. Visibility was good that day at 15 to 17 miles. There were broken clouds with a ceiling of 2,500 feet, varying between six- and nine-tenths. Water temperature was 45 to 53°F. Waves were about four feet high. *Thresher* steamed 98 miles before mooring back, starboard side, to Berth 6A at Portsmouth Naval Shipyard. The time was 1345.

Next morning, at 0735, *Thresher* got underway for San Juan. She steamed 217.3 miles that day and 343.2 miles the next. This was October 19, when at 1155 *Thresher* made rendezvous with USS *Cavalla* (SS-244), a Gato Class diesel-electric submarine, which was to accompany her all the way to San Juan, Puerto Rico. On Friday, October 20, at 1701, Commander Axene gave the order to "rig for deep submergence." This meant *Thresher* should make ready to go down to any depth—1,000 feet or beyond. Carrying out this order involved one specific maneuver in which the ballast trim and drain pump systems were shifted from parallel to series operation. The purpose was to increase air pressure output and shut off sea water systems not essential for operating the ship.

Saturday, October 21, the CO held a Mast for Torpedoman Bither's AWOL, which cost the offender a reduction to the next inferior grade. However, once again Commander Axene suspended sentence—this time for six months. *Thresher* then started calibration runs for USS *Cavalla*, and by midnight covered 203.2 miles.

On Sunday, *Thresher* suffered her first casualty during the San Juan run. At 1926, Seaman Steve Day was lowering the garbage disposal unit when the breech door unlatched and fell on his left hand. He received multiple lacerations of the third and fourth fingers, but luckily no fracture, artery, or tendon damage was involved. Day was treated by the medical officer and placed on the sick list, suffering great pain despite an injection. The day's Log was signed by Lieutenant Commander Raymond E. Engle, then *Thresher*'s Engineer Officer and one of the many among the original crew who were transferred out before she sank.

Playing war games with *Cavalla*, *Thresher* steamed only 107.3 miles on Sunday. Monday she was submerged the whole 24 hours and covered 229.4 miles.

October 25, *Thresher* varied her speed between five and "over" 20 knots, fired a Day-Glo plug from her af-

ter signal gun, conducted an exercise with *Cavalla* called
an S4T firing run, and fired at least two Mk 37
dummy torpedoes. She also went through a "hold contact" sonar exercise while *Cavalla* took evasive action.

Three days later, *Thresher* detached herself from USS
Cavalla and proceeded independently in accordance
with her operational order. Since she left Portsmouth on
October 18 and did not moor in San Juan Harbor until
Thursday, November 2, the trip took her 16 days, which
was a pretty leisurely pace. She could easily have done
it in less than four.

There were, however, one or two other Deck Log
notations worth a mention. October 29, while *Thresher*
was steaming submerged at 11 knots, a "somewhat serious mishap" occurred when at 1840 her trim system
went out of commission. This meant that a precise
amount of ballasting or deballasting (to give her the required degree of buoyancy) was no longer possible.

No one knew better than Axene how critical the submerged trim of a high-speed nuclear submarine like
Thresher could be, yet he ordered the ship to continue
at her set depth while repairs were being effected. They
took 4 hours 38 minutes and so must have been somewhat involved, but finally the job was done. Unper-
turbed, the captain then ordered various changes of
depth so that the planesmen could get some training.

On November 1, the last full day of the cruise, Commander Axene held another Mast, this time on Bryan
McDermitt (Interior Communications Electrician, 2nd
Class). Offense: Violation of Article 91, UCMJ, in
that he willfully disobeyed the order of a chief petty officer and used disrespectful language. Punishment: reduced to the next inferior grade, but the sentence was

again suspended, this time for two months. Despite the
care taken in choosing low-keyed individuals not easily
provoked or bothered with personality conflicts, there's
no way of knowing what personal problem a crewman
may bring aboard, bottled up inside him. This condition, aggravated by the close proximity of other men,
also working in close confines for long periods, is a potential powder keg. Once in a while it causes an explosion that might not occur on a surface ship.

On the morning of November 2, 1961, at 0933,
Thresher moored to portside of Pier Fernandez Junos
Bravo in downtown San Juan, Puerto Rico. Within 17
minutes, her playmate, the faithful USS *Cavalla,* was
moored outboard to the starboard side of *Thresher.* At
1020, as the crew looked forward to some well-earned
liberty in colorful San Juan, the ship was rigged for reduced electrical power, and 15 minutes later her reactor
was shut down to "subcritical."

Normally, electrical power for the ship's needs is supplied by cable from the pier while she remains moored
in port. However, since San Juan did not have this
facility, *Thresher* started carrying the electrical load on
her diesel engine which operated a generator. Lights,
air conditioning, and reduced "housekeeping" chores
were the demands made on this generator, which normally could have coped with ease.

At 2250 that night, however, some 10 hours 15
minutes after starting up, *Thresher*'s diesel engine quit.
The duty section of the second Blue Watch, 2000–2400,
did not immediately pinpoint the trouble. They thought,
at first, that the diesel's salt water cooling system had
become clogged up from saline deposits. In fact, the
problem was more serious. A broken pump shaft was

putting the whole system out of commission. Since the diesel could no longer get any cooling, its very high compression ratio quickly caused it to overheat.

The Officer of the Watch, Lieutenant Commander Mike Di Nola (by then promoted), ordered electricity drawn from *Thresher*'s second backup system—her vast array of storage batteries down on the fourth deck (Frame 40)—while the diesel was being repaired. Since their installation, these batteries had never shown themselves able to take in a full charge. There was nothing like enough "juice" to run the generator while the pump was being fixed. And this in itself was a difficult job.

Axene at once gave permission to restart the reactor, for then, as soon as steam became available, the two small turbines driving the SSTG's (Ship's Service Turbo-Generators) units would provide all the electricity needed. But this was a process liable to take several hours, and meantime *Thresher*'s interior temperature began to soar. There was actually not even enough electricity in the batteries to get the reactor started, and none to spare even for activating the ship's vital circuitry—let alone provide lighting, ventilation, or air conditioning.

In the absence of any air circulation through the ship's crowded interior, and because of the tremendous heat stored by the reactor's steam system, the temperature rapidly soared from 90° to 136°F. At this point the Engine Room duty crew were working stripped to the waist, with perspiration streaming off them. Conditions approximated those of a Turkish bath. Salt sweat got in the men's eyes, blurring their vision. They became dehydrated and dizzy. Their pulse rate went up. Outside, the warm Caribbean night with its still and romantic air did nothing to help matters.

At 2300, Engineman 2nd Class D. J. McCall was overcome by heat exhaustion "due to the high temperature and humidity in the Engine Room spaces." McCall was given first aid, then taken to the Naval Station Hospital in San Juan for "further treatment and observation."

Within 15 minutes "all personnel not necessary for correcting the casualty" was evacuated from the ship. Four men, however, stuck it out to the bitter end under appalling conditions, earning themselves well-deserved Navy Commendation medals. They were Chief Machinist's Mate Donald Wise; Electronics Technician Paul R. Tobler; Electrician's Mate John J. Alaimo and Engineman Ralph W. Gould.

Fortunately, the faithful *Cavalla, Thresher*'s playmate on that long trip to Puerto Rico, quickly came to the rescue. She borrowed electrical cables from the USS *Cadmus* (AR-14), a Vulcan Class repair ship which also happened to be in San Juan Harbor. *Cavalla* was moored close enough to *Thresher* to be able to use those cables as "jumpers" in the same way that a car with a live battery helps another with a flat one. (The cables are clamped in parallel and the healthy battery provides the spark.) *Cavalla* made up the required electrical connections with *Thresher*, then started her diesels to give the crippled sub the electricity she desperately needed.

At 0345, November 3, there was another casualty aboard *Thresher*. Engineman 1st Class R. W. Gillette also was overcome by heat exhaustion due to unendurable conditions "in the Engineering Spaces." Gillette responded to emergency treatment, but obviously things weren't going well aboard *Thresher*.

Finally, at 0402 the reactor was brought back to criti-

cal, high pressure steam became available, and while
one SSTG began recharging the moribund batteries, the
other got the electrical system functioning again. Naturally, there was always the chance that the soaring temperature and heavy condensation might have damaged
some of *Thresher*'s sensitive electrical equipment, but
as it happened, Commander Axene's worries were un-
founded. As soon as the lights came on and the air conditioning began to function full blast, *Thresher*'s interior
quickly returned to normal as the temperature took a
nose dive.

To make up for this unscheduled trouble, *Thresher*
prolonged her stay in San Juan another two days so that
her crew might enjoy some liberty. USS *Cavalla* remained
dutifully moored alongside *Thresher,* to starboard, but
her assistance was no longer required. Finally, Monday,
November 6, 1961, at 1547, *Thresher* got underway
again. The captain was at the Conn, the Officer of the
Deck (OOD) on the bridge and the Navigator, Lieutenant Commander Robert D. Rawlins (who was also the
Executive Officer), in the ship's Control Center. She set
a course of 325°, and by 2312, with her batteries re-
charged, *Thresher* submerged to 200 feet and set a
speed of 20 knots.

Not until the next day did the crew learn of their destination, though they made a pretty good guess at it. The
ship was heading for Cape Canaveral, Florida. Still at
a depth of 200 feet, but now on a course of 318° true,
she remained submerged throughout the day. *Thresher*'s
Deck Log for November 1961 is a substitute one. The
original got lost in the mail, but all the main events for
that month were carefully reconstructed, with the exception of the weather charts. A note to that effect was later

entered by Lieutenant Commander Raymond E. Engle, at that time *Thresher*'s Engineer Officer. No doubt, much of the material was culled from the Quartermaster's Log—a far more complete and detailed document now reposing on the sea bed.

Thursday, November 9, at 1359, four days after her departure from San Juan, *Thresher* moored portside to Pier 1, Port Canaveral, Florida. Between November 11 and 18 she moved about quite a bit, carrying out exercises in the Cape Canaveral Operational Areas, then going on to Port Everglades. While at Cape Canaveral, November 14, Quartermaster 2nd Class, Glenn A. Rountree was hurt. While returning from liberty, Rountree stepped through an open deck plate and fell 15 feet from the first to the third platform decks. Injuries included lacerations and contusions of the head and right shoulder. He was attended to by the ship's doctor and transported by ambulance to the USAF Hospital, Patrick AFB, Cocoa Beach, Florida. At 1747, *Thresher* was again underway, this time to Port Everglades. That day she covered 208 miles in 7 hours 13 minutes, an impressive average of over 18 knots, but far from her maximum sustained capability.

November 16 and 17, maneuvering in local operational areas, *Thresher* fired off four SubRoc missiles she had picked up from the local Naval Ordnance Laboratory. These were instrumented dummies, the same size as the real thing, but without propellant or warheads. The purpose of their launching was to test out *Thresher*'s four torpedo tubes and the compressed air system used to eject these deadly missiles. On Thursday, 13 civilian guests were invited aboard to witness this exercise and were then transferred back to a retriever ship which came alongside. Friday there were no visitors. The ordnance men appeared satisfied. Saturday, *Thresher* made a sortie from Port Everglades but was back at Pier 3 by 1446. Sunday, she went out again and fired two more SubRoc dummies and two Mk 37 Exercise Mines with satisfactory results. The timetable was now complete, and on Monday, November 20, at 0839, *Thresher* began her journey back to Portsmouth, New Hampshire. At 2130 that same day, Lieutenant John S. Lyman relieved Lieutenant Commander R. D. Rawlins as Navigator. Rawlins had plenty of other problems to worry about.

It took *Thresher* 10 uneventful days to reach her home port, but Commander Axene made them busy days and above all indulged his favorite pastime of running submerged. The Log went like this:

Monday, Nov. 20: steamed 112.3 miles.

Tuesday, Nov. 21: 183.4 miles. Conducted stability trials.

Wednesday, Nov. 22: 242.2 miles. Submerged 24 hrs.

Thursday, Nov. 23: 263 miles. Stability trials. Submerged 24 hrs.

Friday, Nov. 24: 274 miles. Submerged 24 hrs.

Saturday, Nov. 25: 149 miles. Submerged fourth straight day. Steamed at various depths. Conducted more stability trials.

Sunday, Nov. 26: 213 miles. Submerged fifth day.

Monday, Nov. 27: 231.4 miles. Surfaced at 2124 because of fire in No. 1 high pressure air compressor. Some 48 minutes later, submerged again and continued air-conditioning tests.

Tuesday, Nov. 28: 135.4 miles. Still submerged.
Wednesday, Nov. 29: 39.7 miles, surfaced.

At 1229, *Thresher* moored portside to Berth 11B, Portsmouth Naval Shipyard, with mooring lines doubled. Actually, since departing Port Everglades, Commander Axene had kept his ship submerged for seven consecutive days, all but 48 minutes while, repairs were made to her high-pressure air compressor. This, for a new ship, and especially since Axene was aware of the risk he took, had to be some kind of a record. Other nuclear submarines (*Scorpion, Triton*) stayed under far longer than this, but theirs were planned attempts scheduled in advance with specific over-all objectives. Axene appeared to "play it by ear."

Now began another of those overhaul periods dreaded and hated by submariners, but which seemed to consume more than two-thirds of *Thresher*'s short life.

First she was moored from November 29 through December 9, a period of 11 days, for "maintenance and repairs." But that was just the beginning. On Sunday, December 10, *Thresher* moved into dry dock and within hours was "resting on keel blocks." She remained there from December 10, 1961, through January 1, 1962, a period of 22 days. Total up to that time, 33 inactive days, plus the usual mess and confusion aboard ship, caused by gangs of workmen who taxed the crew's patience beyond all limits. Once again they set to work restoring order and cleanliness in their loved ship. The smell of wax polish blended with that of various other cleaning agents. Vacuum cleaners, electric polishers, detergents and elbow grease performed the usual miracles.

Luckily, Christmas and New Year's brightened things

up a bit as the crew all got a fair share of liberty and home was on their doorstep anyway. Still, it was galling to realize that *Thresher* was not yet rid of the seemingly endless array of glitches trailing in her wake since commissioning day.

Would she ever be?

On December 23, Commander Axene began a well-earned leave spell that took him home for Christmas and New Year's holidays. He returned from an 11-day furlough on January 2, 1962. *Thresher* had spent her first "active" Christmas undergoing an overhaul; it was to be the same thing the following Christmas, though no one of course had any inkling of it.

Meantime—and this is hard to believe—who went AWOL, December 30, 1961? None other than our friend George R. Townbee, Quartermaster 2nd Class. When, at 0745 that morning the crew mustered at quarters, Townbee was in serious trouble. On the previous day he had been awarded 25 days' confinement in Rockingham County House, Brentwood, New Hampshire, by the civil authorities. That was his sentence upon conviction on a charge of driving while under the influence of alcohol. Since *Thresher* was destined to spend another 30 days at her mooring—January 2 through February 1, 1962—Townbee was in no danger of "missing the boat," but for Commander Axene this must have been hard to swallow.

On January 2 (the day of the captain's return) more trouble developed as *Thresher* began to float clear of dry dock to return to her mooring. With only 55 minutes left of the Swing Watch, she sprang a leak. At 0705, water was reported flowing into the forward compartment escape hatch, and the crew was immediately stationed at collision quarters. This flooding situation was brought under control in less than three minutes, but during that time between 50 and 100 gallons of sea water poured into the ship and had to be pumped out again.

Finally, by 1634, *Thresher* was coaxed back (maneuvering under tug power) to Berth 11C, there to remain for another month.

January 23, 1962, at 0845, the CO again held Mast, with Townbee the first offender on the agenda. So far as the Navy was concerned, Townbee had been AWOL from 0730, December 30, 1961, to 0920, January 22, 1962, while confined by civil authorities. (It seems that he was let out two days early.) Yet Commander Axene, figuring no doubt that Townbee had already been punished, dismissed the truant with a warning. With one exception, none of this high-spirited young man's escapades was serious. He had built up an excellent seaman's record before volunteering for submarine duty. He had been a Boy Scout and was still a churchgoer, and from that time on he no longer shows up in *Thresher*'s Log as an offender.

At 0930 the same day, Paul J. Friburg, Engineman 2nd Class, was the object of a summary court-martial presided over by Lieutenant Commander Engle of the original commissioning crew. At 1300 the court-martial was reconvened to await the action of the convening authority. Two hours later, Friburg was found guilty as charged in violation of Article 92, UCMJ. Sentence: reduced to next inferior rating. Commanding officer and convening authority approved and ordered the sentence executed. Friburg's offense is not stated in the Log, nor is the sentence he received.

Finally, however, on February 2, 1962, following a two-month period of inactivity, *Thresher* once more got underway in accordance with COMSUBDEVGRU-2, Movement Order 262. Her destination was Boston Operational Area No. 5.

THRESHER'S 625 DAYS
February 3, 1962—January 31, 1963

Thresher's itinerary now became a series of local exercises in Narragansett Bay Operational Area Romeo, with several commuting trips that took her from Portsmouth to New London, Connecticut, twice, then to Earle, New Jersey, and eventually Charleston, South Carolina.

Backtracking a little, the Deck Log is brought to life with notations which clearly highlight what can happen aboard a nuclear submarine.

On February 7, while still moored in Portsmouth

Naval Shipyard, Berth 11C, *Thresher* suffered another incident. At 0915, fire broke out in the controller for No. 3 Hot Water Heater. It took five minutes to put out the blaze, and there were no casualties, but immediately following a lengthy overhaul it was something the ship could well have dispensed with.

Two days later, at 2225, *Thresher* dived to 600 feet. Since the Navy, in its profound wisdom, refuses to acknowledge that any of its "nukes" can top 20 knots or submerge to a set depth below 400 feet, this notation must be regarded as exceptional. It could have been a slip of the pen by the officer who made the Log entry.

Saturday, February 10, *Thresher* continued submerged, but at 1240 her battery charge was secured and ventilation interrupted. This was done to wipe away water caused by some heavy condensation in the Fan Room. The job took 2 hours 15 minutes, when the charging of *Thresher*'s pesky batteries was resumed.

Wednesday, February 14, *Thresher* was joined by USS *Conger* (AGSS-477), a *Tench* Class diesel sub, since scrapped, and USS *Entemedor* (SS-340), a Guppy IIA diesel sub, one of 48 converted to "Greater Underwater Propulsive Power" and given an incomplete acronym. *Thresher* used these two ships as "targets" while conducting sonar evaluation tests in accordance with Operational Order 662. She then proceeded independently in Narragansett Bay for three days before making contact with USS *Fairview* (PCE-850), an escort/rescue vessel which transferred some spare parts. *Fairview* was equipped with derricks, and part of her job was test evaluation and training. *Thresher* submerged soon after but reduced speed to keep contact with *Fairview* and run further sonar tests.

February 20, *Thresher* checked off the accuracy of her "magnesium magnetic" compass against the gyro-compass—a good thing to do once in a while. At 0314 she was released by *Fairview* but did not surface until seven minutes after midnight, February 21, still in Narragansett Bay Operational Area Romeo. The rest of that day, *Thresher* remained surfaced as she headed for New London. The ship made several torpedo tube firing tests and again charged her batteries. The Maneuvering Watch was stationed at 1505 and *Thresher* stood by in the navigation channel. An hour later she passed New London Ledge abeam and to starboard, 150 yards distant, and at 1620 was joined by the tugs YTB-438 and 548.

By 1702, *Thresher* was moored starboard side to Pier 12, U. S. Submarine Base, New London, Connecticut. She had been gone almost three weeks and now took a four-day rest, which was welcomed by the crew.

Monday, February 26, she was off again at 0829, headed for Earle, New Jersey. She submerged to 70 feet and stayed under for 11 hours while the on-board tracking stations were manned. At 1850 she made rendezvous with USS *Seawolf* (SSN-575) for a special exercise.

Seawolf, a very good nuclear sub, later fated to be one of the first ships to arrive on scene in the search for the lost *Thresher*, that day acted as target. *Thresher* simulated firing two Mk 37 torpedoes. She then proceeded independently through the night and at 1309 next afternoon moored starboard side to the south side of Pier 2N2, Naval Ammunition Depot, Earle, New Jersey.

Three days later (March 1), with *Thresher* already underway on her return journey to New London, the captain held Mast at 1620 and imposed "nonjudicial" punishment on Albert A. Stonel, Radioman 1st Class, for violating Article 92, UCMJ, and Article 4201.5 of USS *Thresher*. Punishment: reduced to pay grade E-5. Sentence suspended for six months.

The following day at 1248, while *Thresher* was moored portside to Pier 13, U. S. Submarine Base, New London, Connecticut, there was another casualty. Robert E. Johnson, Chief Torpedoman's Mate, received contusions to the left thigh and leg while handling some lines. He was taken to New London Hospital for treatment, and after being medicated and bandaged, was released for duty. Five of the ship's company named Johnson were fated to go down with *Thresher*. Robert, unfortunately, was one of them. Clean-cut, liked by all and a highly capable Executive Petty Officer, Robert Eugene Johnson had been assigned to *Thresher* since February 27, 1961 —a month before the keel was laid. He was first to qualify in this new type of attack ship and was selected as first Chief of the Boat. While holding down a responsible job concerned with all matters affecting enlisted personnel, Robert earned everyone's respect.

Monday, March 5, having taken on a load of oxygen and 20 Mk 53 submarine signal smoke flares, *Thresher* again departed New London. This time it was to be a 12-day "local" jaunt on Exercise Spex-5 in the operational area off the Virginia Capes. For six straight days (and 18 hours of the seventh day) Commander Axene ran submerged. On March 12, however, potentially serious trouble developed at 1802, and 18 minutes later *Thresher* surfaced. A flange connection of the hydraulic system had been carried away so that the ship lost control of her fairwater planes. These were quickly isolated to prevent any damage or loss of hydraulic fluid, but

while surfaced Axene ventilated the ship for good measure. At midnight, *Thresher* was still above water. Some
46 minutes later, with the damage repaired, down she
went again, resuming Spex-5. On March 13, with her
fairwater planes again functioning, *Thresher* remained
submerged and covered 198 miles. Next day, still beneath the waves, she steamed 298 miles, and on March
15, 301 miles. At 0612 the following morning, she was
moored portside to Berth 13S at the New London Submarine Base. Within hours, 17 dummy torpedoes were
taken aboard, but during the weekend the crew got some
liberty.

March 19, *Thresher* made a brief sortie to Narragansett Bay, Operational Area 30. On the day of her departure, a Monday, she kept a rendezvous with USS
Sunbird (ASR-15), a submarine rescue ship which
13 months later (while also searching the area of
Thresher's last dive) picked up some floating debris that
almost certainly belonged to the missing sub. *Sunbird,*
at this time, acted as retriever while *Thresher* fired three
torpedoes from a depth of 80 feet. The first torpedo was
picked up damaged and inoperative. The second was
undamaged and the third only slightly so. Next day,
Thresher continued firing Mk 37 torpedoes while USS
Sunbird acted as bird dog. Axene's torpedomen had a
busy day getting rid of the entire load, and the tin fish
suffered varying degrees of damage, but the crew
gained valuable experience.

Back in New London, March 21, *Thresher* loaded up
another 17 torpedoes, then took a five-day rest, moored
at Pier 13S, receiving AC shore power while her reactor
was shut down.

During her next sortie, which lasted 10 days (March 26–April 4) and again ended in New London, *Thresher* worked even harder. She played hide-and-seek with her old buddy USS *Cavalla,* and on 11 different occasions Axene took the big nuclear sub down to unspecified depths *below* 400 feet. Additional ship's complement included not only COMSUBDEVGRU-2 himself, Captain Frank A. Andrews, veteran Commander Submarine Development Group 2, but also Vice Admiral Pirie, Deputy Chief of Naval Operations, Air, and members of the ASW (Anti-Submarine Warfare) Council. COMSUBDEVGRU-2 hauled down his flag and that of Admiral Pirie was broken out.

The entries in *Thresher*'s Deck Log are meticulously signed, not only day by day, but also watch by watch. The contrast in handwriting legibility is never more apparent than on March 29, 1962, when John Smarz, Lieutenant Junior Grade, signed off the Dog Watch in a strong, neat handwriting, each letter carefully formed. Next came Lieutenant J. S. Agneau (with more of a flourish), followed by Lieutenant John E. McNish. The latter slipped in words or names that were almost illegible, as though he didn't expect anyone to read his Log entry, other than, perhaps, the skipper. Lieutenant Kenneth L. Highfill insisted on signing himself "Highfield" or "Highfeld," with a consistency that would have defied an expert. Lieutenant William T. Hussey was not much better, but it is said that a scrawled signature is often the mark of a man anxious to get on with something else, and who can argue about a young officer who within four years had made full commander?

On April 4, 1962, nearing New London during the Swing Watch, *Thresher* had another fire, this time while surfaced. At 0731 this was determined to be in the electrical breaker on the second platform deck. The breaker was isolated and no additional damage appeared. Six minutes later, Commander Axene ordered the ship ventilated and the crew secured from fire quarters. Next morning saw *Thresher* again underway, this time proceeding to Charleston, South Carolina (via Newport, Rhode Island), where she moored portside to Columbus Street after a five-day trip marked by still more trouble in what appeared to be a rash of small fires. April 8, while submerged at 58 feet, another fire broke out, this time in the Upper Level Machinery Space (indicating that it was electrical). It took one hour, nine minutes to extinguish the blaze and clean up the mess.

Early April 10, *Thresher* began a local demonstration run. Various dignitaries were welcomed aboard, headed by the Commander Submarine Flotilla 6 and the Lieutenant Governor of South Carolina. To a fortuneteller, however, this would have been a sinister date. From the moment she embarked her first visitor on that day, *Thresher* had one year and two hours left to live.

At 1533, after an impressive demonstration (various courses, depths and speeds), *Thresher* transferred her distinguished visitors to the tug *Admiral Dewey* and headed for Onslow Bay, North Carolina, arriving April 11. Later that day she was detached by COMSUBDIV-31 with orders to return independently to Charleston. She berthed there at 1901, starboard side to Pier N2, U. S. Naval Base, for an overnight stay.

Next day she was off once more, this time on course for Groton, Connecticut. The run took four days. April 16 at 0849, *Thresher* moored alongside Pier Charlie of the Electric Boat Company. At 1015, members of the staff of COMSUBDEVGRU-2 came aboard and made a below-decks inspection which lasted an hour and 15 minutes.

Then it was all over.

Thresher was about to undergo another of those interminable overhauls that plagued her short life, already liberally dotted with accidents and incidents, with fires and technical problems. This time they gave her stay in port a different, more optimistic name. "Preparations and modifications for shock testing."

In the light of what was to happen, this particular job perhaps proved a wise precaution.

April 19, *Thresher* was moved from Pier Charlie into dry dock, and an hour later was once more "resting on keel blocks." Commander Axene departed on TAD (Temporary Additional Duty) that evening, visited BuShips in Washington to discuss some of *Thresher*'s problems and was gone for 24 hours.

If we allow for three days of initial mooring, 20 days in dry dock and a further 10 days at Pier Charlie, *Thresher* spent 33 days at Groton in the expert care of the Electric Boat Company. There was the usual mustering of the crew, the routine daily inspections, and customary watches, but although everybody got some liberty and many were able to get back to Portsmouth, it was enough to drive even a saint to drink. Here were 96 enlisted men and 12 officers immobilized and forced into partial inactivity for over a month. And this was the third time since late September the previous year.

Taken very much at random, 28 of the enlisted men boasted a versatile array of spare time talents ranging from archery to woodwork, via gardening, music, photography and sports. Some were avid readers, while others liked to use their hands at creative work. Many of the outdoor skills and sports, such as golf, football, bowling, baseball, exploring, mining and forestry, ice skating, fishing and hunting unfortunately could find no outlet aboard *Thresher*. But a surprisingly high percentage of the crew did turn to off-duty hobbies, while some had highly diversified interests. Among the latter was Chief Engineman Timon J. Arsenault, an amateur radio fan of great skill. Electrician's Mate Ray O. Denny, Jr., an avid reader of books about the sea, who could turn out model ships in minute detail. Norman T. Hayes, also an Electrician's Mate, who loved photography and was adept with languages. Electronics Technician Thomas B. Johnson, who besides being a crack shot with pistol and rifle enjoyed music, sketching and historical books. Machinist's Mate George Kiesecker, avid reader, graceful dancer and an excellent musician who played the piano and organ equally well. Quartermaster Norman G. Lanouette, a cheerful extrovert with a natural talent for MC-ing the crew's social functions. Besides that, he was accomplished at the piano or with a bass fiddle or drum.

Norman's parents, owners of a Fort Lauderdale motel, entertained the entire ship's company during both her visits in 1961 and 1962. As a token of appreciation they were presented with a large picture of *Thresher*, autographed by Commander Axene and everyone aboard. There was also Internal Communications Electrician Richard H. Mann, Jr., keenly interested in antique and model cars and a bug on Civil War history.

The list could go on for pages, but how far can you go, raiding the ship's library, playing cards or chess, writing home or listening to the ship's piped music, which, if you like Beethoven, might turn out to be some kind of Rock, or vice versa?

Everything, however, comes to an end. *Thresher* now had two cruises left before that long and final overhaul which immediately preceded her end. And on each of these trips she was headed for yet more trouble.

Early Saturday, May 19, the powerful, sharklike sub finally got underway for Fort Pond Bay, Long Island, New York, arriving there two hours later. Shortly after noon, May 20, she was on her way to Fort Lauderdale, Florida, or, more precisely, Port Everglades. Four days later she docked starboard side to Berth 16, Pier 3, Port Everglades, after an uneventful journey with her speed seldom below 20 knots and often far above that.

On Friday, May 25, *Thresher* stooged around in local waters but far enough offshore to fire three dummy SubRoc missiles and two X3 mines. With the help of a retriever boat, this was all in the day's work. As has been explained, the versatile antics performed by SubRocs require a good deal of elbow room and, preferably, halfway decent weather, which is the rule rather than the exception in Florida. In fact, the weather report for that day recorded a visibility of 15 miles and the scattered cloud had a 2,000-foot ceiling. Sea waves were only six inches high!

Saturday evening, the first of *Thresher*'s crewmen became involved in a fatal accident while at liberty. His name was Joram Hernandez and he was taken to Holy Cross Hospital, Fort Lauderdale. He was dead on arrival and was not responsible for the accident.

For the next two days, *Thresher* didn't steam a single

mile but consumed 949 gallons of diesel fuel, likely trying to give her batteries a full charge.

May 28 she went out again for a day's SubRoc ejection tests. Four of these deadly guided missiles were fired in the morning and 10 Mk 37 torpedoes in the afternoon. None carried any warheads, of course. *Thresher* spent the night in Port Everglades but next morning returned to international waters and fired two more Sub-Rocs and three Mk 3 exercise mines.

Wednesday, May 30, was a day of rest, but on the last day of the month *Thresher* set off for Port Canaveral, which was then part of a busy coastline with the Gemini two-man orbital program going full blast. Several Mk 37 exercise torpedoes were fired on the way, but on June 1 at 0700 *Thresher* entered Port Canaveral.

Next day she conducted exercises with USS *Observation Island* (EAG-154), a large "Mariner" class merchant ship of 17,600 tons with a crew of 350, converted by the Navy in 1958 for use as a Miscellaneous Polaris Missile Test Ship. Also present was the USS *Thomas A. Edison* (SSBN-610), a recently commissioned ballistic missile *Ethan Allen* Class submarine.

The following morning, at 0844, while maneuvering to berth, *Thresher* was involved in still another accident which might have spelled her end there and then. The commercial tug *Hollywood* of the Port Canaveral Towing Company came up along her portside, forward, moving too quickly. She was unable to steer clear in time and her bow rammed *Thresher*, tearing a three-foot hole from one to four feet below the waterline on the forward frame to main ballast tank No. 3. Inspection revealed that the ship luckily was in no immediate danger but would need major repair before she could proceed. Commander

Axene wasted no time. Eleven minutes later, with *Thresher* moored starboard side to Berth 3, he gave orders for the immediate flooding of the starboard main ballast tank. This caused the ship to list heavily to starboard and lifted her damaged side clear of the water while repairs were made. Since no means were available for dry-docking *Thresher*, this expedient worked very well. It allowed a patch to be welded over the hole while things were generally put together from inside to keep the ship watertight.

At 2130 that evening, Commander R. E. Standard, USN, Commander Submarine Division 42, broke his flag on *Thresher* and presided over the Board of Investigation in accordance with COMSUBDEVGRU Message 1801Z, dated June 3. The board's deliberations began soon after the arc welders had finished a creditable job (some of the most skilled welders were then employed at the cape in connection with NASA's gigantic space effort), but the conclusions were not at once made known. It was clear, however, that the blame lay with the tug *Hollywood* for failing to apply enough rudder as she came up parallel with *Thresher*.

It would have taken more than this to really upset Commander Axene, although he was far from happy. Still, a careful examination of the strain gauges in the ship's hull showed no sign of distortion or other damage. As soon as the welding was completed, Axene ordered the main starboard ballast tank pumped out and the ship settled back on an even keel once more. Meantime, an operational order was received by radio, directing the ship to proceed back to Groton at once, and by 1450 next day she was on her way.

The delay upset *Thresher*'s timetable, since she had

intended to proceed directly from Port Canaveral to Key West for shock testing by depth charges. This would not now be possible until the ship had undergone a complete examination by submarine construction experts. Axene, however, made a very fast trip of it. He allowed the reactor to pump steam into *Thresher*'s powerful turbine so that she was seldom below 20 knots and often going on 30. She ran submerged most of the time, frequently at 300 feet and once in a while at 400 or deeper. The Port Canaveral welders had done a good job and luckily *Thresher* had suffered no damage the crew couldn't handle.

By June 6, *Thresher* was again moored to Pier Charlie, Electric Boat Company, Groton, Connecticut, after a rapid journey. Some idea of her speed can be gained from the 550 miles she covered on June 5. It was the equivalent of 22.87 mph (nearly 20 knots) for 24 hours continuously.

When *Thresher* moored, at 1530, a swarm of experts was waiting to come up her companionway. At their head was Electric Boat's chief hull inspector and his assistant, a welding engineer, and the heads of the radiographic department and quality control division. An hour later she was being moved into dry dock. A thorough inspection was made of all hull fittings and a new plate welded in position. On June 8, *Thresher* was underway again at 1517, headed for Exuma Sound in the Bahamas. It may be that tempers ran a bit short while in Groton, but an hour after sailing the captain held Mast on Karl P. McDonough, Torpedoman's Mate 3rd Class. The charge was a violation of Article 128 —assault. In other words, McDonough must have hauled off and punched someone. The plaintiff was not named, but the defendant was punished by reduction to the next inferior deck rate. Even in a magnificent and roomy sub such as *Thresher,* close confinement can have a cumulative effect as nerves become frayed. Karl normally was a friendly guy with a good disposition. He'd been six years with submarines and held a letter of commendation from the skipper of the USS *Barracuda,* a diesel-type target training submarine to which he had first been assigned. And he'd been with *Thresher* since February 1961, before her first sea trials. He stayed with her to the end.

Two days later, *Thresher* sighted Southeast Point of Eleuthera Island. The time was 1922. Her journey had taken only a few minutes under 52 hours. At 2115, she made rendezvous with MONAB I, (Mobile Norse Analysis Barge 1, a nonpropelled vessel, specially equipped with transducers of variable depth for conducting sound trials), and 20 minutes later, while only 3,000 yards away, she received a small boat alongside and embarked a sound survey team for the coming shock tests. They can hardly have imagined what they were headed for.

Next morning, while in Exuma Sound, *Thresher* transferred Donald Wise, Chief Machinist's Mate, and Richard J. Bartsch, Radioman 1st Class (one of the ship's original crew), to the "Bimini Express." This was a small boat from MONAB I (later to be replaced by the self-propelled MONAB II). Their skills apparently were needed. *Thresher* spent three days in Exuma Sound, conducting various trials, among them some important preshock noise tests. These were intended to pinpoint and catalogue accurately every sound transmitted by the ship into the sea—everything and anything audible relating to machinery, hull, electrical and hydraulic equipment, propeller cavitation—even the snap of rivets or the groan of steel plates under pressure. Nothing was left out, so that *after* the shock tests it would be possible to make an accurate assessment of anything that had worked loose, displaced itself even a fraction or in any manner changed *Thresher*'s "orchestration" while in motion.

Her destination was now Key West, the area where the shock testing was to take place, and at 1610, June 14, with the ship rigged for shock and submerged to a depth of only 50 feet, the first charge was detonated by a surface vessel. Underwater, and especially in the confined spaces of a submarine's steel hull, the noise of an explosion is far greater than on the surface. For safety reasons, *Thresher* stayed near the surface during these shock tests and the charge exploded either to one side or far below. But even to an expectant crew braced for the experience it was an unnerving moment. Every man aboard got a pretty good idea of what kind of hell the U-boat crews of World War II must have endured from depth charges. "Rigged for shock" means that every piece of loose gear or housekeeping equipment must be secured in such a manner that it cannot break loose when the tremendous percussion from the depth charge hits the ship.

All in all, *Thresher* came through that first experience well enough. The crew gained useful knowledge of what to expect in combat, but the intensity of the shock was deliberately kept well below the ship's ability to withstand concussion without being disabled. A total of six detonations was planned for this series of tests, but these were spaced out over 16 days (June 14 through 29, 1962), thus allowing plenty of time to evaluate how much (if any) structural or internal damage *Thresher* might sustain. After each detonation, passive sonar tests compared with the ship's original sound list told their own story.

June 15, *Thresher* entered the waters of U. S. Naval Station, Key West, Florida. At the Outer Mole she moored starboard side to USS *Bushnell* (AS-15), a large *Fulton* Class submarine tender, fully equipped to keep *Thresher* supplied and take care of all her needs. Next day the sub remained moored alongside *Bushnell*, but on June 17 conducted acoustical trials (checking for the possibility of major damage) in accordance with COMSUBRON-12, Operational Order 24-62.

On the morning of June 18 she was moored once more alongside *Bushnell*, but at 1300 next day she again underwent shock testing. No. 2 shock charge was detonated to starboard while *Thresher* was submerged at a depth of 50 feet. But this time, due to a navigation error, she steamed too close to the explosion area where, on the sea bed, a string of HBX dynamite charges were set off.

The entire testing procedure was the brainchild of the Naval Ordnance Lab, who were therefore responsible for seeing that it was carried out properly. There is, however, always the possibility that some part of a sensitive, intricate plan might miscarry, and in this case it did. Unintentionally, SS-593 came closer to the underwater detonation than was intended and, as a result, sustained a shock at least 20 per cent more powerful than that absorbed by any other submarine, before or since, not involved in actual combat. An NOL scientist (before denying his every word while in a manic state of remorse and fear) simply stated that this particular explosion rep-

resented a force of approximately half the design hard-
ness of the ship's pressure hull. Even so (and this
information came from elsewhere) the effect was stunning because of the greatly enhanced sound-carrying
capacity of water, and for a moment *Thresher's* crew
must have thought the world was coming to an end.

In explaining how it evolved its own set of numbers for
the purpose of measuring the severity of underwater
explosions, NOL stated that the actual numbers were
"classified" but had nothing to do with the familiar
Richter scale used for measuring seismographic disturb-
ances. Nor was it an evaluation in decibels. And it was
certainly not related to the so-called Mercalli scale,
which measures the intensity of an earthquake, starting
at "ground zero" and working out in a series of concen-
tric circles called iso-seismal lines. The force of the
shock apparently is, or was—for no subs have been so
tested in years—"determined by the geometry of the
explosive charge." (If this extraordinary revelation
doesn't stand the Russian Navy on its head, nothing
ever will.)

So where did the critical factor of an explosive force
20 per cent over safe test pressure come in? An admiral,
who though unconnected with the NOL project seemed
to have a pretty good idea of the score, expressed himself thus: "It would probably be a scale where 1 would
be the [arbitrary] pressure required to fracture the hull
in terms of pounds per square inch. Over-pressure
would equal water pressure at a given depth, in this case
a shallow one, plus a Delta factor of over-pressure. Thus
while .5 would be a safe over-pressure, .7 would rise 20
per cent over that safe test pressure."

The only thing which today still retains an interesting meaning is what happened aboard *Thresher* immediately following the particular underwater detonation termed by NOL "an intermediate shot." Once again, the reader may be sure, the description of what followed did not come from any official Navy source.

Cabinet doors flew open as the latches fell apart or locks burst. Shelves were ripped off the bulkheads. The glass covering the dials of many instruments was shattered. Sonar tubes disintegrated. The lights flickered, failed, then came on again as the ship's backup electrical system took over. Anything not solidly bolted was hurled across open spaces and wedged into corners. Lightweight panels were torn out of the walls and ceilings. At least one electric clock was put out of action. Temporarily, several panel indicators ceased to function. The periscope sprang a leak and sea valves momentarily became jammed. Papers, books, broken mirrors and personal belongings littered the crew's and officers' quarters. Even the gyro-compass registered an error that called for recalibration. Vibration racked the entire hull like a tremendous shudder. The ship went into a rocking cadence that could not be brought into immediate control even by skilled trimming. It took *Thresher* minutes to settle down again. Probably, only its very strong flexible mounting saved the turbine, reduction gear and propeller shaft from damage. By great good fortune, the ship's propeller, reactor and main hydraulic system also escaped major damage.

Thresher was able to surface, proceed under her own steam at 16 knots, and returned to USS *Bushnell* by 1805. There are very contradictory statements about the ill-fated sub's shock testing. Vice Admiral E. W. Gren-

fell, Commander Submarine Force, Atlantic Fleet, says
(and he should know), *"Thresher* withstood . . . the
most severe shock tests we have ever conducted on a
submarine in service and suffered only minor equipment
failure . . . but she had more built-in protection than
we have ever before achieved."

Even Captain Hushing at his famous press conference of January 11, 1965 (see Chapter 17), held
". . . primarily to attempt to answer those questions
which might have been raised in your mind by the publication of the report of the Joint Committee on Atomic
Energy relative to the loss of *Thresher*," sounded less
than confident on this point.

"Captain Hushing," a newsman asked, "do you think
that the shock trials which *Thresher* underwent had anything to do with the eventual fate (of the ship)?"

"This is a very difficult question to answer," came the
reply, "because I don't know of anyone who knows how
Thresher was lost . . . But I can say this. That the shock
tests indicated again in a few words in the Joint Committee's report were an element to be considered, and it
is obviously possible that the shock tests entered into the
chain of circumstances which led to the loss of
Thresher . . ."

Commander Axene put it on record somewhat differently. There was "no question *Thresher* suffered
damage, but it was relatively minor. The damage we
sustained did not impair the ship's ability to operate,
and much of it, such as the damage to sonar tubes, we
could repair ourselves with our store of spare parts."
This must rank as a considerable understatement, but it
is not inconsistent. What else could the commanding
officer of the U. S. Navy's newest and deadliest killer

submarine reveal without admitting a navigational error that might have triggered off a disaster?

When *Thresher* moored alongside *Bushnell* that afternoon, the crew was probably still recovering from a state of shock. They had never experienced anything like it nor been subjected to a violent noise level of so many decibels.

On June 20, *Thresher* remained moored. The crew was mustered at quarters but there were no absentees.

Next day the big sub steamed out again to conduct some "preshock acoustic trials," which meant take stock of whatever might have worked loose in her machinery without necessarily being audible from the interior. A thorough examination had revealed no serious leaks and she was ready to be put through the wringer once more.

At 1249 *Thresher* submerged to shallow depth, and during the next 42 minutes two more depth charges were detonated in her vicinity. This time, however, there were no mistakes and the force of these underwater explosions was, by comparison, much attenuated. The crew had learned fast and well about "rigging the ship for shock."

There was now an interval of eight days before the sixth and final "special test," which took place June 29 at 1413. Its severity too was carefully controlled, and again *Thresher*'s built-in "protection" served her well. It was on that day, incidentally, that, pursuant to BuPers (Bureau of Personnel) Message 111707Z, Lieutenant William T. Hussey was detached from the ship. *Thresher* did not return to Key West until the following day, June 30, and remained moored alongside USS *Bushnell* for another two days.

Then, on July 3, she was underway once more to Exuma Sound, there to undergo some thorough detection and acoustic trials aimed at discovering precisely what, if anything, had been shaken loose by those violent underwater concussions.

The postshock trials, carried out at various speeds, depths and courses, continued for five days before *Thresher,* her mission accomplished, once more set course for Portsmouth, New Hampshire. She began her return journey July 7 and by July 12 at 0806 moored starboard side to Pier 6C, Portsmouth Naval Shipyard, New Hampshire, with her starboard mooring lines tripled.

Ships present included various units of the Atlantic Fleet and some yard and district craft. SOPA (Senior Officer Present Afloat) was the commanding officer of the USS *Skipjack* (SSN-585).

And that, although not by any means the end of her 625 commissioned days, was the end of *Thresher*'s brief, dramatic and ill-starred life as an active unit of the U. S. Navy.

However, the idea of *Thresher* spending her remaining 266 days between mooring lines or in dry dock, without incident, is a sad illusion. To the very end—to within hours of her last sailing date—she was dogged by troubles of one kind or another.

For instance, during the period under review there were five separate fires, of which the following is a good example.

September 19, the mylar covering the damping material in the midships compartment ignited from the second platform to the first between Frames 36 and 37, starboard side. The flash fire resulting from a burning torch charred four cables behind the Mk 113 Fire Con-

trol Panel. Three crew members (all of them lost with the
ship) and three shipyard workers sustained injuries—in
one case serious. And there were at least two technical
problems, both described elsewhere, the second of which
could have had disastrous consequences. There was also
one absentee, fated to sail on that last cruise. These
mishaps, it is true, occurred over a period of months, but
somehow they were always connected with *Thresher*.

Of the crewmen hurt in shipboard accidents, perhaps
the one who deserves special mention is the unfortunate
George J. Kiesecker, Machinist's Mate, who on Tuesday,
November 6, 1962, at a few minutes after midnight, fell
down the machinery space ladder, injuring his left
shoulder, head and thumb. Chief Hospital Corpsman
Andrew J. Gallant, Jr., soon had him bandaged up and
fit for further duty, but Kiesecker stands out as the crewman with the nightmare premonition about *Thresher*'s
loss, which proved to be entirely correct and cost him his
life.

To all this must be added two changes of officers for
which BuPers came under strong criticism during subsequent congressional investigations into the *Thresher*
disaster. On December 26, Lieutenant Commander Pat
M. Garner, 537183/1100 USN, reported aboard for
duty as Executive Officer, pursuant to BuPers Orders
170108 of September 24, 1962. He was the replacement
for Lieutenant Commander W. J. Cowhill, who, while
not a member of the ship's commissioning crew, had
been with her for some time. On January 4, 1963, pursuant to the orders of the Commanding Officer, Garner
also relieved Cowhill, as Navigator. Pursuant to BuPers
Order 174083 of October 23, 1962, Lieutenant Com-

mander W. J. Cowhill was detached from the ship with orders to report to Deputy COMSUBLANT for duty. This proved to be Garner's death warrant and Cowhill's reprieve.

The second change was that of Commanding Officer of the ship. On January 9, 1963, at 1545, Lieutenant Commander John Wesley Harvey, 532870/1100, USN, reported on board for duty pursuant to BuPers Order 152836 of October 31, 1962.

Friday, January 18, 1963, nine days later, pursuant to BuPers message, Order 211605Z of July 1962, Lieutenant Commander J. W. Harvey relieved Commander Dean L. Axene, 389331/1100, USN, of the command of USS *Thresher* (SSN-593) at a change-of-command ceremony, the momentousness of which fortunately was lost to the participants.

Pursuant to BuPers Order 163796, Commander Axene was detached with orders to report to the Commanding Officer, U. S. Naval Guided Missile School, for temporary instruction. Axene's strenuous objections to his transfer, even though he was already slated to make Captain, have been noted elsewhere.

That day, anyway, the ship's Deck Log was signed jointly by Harvey and Axene, with the latter's name appearing for the last time.

Perhaps the one note of relief during this long and tedious overhaul, punctuated by so many mishaps and destined to achieve nothing but tragedy, was the Deck Log entry made on January 1, 1963, at 0400, the end of the Dog Watch, when presumably a New Year's Eve party was coming to an end. The whole thing was done in the form of verse by Lieutenant J. S. Agneau and is worth quoting in full.

"This entry is dedicated to the unknown, unrated and unnecessary Yeoman at NAVPERS (Navy Personnel), who so faithfully and capably reads, notes, files and forgets by continuing and constant efforts through the Year:

Now read, good Yeoman, and you shall see,
How *Thresher* met the best year yet and first of
   Sixty-Three.
The temperature is Zero, or maybe just below,
And the winds whistle sharply from stern to open
   bow.
The skies are clear, although to the watery west
Appeared a few broken clouds—call it scattered at
   best.
It hardly bears repeating, you must know with the
   weather's eye
That *Thresher* lies in dry dock just as high and dry
As in previous months.
Forgive the cross-overs, please, you'all just this once.
Not a soul is missing, we've mustered our whole flock.
The ship still stands with all hands in Number Two
   Dock.
Or did you believe that we might leave
Our protected spot on New Year's Eve?
Still receiving AC power as reported before,
With Miscellaneous Services brought from the shore.
Units of the Fleets, Atlantic and Reserve,
Are still joined with us in our Private Preserve.
At Dock or on Block, moored with wire or Manila
   hemp,
Spring Line or Breast Line, we're all at Portsmouth,
   Hamp.

There has been no Demotion or significant Promotion,

In this misbegotten, all but forgotten corner of the Ocean.

And the most rancorous and Aeolus is SOPA still you see,

The number, lest your forget, remains ARC-dash-Three*

Thus ends my missive for tonight, the very first this Year,

Though past performance indicates not the very last, I fear.

Your faithful Correspondent, J. S. Agneau, Lt. USN."

* Reference to a cable-repairing and laying ship.

DIPPER SIERRA
AND WAR CLUB
April 9, 1963: 0949—1425

Until that fateful and terrible day of April 10, 1963, probably no one outside the U. S. Navy had even heard of a *Penguin* Class submarine rescue ship named *Skylark,* or of her skipper, Lieutenant Commander Stanley Hecker. Much less did the public know that *Skylark* was acting as escort for the nuclear submarine *Thresher,* or that she had performed the same duty for the same sub at an earlier date, as well as similar duties for other nuclear subs on their sea trials.

In truth, *Skylark* as a surface vessel of any kind was hardly an inspiring sight, nor one to arouse any particular curiosity. She was painted a drab gray from stem to stern and the only thing about her that presented some relief to the eye was the No. 20 in white on her port and starboard bow, close to the anchor heads. Possibly, those with a specific interest in submarine rescue ships would have noted her rather complex stern boom, with the stubby outline of a rescue chamber on the afterdeck.

Launched March 19, 1946, as a fleet tug (ATF-165) named the *Yustaga,* and originally armed with a three-inch gun, this 1,235-ton vessel had been converted 11 years later (1957) into a submarine rescue ship and renamed *Skylark* (ASR-20). Her armament was removed and the conversion involved an extensive retro-fit including powerful pumps, heavy air compressors, helium-oxygen diving equipment, and a McCann rescue chamber. The last was of a type used back in 1939, when 33 men were brought out of the sunken submarine *Squalus* at a depth of 240 feet.

Skylark's other vital statistics were as follows: loaded, she displaced 1,740 tons, her over-all length was 205 feet, beam 38.5 feet, and height just over 15 feet. Her diesel-electric power unit (the diesel engine was built by General Motors) produced 3,000 shaft horsepower, which gave the ship a maximum speed of 14 knots. Her normal complement was 85 men.*

On the day *Thresher* went down *Skylark* had served 16 years as an active unit of the U. S. Navy, including

---

* Among whom, it should be noted, could be found some highly skilled hands able to help a distressed submarine *that could be reached.* Included were divers, machinists, welders, metalsmiths, boatswains and even torpedo-men. Some were so adept they could work by touch alone, even in murky waters.

six years as a submarine escort. She was built by the
Charleston SB & DD Company. Her decommissioning
was delayed until 1973.

Actually, prior to the first two DSRV's (Deep Sea
Rescue Vessels) being put into operation about nine
years after the loss of *Thresher,* the Navy was totally
deficient in ships and equipment capable of doing a
deep-water rescue job. During 1963, for example, one
ASR was deployed in the Western Pacific, another in
the Mediterranean, and a handful more at submarine
bases of the continental United States and in Hawaii.

By stretching her capabilities to the utmost, *Skylark*'s
rescue chamber, under favorable conditions and with
no hitches, could have reached down to 850 feet. But
this was the absolute limit and at the depths to which
nuclear submarines were regularly diving, the term "submarine rescue ship" was something of a misnomer, if
not a grim joke. A *Penguin* Class ship could certainly
not have rescued a distressed submarine of the new type
at her test depth or anywhere near it. She would have
come at least 300 feet short.

It seems, therefore, that the term "escort ship" was
more appropriate and realistic than "rescue," since conditions would have had to be exactly right for *Skylark*
to bring anybody alive out of a nuclear sub. In the days
of diesel boats, which seldom went deeper than 400 feet,
it was another story.

These details of *Skylark* are introduced not merely
for the record, but because they clearly demonstrate that
she was as incapable of helping *Thresher* in the event
of a deep-sea emergency as was NASA of rescuing the
occupants of a spacecraft locked in orbit and unable
to retrofire.

For purposes of identification during the exercises which began Tuesday, April 9, and ended Wednesday, April 10, 1963, with the worst submarine fatality in history, *Skylark,* as noted before, was assigned the code name of Dipper Sierra, while *Thresher* became War Club. During the rest of this chapter, therefore (and most of the next), the two ships will be referred to by their respective code names, particularly since these were the names used in the UQC (Underwater Telephone) Log kept by Dipper Sierra, not only until the moment when she lost contact with War Club, but far beyond that time.

Seven men were involved in the communications loop which kept the two vessels in contact for 23 hours and 28 minutes. Aboard War Club, they were her commanding officer, Lieutenant Commander John Wesley Harvey, her Executive Officer, Patrick Mehaffy Garner, and her Chief Quartermaster, Aaron Jackie Gunter.

In Dipper Sierra, four men performed a similar function: Lieutenant Commander Stanley W. Hecker, the skipper, Lieutenant Junior Grade James D. Watson, Navigator, Roy S. Mowen, Jr., Boatswain's Mate 3rd Class and Wayne H. Martin, Radioman 3rd Class, who recorded much of the telephone conversation with War Club in the ship's UQC Log. To a lesser extent Robert L. Cartwright, Radioman 1st Class.

On September 13, 1972, I received from the Office of the Judge Advocate General, Department of the Navy, a 13-page Xeroxed copy of "Exhibit 16," the (sanitized) version of the Log kept by Dipper Sierra. I was assured that the deletions did not affect the general time sequence of this Log, but were concerned only with classified per-

formance figures (presumably depth and speed). A
minute reading of this Log tends to give a somewhat different impression, yet even though it was released nine
years and five months after the loss of *Thresher,* it is
in a very good state of preservation. In fact a number
of interesting points came to light, besides terminology
with which a layman would be unfamiliar.

On Tuesday, April 9, 1963, there are three entries
of which only the first was of any significance, and that
was untimed. However, one can make a pretty good
guess at the time of origin. All three of these entries and
their replies are recorded in a rather illiterate—or at the
least careless—handwriting. For example "Rendezvous"
is misspelled two different ways, "Rondivieu" and "Ron-
davieu." "Proceeding" appears as "Proceding." The
entries are a hodgepodge of upper and lower case
characters, of handwriting and printing, some of it slop-
ing backward, some of it forward and the rest upright.

If this indicates anything, scholastic qualifications
aside, it shows that the crewman who made the entries
was bored out of his skull with a routine job performed
a hundred times before. And well he might be, since he
must have known that Dipper Sierra could do nothing
more than dance attendance on the fleet's fastest-moving,
deepest-diving and most self-reliant nuclear sub, and
that her McCann rescue chamber and diving gear were
about as much use, right then, as an icebox to an
Eskimo.

The first two entries on Wednesday, April 10, 1963,
were made in the same careless hand, but from just
prior to 0745 onward, someone else (who could have
been Radioman Cartwright) took over, and his handwriting, done entirely in capitals, is neat and meticulous

and so continues through 0754—in other words for a period of about nine minutes.

At this point, the original crewman takes over once again and is so disinterested that he reverses the names of the ship and submarine in the "from" and "to" columns. Thus War Club appears where Dipper Sierra should be and vice versa. The error continues right on beyond the fateful moment of 0917 when the last message ever received from War Club came through garbled and incomprehensible. However, even the neat and meticulous printer let one slip with his spelling of the word "reference," which appears as "refence" in the 0754 entry.

The way Lieutenant Commander McCoole recalls the sequence of events, April 9 and 10, 1963, and his interpretation of Dipper Sierra's UQC Log, just about closes the loop on those fateful two days, the subject of so many inaccurate stories written mainly with sensationalism in mind.

Dipper Sierra (USS *Skylark*, ASR-20) under the command of Lieutenant Commander Stanley Hecker, USN, also got underway from New London, Connecticut, on the morning of April 9. Pursuant to orders of Commander, Submarine Flotilla 2, she was designated to act as escort to War Club (USS *Thresher*, SSN-593) during her sea trials. War Club was a unit of Submarine Development Group 2 and she too was operating under the orders of Commander, Submarine Force U. S. Atlantic Fleet (Administration), Portsmouth, Vice Admiral Elton W. Grenfell.

It was intended that during Tuesday most of War Club's trials should be conducted on the surface, with the exception of one or two shallow dives, those to take place well inside the Continental Shelf, where Dipper Sierra, in theory at any rate, might be able to render assistance were it needed.

At approximately 0949 the two ships made contact in the area 42° 56′ north, 70° 26′ west, in a moderate sea with good visibility. The crew of Dipper Sierra did not even require binoculars to focus on the long, sleek black shape of War Club with her sail well above water.

Since War Club's skipper, Wes Harvey, as we already know, had been appointed tactical commander of both vessels for the duration of the maneuvers, the two ships had little to say to each other throughout that day. The first message in Dipper Sierra's Log obviously was received during the early afternoon. It read, "Change rendezvous point 20 miles east of original rendezvous point for 1200 zulu hours on the 10th."

To the uninitiated, this Zulu business can become confusing, yet it is really quite simple. The globe is divided into 24 time zones of one hour each, or 15° of the sun's travel, thus totaling a 360° circumference. The Meridian (Greenwich Mean Time) represents 0° and is referred to by the world's navies as Zulu Time or 1200 hours. Since the rendezvous was scheduled in zone "R" (approximately 67° 30′ longitude, Western Hemisphere), this corresponded to a local time five hours earlier, or 0700 the following morning.

The actual message from War Club, as it was written down in Dipper Sierra's UQC Log, is worth quoting as a sample of how these communications were recorded.

War Club to Dipper Sierra—"Change 1012002 Rondivieupont to Rondivieu Point 20 miles East of origi. Rondvieu point for 1012002 Break. Over."

It is this kind of ill-spelled, cryptic jargon (appearing

through much of the Log) that Lieutenant Commander McCoole was able to translate seemingly with no difficulty.

The timed messages were as follows:

1406—Dipper Sierra replied to War Club, "Roger, out."

1421—War Club sent out a routine message saying, "Mike speed, 16," which meant that the sub was proceeding at 16 knots but was well aware of her escort ship's speed limitations.

Dipper Sierra immediately acknowledged with another "Roger, out."

1425—About four minutes later, Dipper Sierra contacted War Club with the message, "Proceeding to rendezvous point."

Back came War Club's reply, "See you there."

That ended the conversation between the two ships on April 9. They proceeded independently during the afternoon and night and there was no further communication. War Club had already gone through her full power and maximum speed exercises, and the assumption aboard Dipper Sierra was valid enough. As the wind freshened with the onset of darkness, whipping up some whitecaps, and since War Club was a poor surface ship, given to wallowing, Harvey took her down to shallow depth and kept her there for several hours, running in smooth waters, still over the Continental Shelf. At the same time he took care not to outstrip his escort by many miles.

That evening Dipper Sierra's off-duty crew, not having much choice of entertainment, probably tuned in to those time-honored but still-popular newscasters, Huntley and Brinkley.

"Good evening. In the news tonight!

"The U.S. favours an end to the Moon Race with the Russians, according to a recent nationwide poll. The prestige of being first is not worth the almost certain casualties. LOR (Lunar Orbit Rendezvous), however, remains the odds-on favorite, though NASA is still undecided. David?"

"This word just in. Pennsylvania's unemployment situation continues as the worst of any big industrial State in the U.S., according to the Bureau of Labor Statistics. Total workless have now reached 400,000 or 9 per cent of Pennsylvania's work force . . . Chet."

"President Kennedy today signed at the White House a bill making Sir Winston Churchill an honorary U.S. citizen. The ceremony, scheduled for tomorrow, will be shown live on TV. Mr. Randolph Churchill will attend in his father's place."

We come now to April 10.

On that calamitous day, the Log (not all of which was written down because things happened too quickly) goes as follows:

0700—War Club to Dipper Sierra, "Radio check." The sub was trimmed to neutral bouyancy, which kept her just close enough to the surface so that her radio antenna (whip) stuck out and she was able to transmit and receive messages and also use her periscope.

0702—(estimated) Dipper Sierra replied, "Over." War Club and her escort were establishing communications for the day. During the next few minutes, according to the Log, the two ships exchanged information which was considered "classified" and was therefore deleted from the record by the Judge Advocate's office.

Then the curtain lifts once again.

0745—War Club picked up Dipper Sierra (presumably using her sonar) in the vicinity of 41° 46' north and 65° 03' west on a bearing of 147° true, at a range of 3,400 yards. She transmitted this information to her escort ship.

Within the same time frame, that is to say, immediately, Dipper Sierra replied, "Roger and out."

Soon afterward, many of Dipper Sierra's crewmen clustered on her afterdeck. They got the last view of War Club that they would ever have, as slowly, almost reluctantly, first the diving planes sticking out either side of her sail, then the tall rudder with its painted numbers, slipped beneath the waves. She was already picking up speed as evidenced by the turbulence about her sail and rudder, but the latter seemed so far astern that it moved along almost like a separate entity, detached from the rest of the long, sleek hull.

As a matter of routine, Lieutenant Commander Hecker adjusted his binoculars to follow more closely every detail of SSN-593's descent below the surface. It was, to him, a familiar sight, but never a dull one. Almost at once you could tell that War Club's increased speed meant she was being "driven under" by sheer power. She had yet to be trimmed to the exact degree of negative buoyancy. But this was pretty much a routine procedure with submarines, especially the nuclear-powered giants that were fast becoming the order of the day. Seconds later, War Club was totally engulfed by the restless but not rough seas off the coast of Maine.

The only thing that none of the 85 men aboard Dipper Sierra even remotely suspected was that War Club had disappeared forever.

0747—Two minutes later, War Club alerted Dipper Sierra, "Starting deep dive." This meant she was heading down almost certainly to test depth, assuming no problems arose.

The immediate reply from the submarine escort was, "Roger."

0748—Dipper Sierra thought it proper to inform War Club, "Will be making 10 to 20 rpm to maintain steerage way." The message indicated that the surface vessel would be putting just enough propeller wash across her rudder to keep the steering effective.

War Club acknowledged this at once with, "Okay to maneuver as long as you remain in present position." The escort ship made no direct reply to this injunction, but two minutes later came up with a request of her own.

0750—Dipper Sierra to War Club, "Request Gertrude Check every 15 minutes." This meant a UQC or underwater telephone report, since the submarine was no longer able to use her submerged radio whip, although she could still transmit in Morse code.

Within that same minute, back came War Club's "Roger and out."

0752—War Club informed Dipper Sierra, "At 400 feet and checking for leaks." Having attained that depth, War Club would remain there until all her equipment, salt water system, and sea valves were checked out and every compartment reported watertight integrity.

Equally promptly, Dipper Sierra acknowledged this information and signed off, "Roger and out."

0754—After a further two-minute interval, War Club told Dipper Sierra, "My future reference to my depth will be Test Depth." This did not actually make sense, but translated it meant, "Future depths will be in reference to my test depth." Thus you could have, for instance, "Test depth minus 400 feet," or whatever. The object was of course not to reveal War Club's true test depth over an open communications channel. The Russians too often displayed not merely an annoying but a dangerous curiosity.

Seconds later, Dipper Sierra replied as before, "Roger and out."

0800—The recording crewman who was listening in on UQC continued to reverse the "from" and "to" columns, but for purposes of the present record the error has been corrected.

Dipper Sierra informed War Club (and not the other way round), "My course is 180 degrees."

0801—War Club to Dipper Sierra, "Roger, out." At the same time the submarine announced, "Corpin 270," which meant, "My course is 270 degrees." As certain words do not transmit well by underwater telephone, and are liable to create confusion, the Navy uses "Corpin" for "Course." This is a more easily decipherable sound.

0807—The escort ship acknowledged with the usual, "Roger, out."

Before that minute expired, War Club came through with an important message. "Am proceeding one-half set distance." Recorded in those words, the message doesn't make any sense. What it meant to convey was, "Am proceeding to one-half my test depth.

0815—For some unexplained reason, Dipper Sierra waited eight minutes to reply, "Roger, out."

As on several previous occasions, the recipient of a

message came back with a further communication. War Club now announced, "Corpin north, 000 degrees."

0819—Dipper Sierra acknowledged, "Roger, out," but in the Log this appears as "R. AR." Again, however, the reply took so long that another message from the sub followed. "Course [or Corpin] 090." Still, this was fairly rapid maneuvering and suggested the start of another circle with a tighter radius.

0824—Seemingly in no great hurry, Dipper Sierra responded with the customary, "Roger, out." The delay may have been caused by the escort plotting the sub's position on her chart and generally evaluating the situation. War Club seldom announced her speed, but Dipper Sierra's sonar would be of help in getting an accurate estimate.

War Club's final word at this time was, "Corpin 180." She was indeed navigating a tight circle.

"A HOLLOW, LIQUID SOUND"
April 10, 1963: 0835—0917

Up to this point, Hecker had the entire duty diving crew
on standby and the equipment ready for instant use, but
experience must have told him that War Club was fast
approaching the point of no return. She was at a depth
where Dipper Sierra would no longer be able to offer
any useful help. He already knew that the sub was describing a downward spiral which was taking her deeper
and away from that last toehold of safety, the Continental Shelf. Poring over a depth chart, Hecker and his
navigator, stocky James Watson, had a pretty good idea

of how far down the ocean bed suddenly dropped from here on out. But if Harvey was to go to test depth, he had little choice off the coast of Maine between an area that was too shallow and one that was too deep.

0835—Following an 11-minute interval, Dipper Sierra transmitted her customary acknowledgment, "Roger, out."

There was scarcely a pause before the first crucial message came through from the big sub. "Proceeding to test depth." She was now past the halfway point, or more than 600 feet down, groping her way ever deeper into the cruel sea.

0842—Presumably the skipper and navigator were again busy with their chart, deciding which course to steer so as to keep station with War Club. This led to a seven-minute delay before Dipper Sierra answered, "Roger, out." No sooner did she receive the escort ship's reply than War Club came back with "Corpin 270." She had completed three segments of her spiral in 27 minutes.

0843—Dipper Sierra to War Club, "Roger, out."

Everything at this point seemed to be going normally. There was cause for no greater concern than usual. Lieutenant Commander Stanley Hecker, a trim, conscientious, worried-looking man with a crew cut and a barely perceptible cast in his right eye, experienced pretty much the same reaction as he did every time one of his charges ventured into ocean depths where salvage would be out of the question. For then he knew that until they surfaced his usefulness would be reduced to one of acting as a communications relay.

The present inference was clear. War Club was proceeding to test depth on a course of 270 degrees. She would level out at a depth where never before in her life had she attempted to blow tanks. It was very unlikely that she had even gone down that far. The best that Hecker could do was try to second-guess War Club's skipper, since Harvey was making his own rules for this particular exercise.

"Roger, out," was all that Dipper Sierra could offer before War Club again cut in with "Course 000 degrees," which in the Log appears as "Corpin ∅∅∅." This indicated that the sub was steering toward the completion of her second spiral.

0853—Ten minutes later, Dipper Sierra sent out her usual reply, "Roger, out." The submarine then repeated, "Proceeding to test depth," but gave no further change of course. What was her intent now? Watson pondered. Would she begin yet another spiral or continue straight ahead for a while, increasing depth more rapidly? The chances were in favor of the former maneuver, for in that way she would not stray too far from the position of the surface vessel. Hecker really had little to go on. The decision in no way rested with him. His evaluation of War Club's performance characteristics was based largely on hearsay, though to some extent, also, on having acted as escort during the sub's original sea trials. At the time, a number of potentially dangerous weaknesses had come to light, but, that aside, one captain's reactions and decisions would not be the same as another's.

0902—The Log entry made by the enlisted man slips into a kind of shorthand. "R out," for "Roger, out." Immediately following, War Club did make known her decision. She announced a further change of course which indicated a clear intent to continue spiraling. This is entered as "Corpin 090," followed by a question mark, as if the message were unclear. Whoever was now speaking from War Club's Control Center, his voice came through with a hollow, liquid sound that camouflaged all identity. There could be several reasons for this, none of them alarming. The most likely would be a low temperature thermal barrier tending to blank out communication. It was a not infrequent occurrence.

0912—Dipper Sierra was back to War Club on the UQC. "Gertrude Check, K." A request to restore communication between the two vessels. The symbol "K" meant "Over."

The next two messages from Dipper Sierra are not timed, but probably went out only seconds apart. They are a repetition of the "K" symbol—a more urgent way of saying, "Over . . . Over?" An invitation to War Club to make some reply through the underwater telephone.

Unknown to Dipper Sierra, the giant sub was already involved in a dangerous situation.

0913—War Club did finally re-establish contact, but what she had to say, though guarded and seemingly casual, must have come as a shock to those on watch aboard the escort ship.

". . . Have positive up-angle. Attempting . . ." The first and final parts of the message were not recorded, although they were heard both by the skipper and the navigator. It can be assumed that the man on duty at the UQC became confused and could not get the words down fast enough, or that he was uncertain as to what he did hear. As later reported both by Hecker and Watson, the complete message sounded something like, "Experiencing minor difficulty. Have positive up-angle. Attempting to blow . . ."

Seconds later, according to the testimony of both officers, the loudspeaker carried up sounds of War Club trying to close her water vents and blow compressed air through her manifold system in an attempt to surface. This lasted "two or three seconds. There was the sound of air under pressure." Dipper Sierra would indeed probably have been able to pick up the peculiar hissing of air going into the ballast tanks.

0914—Dipper Sierra, now very much on the alert, responded to War Club, "Roger, out," which was written down as "R. Out." Within seconds, the surface vessel followed the acknowledged practice between an escort ship and a submarine attempting to surface, by saying, "No contacts in the area." In other words, the sea was clear of shipping which might constitute a danger to War Club were she to "bounce" out of the water.

0915—Dipper Sierra to War Club, "My course 270 degrees. Interrogative range and bearing from you?" The escort ship's heading was now the same as that last given by War Club. The Log entry reads, "My Corpin 270. Int R & B fm U?" Dipper Sierra was asking the submarine to give her range and bearing, which under normal circumstances, using her sonar and gyro-compass, would have been no problem at all. The big question now loomed, were circumstances normal with War Club?

There was no reply, and a few seconds past 0915, Lieutenant Commander Hecker himself took over the UQC mike. Immediately, he sent out the query, "Are you in control?" Attempts also were made to locate War Club by sonar and radio, with no better success.

0917—With War Club now in imminent danger of total destruction, although her escort had of course no inkling of it, the Log shows a confusing entry which was the last transmission from War Club ever noted. It is simply "900 N" followed by a question mark, as though the recipient were uncertain of what he actually heard.

He could well have become confused.

Calculations by scientist Chester L. Buchanan (Naval Research Laboratory) explained the garbled, disjointed nature of *Thresher's* last transmission. The UQC between *Thresher* and *Skylark* would suffer a 110-decibel loss at 10,000 yards—maximum range. This strengthens the belief that the sub's last transmission was within five miles of datum. In fact, "900" could have been an event number to which the Navy alone—or perhaps the submarine service alone—held the key. For example, event "1000" means that a submarine is presumed lost. Beyond doubt, during the test period of a "nuke," each event or maneuver is assigned a number. On the other hand, as thus recorded, the transmission had little or no meaning and no one has thus far suggested any meaningful transmission which might have been misinterpreted as "900 N," coming from War Club. If, however, "900" stood for the coded event number which indicated that the ship had reached test depth, while "N" was an abbreviation for "Negative," in reply to the question "Are you in Control?" then some sense can be made out of this cryptic message. What War Club might have been trying to say was that she had reached test depth but was no longer in control. The reason for surmising that "N" stood for "Negative" was that War Club had already told Dipper Sierra she was "attempting to blow tanks." And under those conditions you no longer are in control of the ship.

When the commanding officer of Dipper Sierra took over the UQC, apparently messages were passing so rapidly back and forth and things were happening so fast that they could not all be recorded. This was especially true during the period 0916 to 0920.

Another point worthy of note is that, while Dipper Sierra's Log clearly shows reception from War Club of something that must have sounded very like "900 N," it was not mentioned by Hecker at the Navy Court of Inquiry. Or he was not questioned about it. Or if he did testify, not a word of what he had to say ever got into print. Instead, we have him telling the Court that a few seconds after 0917 he picked up a garbled message which ended ". . . test depth." Even though it went unrecorded, or at all events is not shown in the Log, this was the last message of any kind received from War Club. Worse, the words were so indistinct that listeners found it extremely difficult to decipher, and tests have shown that even a clearly expressed communication heard only once is subject to all kinds of misinterpretations.

Many years ago, a message was sent along a line of 50 British Scouts, each boy relaying the words as he thought they sounded, but not repeating them. The message started out, "Please send reinforcements to our aid as we are in a tight place [spot]." It ended up, "Please send pork pie, lemonade and a boot lace."

Still, long experience in listening to the metallic outpourings of the loudspeaker on Dipper Sierra's bridge was certainly a plus for Hecker, Watson, Mowen and Cartwright. And at least the first two agreed on the phrase ". . . test depth," and on the reasonableness of assuming that it was prefixed by the word "Exceeding . . ."

Given "Exceeding test depth . . ." *after* reception of

the mysterious message "900 N" begins to make sense, but little more can be said than that.

As to what was heard next, "a dull, muted sound like that of a ship breaking up," both men recognized this from World War II experience as "the sound of a compartment collapsing." However, Lieutenant Commander McCoole casts some doubt on this interpretation of what was heard. The receiving equipment, in his opinion, would probably not cover the frequency range of "breaking up" noises. It could, however, pick up a positive explosion. Or if there was a thud of any kind (another description of what the men recalled), it might have been a main sea water suction valve slamming shut in order to isolate a component or system. These are very large valves which meet the contour of the hull and they are hydraulically operated. A distress flare from a signal gun, or a smoke signal to warn anyone on the surface to clear the area for emergency surfacing, would also produce a thud within the frequency limits of the surface vessel's listening equipment. But at no time did Dipper Sierra observe either a flare or a smoke signal breaking the surface of the ocean.

0920—The escort vessel requested a "radio check," and from this time on, during the next 46 minutes, Dipper Sierra tried 38 times to re-establish communications with War Club. Most of the transmissions were made at one-minute intervals, but there was no reply.

0921—According to evidence given by Hecker at the Navy Court of Inquiry, Dipper Sierra established her own Loran position as 41° 44' north and 64° 59' west, and supposedly recorded this information, but it probably would not have gone into the UQC Log. What the Log does show is the symbol "K" for "Over" repeated 19 times. There are also 19 requests for a radio check, presumably in Morse code.

0931—Under the symbol "K" is the notation "Radio check every 60 seconds. Unable to raise War Club."

1006—Dipper Sierra transmitted to the sub what appears in the log as "QQQ-K." This translates into "Quebec, Quebec, Quebec—Over," meaning "Fire a smoke bomb or flare to indicate your position."

By then, of course, War Club, over 4,300 tons of the most sophisticated undersea equipment available to the Navy, had long since crashed to the sea bed, a broken hulk, and partly buried herself in the silt, 8,400 feet below, carrying with her 129 able-bodied men, most of whom were dead long before the final impact—if not every last one of them. Even had the entire U. S. Navy and Air Force combined, appeared on the spot one minute after 0917, they could have done absolutely nothing to help—or one minute sooner, to prevent—this awesome tragedy.

1040—Lieutenant Commander Hecker ordered the crew to start dropping a series of hand grenades overboard which would indicate to War Club that she was to surface immediately. Even at that point, Hecker was very reluctant to believe the worst and somehow clung to the forlorn hope that War Club had suffered nothing more than a communications breakdown. Everything was going to turn out all right. In those depths, anything else was unthinkable. There was also the outside chance that the sub, having experienced trouble in surfacing, was now headed at full speed on a westerly bearing. In that case, she had recrossed the edge of the Continental Shelf, where rescue might still be possible.

1045—Two events took place at this time. Dipper

Sierra's UQC, which had been working intermittently for a while, quit completely during a three-minute interval. The Log reads, "UQC fails to transmit on CW [pulse code or Morse]." Meantime, Hecker came to a decision. At 1104, he ordered his operations officer to radio New London and report loss of contact with War Club. Here again there were complications. Although the escort ship had been in touch with base earlier in the morning, on routine radio tests, serious difficulties were now encountered in getting even the dot-dash radio to work. However, after several attempts which took 1 hour 40 minutes, with interruptions and requests for repetitions, the following message did get through to COMSUBLANT:

"Unable to communicate with Thresher since 0917R. Have been calling by UQC voice and CW, QHB, CW every minute. Explosive signals [grenades] every 10 minutes with no success. Last transmission received was garbled. Indicated Thresher was approaching test depth. My present position 41° 43' north, 64° 57' west. Conducting expanding search."

1121—With the underwater phone again operating and only the radio behaving erratically, Hecker transmitted the following in pulse form (Morse code).

"Indicate your position, prepare to surface. Acknowledge. Initiating event SUBMISS."

1129—The following message was entered in the escort ship's UQC Log. "Have initiated SUBMISS. Indicate your position. ACK. K." This meant, "Acknowledge, over."

1245—New London (DBL) finally receipted for Skylark's message and at once set about alerting every ship within a reasonable distance to head, full speed, toward the co-ordinates where *Thresher* had made her last dive. All submerged submarines were ordered to surface at once, and any unit of the underwater fleet that was close enough was directed to join in the search.

From 1245 until the Log ends, that is a time span of 4 hours 21 minutes, the now despairing appeal "QQQ-K" appears in the Log 69 times.

1302—Hecker's message was handed to Captain J. Sneed Schmidt, COMSUBFLOT-2, on his return from lunch. This was 3 hours 45 minutes after *Thresher*'s last message.

1704—Dipper Sierra is still calling, "Event SUBMISS. Surface, surface. Over," with a sort of numbed desperation.

1706—"Same as usual."

By then, the concentrated search was rapidly taking shape and not even Hecker or Watson held out any hope that *Thresher*'s silence, which had already lasted 7 hours 49 minutes, could portend anything but her loss. But even at that point there were no means whatever of evaluating the nature and extent of the worst submarine disaster in history.

The U. S. Navy, however, perhaps already sensing the nationwide publicity it would have to face (and possibly the urgent need of some kind of scapegoat), was rapidly tempering its initial shock with a state of indignation. The opinion expressed at admiral level (a dangerous level for anyone below) made this abundantly clear. "Skylark's message did not convey to operational commanders the full extent of the information then available, nor did Skylark's subsequent reports include such additional information. Moreover, Thresher's last messages were not disclosed to higher authority until April 12, when Lieutenant Junior Grade James D. Watson, navigator of Skylark, boarded the USS Blandy with the Underwater telephone log which was examined by Deputy Commander, Submarine Force, U. S. Atlantic Fleet, Rear Admiral Lawson P. Ramage."

But for the stubborn curiosity and spirited intervention of Senator Hickenlooper at the subsequent Congressional Hearings (about whom more will be heard), it would be fair to say that the guillotine was poised and ready. Only the slenderest of threads prevented Hecker's head from rolling into the basket.

Provoking the wrath of admirals is not a healthy pastime, while to "irritate" the Secretary of the Navy is about as far as anyone can go. The door of sweet reasonableness, however, was left open just a crack. The Naval Court of Inquiry, although it made Hecker an "interested party to the proceedings" (indicating that he was legally involved), reluctantly concluded that discretion might be the better part of valor.

"Skylark's commanding officer's failure to promptly notify higher authority of all the information available to him pertinent to the circumstances attending the last transmission received by Skylark from Thresher, April 10, as it was his duty to do, did not contribute in any way to the loss of Thresher and was not materially connected therewith."

As if the skipper of a submarine rescue ship, holding the rank of Lieutenant Commander and with many years' experience behind him, could be so stupid, incompetent, and callous as to "contribute in any way" to the death of 129 of his fellow Servicemen and the destruction of $45 million worth of Navy property.

Such a proposition is absolutely outrageous.

THE LUCKIEST MAN ALIVE
The Recollections of Lieutenant Commander
Raymond A. McCoole USN (Retd.)

THE LUCKIEST MAN ALIVE
July 1962—January 1963

Countless people would wear with a feeling of distinction
the title of the "Luckiest Man Alive," and I can well understand how the press throughout the world was quick
to pin that label on me. When you consider the combination of circumstances, coming at exactly the right
time and at the penultimate moment, which conspired to
save my life, I suppose I could be considered the luckiest
of mortals. Thanks to what turned out to be an
unpleasant but relatively minor accident to my wife,
Barbara, and thanks also to a sudden compassionate de-

cision on the part of *Thresher*'s skipper, Lieutenant
Commander Wes Harvey, I was ordered off the ship with
no appeal just 13 minutes short of 24 hours before she
sank to her doom, carrying with her every last crew
member who did sail. Not only that, but she also claimed
the lives of 21 passengers, Naval and civilian, who were
aboard as observers.

Long after *Thresher* was given up as lost, or "Stricken"
from the Navy's roll of ships, reporters and radio net-
work men pursued me at every turn, brandishing mikes
in front of me and saying, "Don't you realize what a
fantastic escape you had? Why, you must be the luckiest
guy that ever lived!"

Barbara doesn't look upon it that way and never did.
She's convinced there was a good reason why Raymond
A. McCoole, *Thresher*'s Reactor Control Officer, didn't
go down with his shipmates—even if we never find out
what that reason was. It's not fatalism, but rather a
religious belief that, if I escaped the worst disaster in
submarine history on April 10, 1963, it was so ordained
and could not have happened any other way. She's
naturally glad our large family was not deprived of father
or husband, but content to leave it at that, amazing as my
survival may seem.

With the passing years, I have leaned more and more
toward my wife's viewpoint and certainly respect it. Endless speculation as to why a certain thing happened in a
certain manner, no matter how extraordinary the event,
is not a profitable way to occupy your time. For example,
if I was a very lucky guy, we might as well try to figure
out why the *unluckiest* man aboard had to go down with
Thresher. He must surely have been 29-year-old Alan
Dennison Sinnett, an experienced swimmer and skin

diver. What was it that prompted Alan to apply for transfer to the Navy's Fire Control Technician's School and graduate when he did? Why was he then ordered to report to *Thresher* April 4, 1963, less than a week before her fatal dive? But he was.

Or we could ask ourselves why three other crew members were taken off *Thresher* at the time they were—only a short while before she left dry dock, ready for her last trip. As I recall, these men were Frank DiStefano, Garron S. Weitzel and Raymond Mattson. DiStefano, also 29, a machinist's mate, was ordered to Washington April 8, the day before *Thresher* sailed toward her tragic fate. He was slated for an interview with Rear Admiral Rickover (now Admiral, retired but still active), prior to reassignment to the Navy's nuclear reactor program. I knew him well and he deserved the break, but it could hardly have come at a more opportune time. Weitzel, 27, an electrician 2nd class, received orders in January for a temporary transfer to the Navigation School at Dam Neck, Virginia, but was due to rejoin *Thresher* in June. Mattson, 34 years old and a torpedoman's mate 1st class, developed a nervous problem and was excused from sea duty and ordered ashore for observation and treatment. I also recall Dick Podwell, only 24, a machinist's mate with a happy-go-lucky disposition, who had only been married 18 months. And Charles Wiggins, 30, one of our fire control technicians, who had one great love after his baby daughter—*Thresher*. He was very proud to be serving aboard our ship and had been with her since January 1962. These men, and others, pose a strange, bewildering question as to why things happen at times that are inexplicable, not to say illogical, but the fact remains that they do happen that way. The *Thresher* tragedy stands out all the more because it presents so many instances of this kind, seemingly without rhyme or reason.

Better, perhaps, to take things as they come and not ask too many questions.

In late April 1962, I received orders from the Bureau of Naval Personnel, transferring me from the Nuclear Power Training Unit, Idaho Falls, Idaho, to report to a submarine in New London, Connecticut. The orders granted me 15 days' travel and, in addition, 30 days' leave. Since I had spent three years in Idaho, passing first through the nuclear reactor school, then taking over as officer in charge of the training program, this leave was most welcome. The whole family pulled up stakes, but on arrival in New London I found that my orders had been changed. They now directed me to report aboard USS *Thresher* in Portsmouth, New Hampshire, as Reactor Control and "E" Division officer. When I reached Portsmouth Naval Shipyard, I was informed that *Thresher* was still at sea and would not be back for a couple of weeks. The two weeks stretched into nearly three, but during that time I got my family settled in Dover, New Hampshire, which happened to be my wife's home state. After the long trip from Idaho, she was delighted to be home once more, among the pines, oak trees and rolling hills. At that time, in the summer of 1962, we had four sons, nicely spaced out at two-year intervals. Kevin, the eldest, was eight years old, followed by Tim, six, Mike, four, and Dan, our two-year-old. Barbara was then expecting our No. Five son, who was born August 9, less than a month after I reported to *Thresher*. His name was about to be Kerry.

The first time I set eyes on *Thresher* (SSN-593) was

July 11, 1962, when her long, sleek black form came gliding up the Piscataqua River with tugs fussing alongside. She made a smooth, uneventful landing and moored at Pier 11C, Portsmouth Naval Shipyard. I reported on board, first to her commanding officer, Commander Dean L. Axene, whom I had not set eyes on since our *Nautilus* days when he held the post of Executive Officer. That had been seven or eight years earlier, but Axene was little changed and remained the same impressive naval officer, a bit more mature perhaps, and a rather stiff-collared and polished career man. Once you got to know him, however, the picture came into focus of a very sharp, aware and personable individual who knew exactly what was going on aboard his ship at all times.

There were details you might think would be of little interest to the commanding officer of the Navy's most advanced nuclear attack sub, but this was certainly not the case with Axene. He kept track of the smallest detail in the running of his ship, and even when she was safely berthed he did not let go the reins for a moment. As I was soon to find out, if any problem occurred, Axene was right on top of it, getting things sorted out with a minimum of delay, although at times even he couldn't buck The System. That's to say the way things were done at the Navy Yard and by the Navy in general. Still, since Axene never gave an order which he couldn't carry out himself, he insisted that his officers live up to those standards.

The CO greeted me cordially, made me welcome aboard and added, "By the way, an old friend of yours knows you're expected, Ray. He's looking forward to seeing you again."

"You mean John Smarz, sir?"

"Who else?" Axene smiled.

Lieutenant John Smarz was indeed an old and close friend. We had served together in the submarine service since 1952, when we were both presented at the commissioning of USS *Gudgeon* (SS-567). We had shared experiences aboard this diesel boat, then gone on to a nuclear power school together and thence to *Nautilus*. Now, he was *Thresher*'s "A" Division Officer in the Engineering Department, in which capacity he also acted as Diving Officer.

John lost no time introducing me to the Executive Officer, Lieutenant Commander John Cowhill, who in turn made sure I met all the officers on board, then showed me to my stateroom. This consisted of three comfortable bunks, arranged in tiers, with individual lockers and a desk. It was known as a Wardroom/Stateroom (WRSR), and I found myself sharing space with Lieutenant Commander John Lyman, the Engineering Officer, and Lieutenant Junior Grade Jim Henry, my assistant-to-be, who had actually served in *Thresher* since November the previous year. Lyman occupied the middle bunk, with Henry below him and myself in the upper bunk. Only the Commanding and Executive Officers had their own staterooms.

At first, I must admit that I felt a bit like excess baggage, although I met with nothing but cordiality. This was because everyone was very busy planning the many tasks ahead that would make it possible to end *Thresher*'s PSA (Post Shakedown Availability)—her in-port visit—within the intended period of six months and perhaps sooner. Even so, that would bring us well into December, not the best time to start on sea trials.

Naturally, when you come aboard a new ship, certain impressions tend to register rather strongly. I must say that my first impression of *Thresher* was very good and I found her absolutely outstanding, even allowing for the fact that I was naturally elated at being accepted for duty aboard this ship. I at once got the feeling that *Thresher* was far superior to any submarine in the fleet. The layout, equipment and accommodations were something that had to be seen. In my estimate, the amount of space per capita was perhaps tenfold that available in earlier nuclear ships which I had known well, having served in *Nautilus* for several years and in diesel-type submarines before that.

I was particularly impressed with the interior appointments of *Thresher*, the handsome décor throughout the ship and the air of spaciousness and comfort. The key color was beige with white ornamental ceilings, deeper beige formica table tops and brown patterned linoleum covering the floors or decks. The only drawback was that to get at the mass of complicated piping that pursued its course throughout the ship meant having to remove various panels in those handsome ceilings. The consequent loss of time involved in case of having to locate some defect or failure can well be imagined. This was a thing that I soon discovered to be a source of unease to Commander Axene. He would willingly have sacrificed some of *Thresher*'s streamlined interior artistry to less beguiling and more accessible means of reaching vital components.

Much stainless steel went into the ship's interior, while the engineering spaces were almost entirely done in white. At the time, *Thresher* was beyond doubt the most luxurious and comfortable submarine I had ever served in. She also boasted an entertainment system that was very comprehensive. Tapes and platter-type records piped music throughout the ship to every stateroom and bunk, as well as the Officers' Wardroom and the Crew's Mess. Every evening, a different movie was shown. This took place in the Crew's Quarters, where the tables were ingeniously designed for quick conversion into something approximating armchair seats. The movies were full length with color Cinemascope and the general effect was not much different from your local movie theater.

In fact, the day I reported aboard *Thresher* and for less than a week thereafter, the effect was very pleasing and sanitary, with everything spotlessly clean. But that was before the Yard workmen began swarming all over the ship, tearing everything apart and creating an unholy mess that was to last not six, but an inexpressibly dreary nine months.

But we'll come back to that.

As soon as I was introduced to Lieutenant Commander John Lyman, the ship's Engineering Officer, he gave me my job and told me to get into some working khakis. Although John and I soon became close friends, he was not one to waste time and we at once sat down and had a long discussion about the problems in the "E" (Electrical) and "RC" (Reactor Control) Divisions. I took a bunch of notes, but it was apparent from our talk that I had plenty of work ahead of me. However, there was no lack of skilled help available to back me up. I knew that almost from the moment I met the Division Chief Petty Officers, one of whom was Chief Roscoe C. Pennington, Electrician's Mate and Chief Petty Officer in charge of the Reactor Control Division. There were also the brothers Benjamin N. and John D. Shafer. Ben was an electrician's mate, Master, and the over-all Department Petty Officer. John was an electrician's mate, Senior, in charge of the electrical gangs.

I had already been assigned my in-port Watches by Lieutenant Commander Mike Di Nola, *Thresher*'s Main Propulsion Assistant and the most senior officer in the Engineering Department under the Engineering Officer himself. Mike had been aboard *Thresher* since prior to her commissioning. So he really knew the score. In fact, at that time he was the only other officer, besides the skipper, qualified to command a submarine. Di Nola and I were also to renew a close friendship of long standing as the weeks wore on, but business came before pleasure and the first step in carrying out my duties was to learn the ship and her capabilities and requirements while in port.

At the earliest opportunity, I sat down with Jim Henry, who had been acting as Reactor Control and "E" Division Officer prior to my reporting, and discussed with him the problems that the ship had experienced with her reactor and those it was now facing. We also batted back and forth the approach that would solve these problems. At the time I was impelled with a sense of urgency because, as I have said, we figured that the time allotted to us to supervise any work on the reactor might be cut down if we really put our backs to it. In turn it would mean being able to put to sea that much sooner.

Henry was an earnest young man of 25, tall, pleasant-looking, and with a head crowned by thick and wavy dark hair. What he lacked in experience he made up in his eager quest for knowledge and his willingness to undertake any task I set him.

During the week that we remained aboard *Thresher* after she docked, I had an opportunity to become attuned to many facets of shipboard life and routine. For example, in the wardroom generally there was a congenial atmosphere, despite the fact that all officers showed a tremendous amount of ego drive, generated perhaps by Commander Axene. The food, however, was excellent, as in virtually all types of nuclear submarines. It was in fact so plentiful that a man could spend his entire leisure hours eating! The facilities were there, and if you wanted to prepare your own meal, there was nothing to stop you from raiding the open-food locker or freezer at midnight. You could, for instance, choose a thick, juicy porterhouse or T-bone steak and cook it yourself, just the way you liked it, complete with trimmings. You could eat just about anything you wanted at any convenient time throughout each 24 hours. You knew that the Navy had spared no expense to keep your tummy happy, realizing how important good eating is aboard a submarine. The reason is of course that even in the roomiest sub space is so confined that both officers and men can hardly turn around during duty hours without rubbing elbows. Under these conditions, which sometimes continue in a totally confined environment without a break for perhaps a month at a time, while the ship runs submerged, any kind of irritation assumes explosive proportions.

But besides freedom to raid the icebox at will, there are the cooks who prepare three ample meals a day. Breakfast is at 8 A.M., lunch at noon, and dinner at 8 P.M. In addition, there is a 4 P.M. "soup call" (coinciding with the end of the second Dog Watch), and at

midnight those coming off duty from the second Blue
Watch can enjoy midnight rations, generally called "midrat."

To simplify choice in the variety of food available
during the regular meals, menus are given standard
designations. For example, "J5" may be steak night. Item
"Q14" would indicate sweet peas, and so on. Contrary to
what many people believe, it is not the Quartermaster
who is in charge of food—he has nothing to do with it—
but the Commissaryman, or Storekeeper. And as if all
this fare were not enough, food is constantly available
in the form of sandwiches, hot stew, coffee, or anything
else your heart (or rather your palate and digestive
organs) may desire.

Submariners are especially proud of the excellent
coffee they drink and consume incredible quantities of
it in a variety of ornamental mugs that are strictly the
property of the individual. These can be identified by a
wide selection of devices which seldom fail to include the
owner's name or initials. One of the commonest "small
talk" remarks you hear aboard a sub when people are
drinking strong, hot coffee is: "This stuff sure beats the
bilge water that passes for coffee ashore!"

Another highly important factor in a submarine is the
air you breathe—the atmosphere generally, and that includes temperature. Powerful air conditioners maintain a
comfortable, easy-breathing shirt-sleeve atmosphere of
68 to 72°F., regardless of how cold the sea water may
be, just the other side of the ship's confining steel hull.
They get some help, of course, from the heavy cork insulation lining the walls of the ship. Carefully regulated
air conditioning on a 24-hour basis in a submarine the
size of *Thresher* consumes a tremendous amount of

electricity. Two backup systems are therefore available besides reactor power, but even they can sometimes fail. In warm climes, a breakdown of the air-conditioning plant would soon turn the interior of a submarine into a furnace of suffocating heat. (*Thresher* had once experienced such a failure while in Puerto Rico.)

Without exception, the air in a nuclear sub is far cleaner and fresher than the atmosphere in any city, or even way out along our super highways. This has to be so because of the constant smells generated by cooking, smoking, hot oil and metal in the Engine Room, a variety of chemicals and last but not least the normal exhalations from perhaps a hundred human bodies in close proximity. *Thresher* at that time was not equipped with carbon-scrubbing air revitalization machines, but would have been had she survived. There was, however, ample means of "bleeding" fresh oxygen into the polluted atmosphere each time it was recycled through the ship.

Approximately a week after I reported to *Thresher,* on July 16, 1963, our living and working quarters (in so far as paperwork was concerned) were transferred to a barge at the Portsmouth Naval Shipyard. This was then brought alongside the sub for convenience, but the move still required packing and transportation of reams and reams of documentation paper from *Thresher* to the barge, and this was a monumental task in itself. The move resulted in the loss of several valuable days which could otherwise have been devoted to the overhaul of the ship. However, it sure paid for itself in terms of comfort for all concerned. But before the gangs of Yard workmen were turned loose aboard *Thresher* to dismantle her insides and tear out just about everything that did anything, we also had to dismantle and remove every single

FIG. 1
Rear Admiral Dean L. Axene, USN,
Thresher's first commanding officer, probably
knew that temperamental—and at times
appallingly dangerous—nuclear submarine
better than anyone else aboard. Never for a
moment turning his back, Axene coaxed some
extraordinary performances out of SSN-593
during his 17 months as her captain.

FIG. 2
Lieutenant Commander John Wesley Harvey,
USN, 36, second and last commander of the
ill-starred *Thresher,* went down with his ship.
Though he was a dedicated submariner of
great experience, this was Harvey's first
command of a nuclear submarine. He had
relieved Commander Axene only three months
earlier and had never before put to sea in
Thresher.

FIG. 3
Lieutenant Commander Raymond A.
McCoole, *Thresher*'s Reactor Control Officer,
dubbed "the luckiest man alive." McCoole was
the only member of the crew to survive
SSN-593's disastrous sea trial. A million-to-one
combination of last-minute injury to his wife's
eyes, an already overcrowded ship, and a
stubbornly compassionate captain kept him
home despite his tremendous eagerness to sail.

FIG. 4
Captain H. P. Rumble, USN, shipyard
commander at the time of *Thresher*'s launch
(July 9, 1960), holds the traditional (dented)
champagne bottle with which Mrs. Frederick
B. Warder (center), the ship's sponsor,
performed the christening. At left, her husband, Vice Admiral F. B. Warder, USN,
Commandant Eighth Naval District.

FIG. 5
Launch of the tragically fated *Thresher*, July
1960. The 127th submarine built at Portsmouth Naval Shipyard, SSN-593 broke trad
tion by going down the slipway bow first. Th
need was dictated by *Thresher*'s difference i
distribution of buoyancy and the depth of th
water at the end of the building ways. Ironically, she sank to her doom stern first.

Jnusual dead astern view of *Thresher* (sur-
aced) during her builder's trials, July 1961.
he ship's great length (over 278 feet) and
moothly rounded hull are clearly apparent.
Draft markings enabled rudder to be identified
m sea bed almost two miles below the surface.

3. 7

e ill-fated *Thresher* (SSN-593) on the
rface during her precommissioning builder's
als, July 1961. Photo was taken about 45°
 the starboard bow.

FIG. 8

Vice Admiral Harold T. Deutermann, USN, Chief of Staff and Aid to the Supreme Allied Commander, Atlantic, on his way to the *Thresher* commissioning ceremony with Rear Admiral Carl F. Espe (right), USN, Commandant First Naval District. Deutermann gave the main address; Espe read the Navy Department Orders to commission SSN-593.

FIG. 9

Rear Admiral Carl F. Espe, USN, Commandant First Naval District (standing, left) salutes Commander Dean L. Axene, *Thresher*'s first commanding officer prior to reading of Navy Department Orders commissioning the ship, August 3, 1961. Commander Axene returns

salute. Seated (left to right), Vice Admiral Harold T. Deutermann, senior officer present Vice Admiral Elton W. Grenfell, Commander Submarine Force, U.S. Atlantic Fleet (hidden by lectern); Rear Admiral Charles J. Palmer Commander Portsmouth Naval Shipyard (behind Axene) and Commander K. G. Peterson, Navy Protestant Chaplain. Extreme left (seated), Lieutenant Commander John Fay, CHC, USN; civilians Robert Whalen Chairman Military Affairs, Portsmouth Chamber of Commerce, and Lewis R. Watson President Squalus Memorial Chapter, Submarine Veterans, World War II. Watson's presence was to become a tragic coincidence since the deep-sea retrieval of half the *Squalus* crew marked the greatest submarine rescue operation ever undertaken.

10

mander Dean L. Axene (now Rear
niral) reads the Navy Department Orders
cer, August 3, 1961. Background (standing,
to right) Rear Admiral Carl F. Espe USN;
pointing him *Thresher*'s first Commanding

Vice Admiral Elton W. Greenfell (behind
Axene); Rear Admiral Charles J. Palmer;
Commander K. G. Peterson, CHC, USN.
Seaman (right) holds up commissioning pen-
nant and Vice Admiral Deutermann's personal
flag.

11

d up in an impressive display of immacu-
summer whites was *Thresher*'s entire
nal commissioning crew—10 officers, 17
petty officers, and 74 enlisted men (later

increased to 96). Total complement, August 3,
1961, was 101. Of the ship's original company,
only two enlisted men, eight chief petty officers,
and three officers were with her at the end.

FIG. 12
Cutting the cake, following "593's" commissioning ceremony. Commander Dean L. Axene (right, holding sword hilt), *Thresher*'s newly

appointed Commanding Officer, is assisted Lieutenant Commander Robert D. Rawlir ship's first Executive Officer. Mrs. Axene on at right; Mrs. Rawlins at left.

FIG. 13
Thresher's device, depicting the killer shar after which she was named, was indeed we chosen. This nuclear ship was then the wor deadliest attack submarine (and for that m still is). Her motto, "Silent Strength," also highly appropriate.

resher moving at high speed on the surface
ing her postcommissioning trials. Photo
s taken near the sea buoy KR in the Ports-

mouth, New Hampshire, operating areas, off
the Isles of Shoals. Figures are still discernible
on the bridge, but the ship is obviously about
to be "driven under" in a shallow dive.

15

S *Barb* (SSN-596) a sister ship of the lost
resher, launched February 12, 1962,
months later. Standing on her port diving
ne (extreme right) is the brilliant, highly
ntroversial Vice Admiral Rickover, "father"
the nuclear-powered sub. Rickover was
oard every "nuke" undergoing her builder's
ls—save two while he was hospitaiized.

Courtesy Ingall's Shipbuilding Division, Pascagoula, Miss., who built the USS Dace.

FIG. 16

Weapons Control Panel in the Torpedo Room of USS *Dace* (SSN-607), sister ship of the late *Thresher* and the eighth nuclear attack submarine to be launched in the Permit Class. These ships had identical weapons systems. Following target detection, the sub's Attack Center computes course, range, speed, and bearing and passes the information to the Weapons Control Panel operators. The flick of a switch can now send a deadly SubRoc missile on its errand of certain destruction. A chief petty officer looks on while drill is in progress. Space, here, is at a premium.

FIG. 17

Operational Control Center of USS *Dace* (SSN-607), also identical with that of the l‑ *Thresher*. Located directly below the sail, t‑ duty crew here keeps the ship on her correc‑ course. Seated at their respective controls a‑ the Planesman (nearest camera) and Helms‑ man. While surfaced, commands are receiv‑ from the Officer of the Deck on the bridge. When submerged, radar and other sensors serve as the eyes of the sub, to keep her on course at set depth. The Diving Officer, sta‑ ing between the two operators, keeps an eye‑ the situation. To his left is the ship's ballast control system—critical for diving and surfacing.

FIG. 18

Tongue of the Ocean (TOTO), a vast coral basin east of Andros Island, Bahamas, where (in August 1961) on her first commissioned

cruise, *Thresher* underwent sonar and weap‑ tests in this unique location. She returned fc‑ acoustic tests in June 1962.

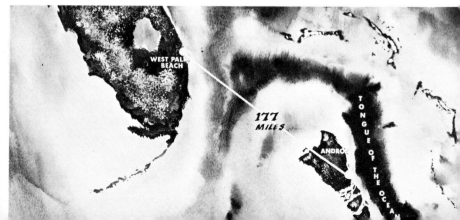

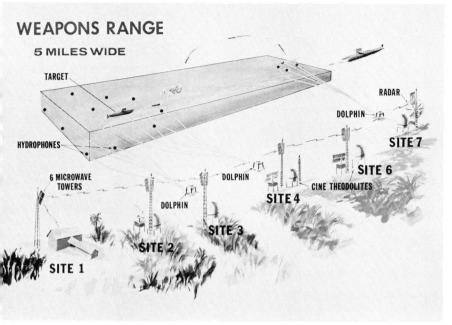

WEAPONS RANGE

5 MILES WIDE

TARGET

RADAR

DOLPHIN

SITE 7

HYDROPHONES

6 MICROWAVE TOWERS

DOLPHIN

CINE THEODOLITES

SITE 6

DOLPHIN

SITE 4

DOLPHIN

SITE 3

SITE 2

SITE 1

19

pons Range at AUTEC (Atlantic Undersea and Evaluation Center), a joint U.S.-ish antisubmarine warfare testing facility in Bahamas. It was here that *Thresher* fired sophisticated subsurface-to-subsurface Roc missiles—the world's most advanced orne torpedo and the deadliest.

FIG. 20

Thresher's long, lean, and graceful silhouette tied up alongside USS *Bushnell,* a large submarine tender, at Key West, Florida. Photo was taken in June 1962 during 593's recuperative breaks while undergoing a series of severe underwater shock tests.

FIG. 21
The renovated but antique USS *Skylark* (ASR-20), ordered to accompany *Thresher* on her last and tragic sea trial. In this case, the 17-year-old *Skylark* was more suitable as an escort ship than as a rescue vessel to the doomed sub. The maximum rescue depth of 25-year-old McCann diving bell was 850 feet under ideal conditions—utterly useless off the Continental Shelf.

FIG. 22
Lieutenant Commander Stanley M. Hecker, commanding officer of the submarine rescue ship *Skylark*, ordered to accompany *Thresher* on a two-day sea trial which ended in the worst submarine disaster on record. Hecker, though he had nothing whatever to do with *Thresher*'s tragic loss, narrowly escaped the icy wind of the wrathful Navy Brass in search of a scapegoat.

FIG. 23

erial view of the position where *Thresher*'s
oken hulk, carrying 129 dead men, finally
me to rest at the foot of the Continental
elf, 8,400 feet below. Circling the spot clock-
se (approximately 41° 45' N, 64° 36' W)
e the diesel submarine USS *Redfin* (SSN-
2), submarine rescue ship USS *Sunbird*
SR-15), ballistic missile nuclear sub USS
omas Jefferson (SSBN-618), and the de-
oyer *Warrington* (DD-843), foreground,
gship of the group.

FIG. 24

On May 28, 1963, USNS *Conrad,* one of the
armada of surface vessels trying to locate
Thresher, dredged up what could be considered
the first positive identification. Some 19 packages were retrieved from deep water, each
containing "O" rings used for pipe flange
connections. Of the three samples here shown,
two could have come from a destroyer, but the
third was uniquely for submarinoe use and
almost certainly had been aboard the lost sub.
"O" rings are on top of the individual packages
containing them.

. 25

NS *Conrad*'s deep-sea cameras, helped by
liant lighting of the ocean's deep water
ckness (below propeller-shaped shadow),
tographed this intact compressed air bottle
ding on the ocean floor, 8,400 feet deep.
ile it could have come from a Navy surface
, there was little doubt that it was, in fact,
of *Thresher*'s equipment.

FIG. 26

Not to be outdone, RV *Atlantis II,* of Woods
Hole Oceanographic Institution, retrieved this
badly damaged six-inch section of battery
plate on June 24. The feat was all the more
remarkable since a makeshift dredge was used,
fashioned from baling wire and coat hangers.
A Navy contractor positively identified this find
as part of *Thresher*'s huge Exide battery bank.

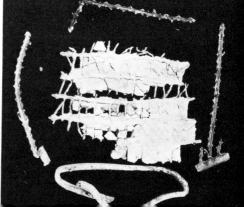

FIG. 27

Atlantis II, which made a major contribution in locating *Thresher,* was diverted from her maiden cruise at the Navy's request to assist in the search. Product of a Baltimore, Maryland, shipbuilder, she carried a direction finder, gyrocompass, echo-sounding, and position-fixing devices, radar, a medium frequency radiotelephone, and a 12-ton stern crane.

FIG. 28

Unloading the *Trieste* at Boston, Massac setts, from USS *Point Defiance* after long journey from San Diego, California, via Panama Canal. Bathyscaphe's striped hul reality a huge (34,000 gallon) gas tank w gondola slung underneath. Y.D. 196 (d below *Trieste*) indicates Navy floating cr with derrick.

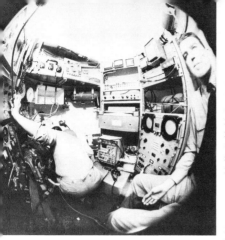

FIG. 29
Lieutenant Commander Don Keach (right), *Trieste*'s Officer in Charge, and Lieutenant jg Robert Claypool of the Naval Photographic Center (back to camera) aboard the cramped Bathyscaphe gondola, only 78 inches in diameter. Complex and tightly packed instrumentation includes closed circuit TV, depth measurement devices, sea-bottom samplers, deep-sea cameras, sonar and some highly sensitive acoustic devices. Controls for a mechanical arm were later added.

FIG. 30
Trieste, riding low in the water and readied by her maintenance crew, awaits the arrival of the small boat carrying the Officer in Charge, before start of deep-sea dive in search of the lost *Thresher.*

31

gh weather and fog delayed the first dive *riest*'s second series until the afternoon of ust 23, 1963. Nevertheless, several excel- photos of *Thresher* debris were obtained

from the sea bed. Here, part of the lost sub's bow-mounted sonar equipment is identified. At top left are the remains of a junction box for electrical circuits.

FIG. 32
Another startlingly sharp photo taken from *Trieste,* August 23, revealed *Thresher* debris scattered on the ocean floor. Bottom (left) is a small-diameter bent and twisted pipe torn out of the sub, while at right may be seen some of the rock wool thermal insulation of vital importance in lining the ship's interior.

FIG. 33
On August 23, 1963, during the first of *Trie* second series of five dives, this close-up, de sea photo, taken with the gondola's underw camera, revealed a manhole cover from one *Thresher*'s steam generators. (Picture was wrongly identified by the Navy's Photograp Center as that of a "water-tight bulkhead door.")

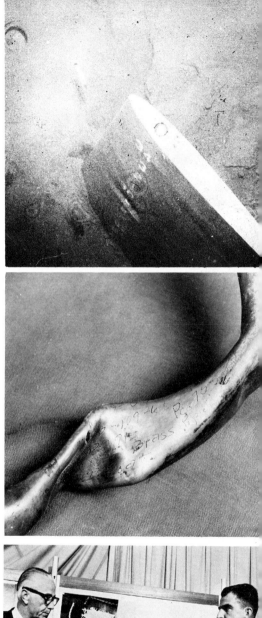

34

...nmanned, towed deep-sea vehicle from the
...al Research Laboratory obtained this re-
...kable photo of *Thresher*'s upright rudder
...he first day of renewed search operations in
...4. Picture was the result of a random pass,
...the NRL vehicle used three cameras, a
...netometer, and a highly successful track-
...system. Plainly visible stern draft numbers
...*Thresher*'s rudder provided certain identi-
...ion.

35

...s length of twisted brass piping ended
...greatest hunt of all time for a sunken sub-
...ine. Recovered by Lieutenant Commander
...ch, USN, using a mechanical arm operated
...n inside the Bathyscaphe's gondola, it was
...ught up August 28, 1963, during *Trieste*'s
...d dive of the second series. Stamped on the
...with a vibrator drill were the job and serial
...bers and the momentous inscription
...Boat."

36

...all over!" At a Pentagon press conference
...September 5, 1963, SECNAV Fred Korth
...s the microphone as Lieutenant Com-
...der Don Keach tells of his dramatic deep-
...ecovery which ended the *Thresher* search.
...h is holding the brass pipe (57 inches long,
...ht 10 pounds) which was identified as part
...hot water flushing line in the lost sub.

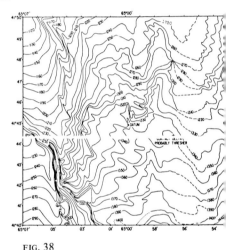

FIG. 37
The search for *Thresher* encompassed an original area of 10 square miles. Well over parallel (north to south) survey lines, each spaced about 250 yards apart, were covered using echo sounders and precision depth recorders. Four ships were assigned to this high precision systematic echo survey, which took from May 5 to 16, 1963. The vessels were USNS *Mission Capistrano,* an ex-T–2 tanker USS *Alleghengy,* a small seagoing tug; USS *Rockville,* a converted patrol craft; and USS *Prevail,* a converted minesweeper.

FIG. 38

FIG. 39
The approximate location of *Thresher* on the continental slope east of the Gulf of Maine.

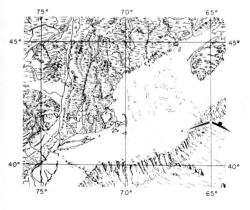

FIG. 38
The outcome was doubtless one of the most precise, detailed, and thorough bottom survey ever made of the sea floor beyond the Continental Shelf—or, for that matter, of any area of ocean bed. The data obtained (bottom contours and depth variations in fathoms) produced the above picture. Datum point of echo search (center) first determined its are and size. This datum was located at 41° 45′ north and 65° 00′ west, the last known position of *Thresher* during her fatal dive. Contact point DELTA (right), at first thought to be sub's wreckage, was not far off actual debris site. This bathymetric survey compiled by the University of Miami (interpretation by R. J Hurley, June 1963) even gave precise detail of sea bed topography as regards sediment, rock, vegetation, etc.

item of equipment susceptible to theft or damage through carelessness.

My days fell into a routine of normal division officer duties, and like anyone else with specialized skills I had to be available at all times for consultation with Yard foremen, work superintendents and other people directly in charge of the overhaul. The incredible scene of upheaval that quickly transformed into an unspeakable shambles the normally spotless and orderly interior of *Thresher* would be hard to describe. Empty milk cartons and sandwich bags were stuffed into every available corner. Panels torn out to get at the wiring or piping bore dirty finger marks. Loose screws and pieces of wire and insulation were tossed unceremoniously on the floor where no one bothered to pick them up. There were even odd tools which the workmen forgetfully left behind at the end of each day, along with muddy footprints and outdated newspapers sopping up half-dried pools of urine. The ship's crew at first viewed this encroachment of dirt and confusion with disgust and bewilderment, but their feelings soon crystallized into a strong resentment of the sometimes downright filthy workmen who were despoiling our beautiful ship and ruining its civilized amenities. As time dragged slowly by and the days lengthened into weeks and then into months, there were occasions when the atmosphere grew pretty tense. However, we all knew that it was the Commanding Officer's wish to have us avoid any direct confrontations with Yard personnel, and in this he was right. Complaints lodged through the usual channels were one thing, but in order to get the work done properly and completed as soon as possible, Commander Axene realized that our only hope lay in maintaining good relations with the shipyard.

Thresher's CO and sometimes her officers (at least the Exec and those of us who held divisional billets) had to deal with four different levels of people in the Portsmouth Naval Yard's chain of command. Working downward, *Thresher*'s entire overhaul was in charge of the production officer. Then came the repair superintendent. Under him were the ship's superintendent and his assistant. Axene, who was suave but very persuasive because he conveyed a strong feeling of authority, managed to get along pretty well with these Naval officers, but even so he could not accomplish miracles. As for us, *Thresher*'s officers, we were frequently outranked by people in the same service, and that was one sure way they could put an end to any arguments or objections. On top of that I recall wondering with some dismay how in the world *Thresher*'s overhaul was ever going to be completed in any kind of sequential manner. In November 1962 they replaced the ship's assistant superintendent, and in December the chief superintendent. Trying to communicate with their replacements naturally set things back further, although the new men were in no way to blame.

The final arbiter on all matters pertaining to the Portsmouth Yard's overhaul facilities and its supply problems was Rear Admiral Charles J. Palmer, the commander. He obtained information and took "advice" from numerous sources, but the final decision on whether or not to send a ship to sea rested with him alone. It was also his responsibility to react to information or orders handed down to him by the Bureau of Ships. How well this highly placed officer fulfilled his responsibilities in regard to *Thresher* and other ships entrusted to him is discussed further on in this book. I prefer to withhold my opinion.

As for myself, to get back to our routine, I was faced with a long day of seldom less than 12 hours. After I had finished poring over blueprints or reading and writing lengthy reports, making telephone calls and visiting *Thresher* for the regulation eight hours, I would stretch my workday by another four hours to find time to study my own qualification. This, as I have said, meant learning all about the ship and thoroughly familiarizing myself with its complex structure. Like the rest of the crew, I still clung to the pipe dream, during those first few months, that we might be able to sail on time, escape from the shipyard, and actually see *Thresher* once again in operation. How mistaken we were became evident toward the end of December, when the end was nowhere in sight. Instead of getting better, the multitude of problems in obtaining material and new equipment for the ship, and having it correctly installed, seemed to pile up on one another. Even replacement parts needed to repair tired components took forever to reach their destination. In fact delays became the rule rather than the exception. These exasperating holdups eventually stretched out to nine months which seemed more like nine years. The only cheerful note that injected itself into our often miserable situation was the opportunity I was afforded of reviving old friendships and cementing new ones.

I have many times been asked to portray character sketches of my closest shipmates aboard *Thresher*—the men I came to know intimately—and this seems like the appropriate place to do so, if only as a tribute to a fine crew that never came back.

Of course, like everyone else, I used every available opportunity to spend time at home with my family, but when you live for a long period in close proximity to a number of people, you soon get to know their quirks and peculiarities—the things that attract you or have the opposite effect. One man might be superstitious to the point of absurdity. Another might have a low boiling point, while a third would be blessed with a keen sense of humor, and so on.

I've mentioned John Smarz, Mike Di Nola, John Lyman and Jim Henry in particular, but these men have stayed with me as something much more vivid than just names. I still regard them as people, real and three-dimensional as when they were alive. People whose memory will stay with me and with my wife for as long as we draw breath.

One man in particular to whom I grew closest during my stay with *Thresher* was Mike Di Nola. He was dark-complexioned, about 32, heavy-set and good-natured. Tipping the scales at perhaps 200 pounds for a height of five feet nine inches, I guess Mike was somewhat overweight but somehow managed not to look it. He had thick black hair, lively brown eyes and a friendly, easy-going manner which hid great resources of unusual skill at his job. But above all else he enjoyed his food. In fact, Mike was no mean cook and would often regale us with fantastic dishes prepared on the spur of the moment. What was more, they were always good, although I am fairly certain he never would have been able to reproduce any of them exactly. They just came off the top of his head and he would think of appropriate names for them. All we were expected to do was sit down and enjoy his cooking, which certainly was not difficult.

Despite his poundage, Mike did not give the impression of being fat—probably because of Admiral Rick-

over's feelings about the men under his command, and
certainly thanks to Commander Axene's rigid requirements in calisthenics. He was a bug on physical fitness,
and some of us who were getting a bit older didn't exactly
appreciate being made to do a dozen pushups on a cold
morning. Still, I must admit that we felt better because
of these rather arduous sessions.

Then there was Lieutenant John Smarz, easily my
oldest friend in terms of years and about the same age
as Di Nola. John was fair-haired and had the light complexion of a Pole—which indeed he was. He filled every
minute of his waking hours either working his head off
or partying full bore. Whatever John did, he threw himself wholeheartedly and unsparingly into it. For him
there was no transitional break between working and
partying. He went from one to the other impulsively and
hated a vacuum. If ever things got quiet, which was not
often, John would throw a party. Or else he would stage
some practical joke on those nearest to him, undeterred
by rank or anything else. I don't know whether he would
have had the nerve to pull anything like that on an
admiral, but no one aboard was safe from John's practical jokes, which he, at least, found absolutely hilarious.
To describe John in a sentence, he was an able, likable,
and spontaneous fellow with a great zest for life. The
wives of both Mike Di Nola and John Smarz, Edna and
Joyce, were particular friends of Barbara's.

Lieutenant Commander John Lyman, who was 32
when he went to his death, also became a good friend of
mine during those trying weeks and months while work
aboard *Thresher* dragged on endlessly. He was a very
capable officer, even though of relatively limited experi-

ence, and had qualified both on submarines and as a nuclear reactor operator. *Thresher* was his first atomic sub, but he had been with her since the beginning, assigned to the commissioning crew. Beyond doubt, Lyman was totally dedicated to his job. I would seriously question whether he averaged more than four hours sleep a night, yet his constitution seemed to stand up indefinitely to this kind of abuse without ill effects. In complete contrast with Smarz, Lyman was not an ebullient character, but for all that there was a staunch quality about his friendship that gave you to understand right away it was worth cultivating.

My friendship with Lieutenant Junior Grade Jim Henry was particularly fortunate because, at only 25, he was serious, dependable and mature beyond his years. This made him an ideal assistant during our long working hours, as well as a pleasant boon companion, always ready to join in the fun.

In addition, it was reassuring to know that several crew members had served on other ships with me prior to that time.

However, as the months passed, there were some important changes in our personnel structure. In January 1963, our Executive Officer, Lieutenant Commander John Cowhill, was transferred out and his place taken by Lieutenant Commander Pat Garner, a slender, poker-faced Irishman who, in a sense, was responsible for saving my life. John Cowhill was needed on the staff of the Deputy Commander, SubLant, as the qualified nuclear officer on that staff. Since he was also a classmate of *Thresher*'s intended new CO, Lieutenant Commander Wes Harvey, it was thought advisable to transfer him at about the same time as they brought in Harvey. That, at least, was the rationalization of Vice Admiral William R. Smedburg III, Chief of the Bureau of Personnel.

Garner was a highly capable officer who, including the skipper, of course, turned out to be the third man aboard fully qualified for submarine command. I really did not know him well because we had little time to get acquainted, but in any case it was difficult to read Pat's true feelings about anyone or any situation. To further confuse the onlooker, he gave the impression of being totally carefree. Nothing ever rattled him and he took whatever came along in his stride.

That same month, Commander Axene (who had already been selected for captain) received a letter of transfer. This granted him leave, then required him to report for duty as Officer in Charge, *John S. Calhoun* (SSBN-630), for her builder's trials, and following her commissioning as Commanding Officer (Blue Crew).

John S. Calhoun was one of the new *Lafayette* Class Ballistic Missile (*Polaris*) type submarines. This giant ship, 425 feet long, then nearing completion at Newport News, Virginia, was of course nuclear-powered and equipped with a "Sherwood Forest" accommodating 16 atomic warhead missiles, each capable of hitting a target 2,500 miles away.

While our skipper was no doubt flattered, at the same time he took a dim view of his orders and protested them with good reason, it seemed to us. As a matter of fact, three months earlier, in November 1962, *Thresher*'s Commanding Officer had written a detailed report on the ship's first year of operations. He called her "the best ASW ship afloat today," but also highlighted a number of her deficiencies. *Thresher* was too complex in certain areas and had a vulnerable auxiliary sea water system. He was also concerned about the fact that in too many places accessibility to vital components had been sacrificed to appearance. In other words, function should have come before beautification. "In my opinion," he concluded, "the most dangerous condition that exists in *Thresher* is the danger of salt water flooding at or near test depth."

Having put his opinion on record for the benefit of COMSUBLANT, BuShips and COMSUBDEVGRU-2, to which *Thresher* belonged, Axene rightfully felt he had an ax to grind. He had been with *Thresher* from the very beginning—even prior to the time her keel was laid —and had seen her safely through a variety of troubles. Now, when his letter of transfer came through, Commander Axene wrote to the Bureau of Personnel objecting to this on the grounds that a supervisory change would not be good at this time. More so, since the difficulties which *Thresher* had experienced under his command had not yet been corrected. He wanted to see the job through, and once the overhaul was completed, to take the ship out to sea and make sure that all was well before handing her over to a new skipper as a going concern. I think he was pretty much on solid ground, but his objections were overruled.

Still not satisfied, Axene appealed directly to his immediate superior, Captain Andrews, then Commander of Submarine Development Group 2. Andrews again protested the orders to BuPers, but with no better success. The decision had been made by Admiral Smedburg and the order stood. The reason for this, apparently, was that, while the *Polaris* program then had top priority with the Navy, there was a critical shortage of experi-

enced officers capable of commanding these new subs.
The most competent officer slated for such a billet, Smedburg believed, was the Commanding Officer of *Thresher.*

At that point, Axene decided not to press matters any
further. He had stated his point clearly, his protest was
on record and that was as far as he could go without
damaging his career. Anyone can develop 20/20 hindsight, but how right Axene turned out to be was tragically
demonstrated not only by the loss of *Thresher,* but subsequently by a statement from Secretary of the Navy
Korth, during Congressional Hearings on the disaster.

"Actually, I have not yet cleared up in my own mind
at what point a commanding officer, if he is to be rotated
to another position, should be moved out. In other words,
he comes back with a submarine after shock tests and
perhaps knows more at that time about what faults and
what shortcomings there are in this particular sub. He
should therefore stay until after these shortcomings have
been corrected.

"If he then gets orders to move on, he should not do
so until he is certain that when the submarine goes out
again, it is in proper condition. In other words it can be
said that he supervised the work."

That, as I recall, was precisely Commander Axene's
thinking, but those who could have done something
about it wouldn't listen, while the far greater number
who concurred with him were powerless. Still, that was
perhaps what saved his life, too, and opened the door
to further promotion, for he is now a vice admiral.

Oddly enough, there was another man slated for transfer from *Thresher* to the *John S. Calhoun*—an enlisted
man of great promise. He was Machinist's Mate Donald
J. McCord, 33, recipient of a letter of commendation

from Axene for outstanding performance on duty. He had been with *Thresher* just under a year, and his orders would come through after the ship completed her sea trials.

He never made it, either.

THE LUCKIEST MAN ALIVE
January 1—April 9, 1963

When Commander Axene handed over *Thresher*'s command to Lieutenant Commander Wes Harvey in January 1963 (I shall never forget that ceremony, for Dean Axene was deeply moved and hard put to it to control his emotion), another continuity link was forged with *Nautilus*. Harvey had been Reactor Control and Engineering Division Officer aboard *Nautilus* while Axene was the Executive Officer, and I had worked very closely with him then. Now that he was taking over *Thresher* from Axene, I was assigned to his old job in the new ship. As he settled down to his first command, I probably got to know John Wesley Harvey even better than I had when we both served aboard *Nautilus,* and certainly as well as any officer on a ship can get to know the captain.

Much has been written about Wes Harvey, most of it at the time of the *Thresher* disaster, and his name was to appear repeatedly at the (unpublished) Navy Court of Inquiry and during subsequent Congressional Hearings by the Atomic Energy Committee. But his true personality did not emerge very clearly for all that, because he was no longer available for interviews and pen portraits. He was gone forever.

As I recall Harvey, he was a kindly, considerate man of 36, about five feet nine inches tall, stockily built, with a light complexion and light brown hair. You could have called him a very serious man, technically oriented because his consuming interest was submarines, and not because submarines had become his career. He was as much of a stickler for detail as Dean Axene, but in a different way that immediately made you aware of his deep preoccupation. He had many scholastic achievements behind him as well as a great deal of Navy experience. About 17 years of it, as I recall. His career began at the Naval Academy in September 1946 and he graduated eighth in the 1950 class, when he was sworn in as midshipman. During his Academy years he played football with distinction—a game he loved—and was guard for the Navy Eleven. Wes proudly bore No. 67 on his sweater and had some good action photos of himself which he cherished. In fact, when he wasn't talking subs, he liked to talk football. But he was also a devoted family man who married his childhood sweetheart, Irene

Nagorski. At the time of his death, Wes was the father of two fine boys, John, Jr., 11, and Bruce Walter, 8.

In 1951 he graduated from submarine school, standing third in a class of 77, and was picked for A-subs two years later. His father, Manning Harvey, a nattily dressed retired TV salesman, didn't think so much of that. He advised Wes against getting mixed up with submarines. His mother, a lady of strong religious beliefs, had a more philosophical view. "The Lord will take care of him," she said of her son.

If I've contrived to give the impression that Harvey's experience with nuclear subs was confined to *Nautilus,* or that he came straight from *Nautilus* to *Thresher,* this was far from being the case. He was first exposed to submarines aboard the diesel-powered *Sea Robin,* (SS-407), where he qualified as a submariner. Following this tour of duty, he was selected for advanced training in the nuclear program and went to Idaho Falls, Idaho, to study the reactor there. He reported to *Nautilus* in July 1955 and stayed with her for three years, which was when we saw a great deal of one another. While aboard *Nautilus* (Commander William Anderson, who later made captain and on his retirement became a Senator) we both took part in her two historical transpolar journeys under the pack ice, after which, having graduated from a chief to an ensign, I went off to officers' school at Newport, Rhode Island.

Wes Harvey continued from strength to strength. When he left *Nautilus* in August 1958, it was to become First Engineer of a land-based reactor in Windsor, Connecticut, where he stayed a year. He was then assigned to USS *Tullibee* (SSN-597) as Engineering Officer. In May 1961 he was selected for Executive Officer with

USS *Sea Dragon* (SSN-584), his second highly responsible job in a nuclear submarine. *Sea Dragon* made a historic rendezvous with *Skate* (SSN-578) at the North Pole in 1962, and Wes earned a citation for service under the ice aboard *Sea Dragon*. It was to have been presented to him on his return from *Thresher*'s last cruise, but his wife, Irene, received it instead in July 1963.

One thing stood out very strongly about Wes Harvey. He was aware that *Thresher* was his first command and he was keen as mustard to make good—to prove himself capable of handling this new and heavy responsibility. No man ever worked harder at his job than did Harvey, nor took it more seriously.

I must say, though, that by the time *Thresher* was finally ready to go to sea again, the thing I liked least about that fine ship had come through loud and clear. Looking back, you couldn't help but wonder about her frequent and extended stays in shipyards—her ever-present need of overhauls and inspections. Somehow, she never seemed to make a clean cut of the umbilical cord that tied her to moorings or else put her in dry dock. This, as we shall see, continued until the very end.

And that brings us to *Thresher*'s first postoverhaul "fast cruise," after nine inactive months in Portsmouth Naval Shipyard.

A submarine's "fast cruise" has nothing to do with speed. It starts when she has been determined by the shipyard to be ready for sea but is still moored at her berth. All shipyard workers depart and the crew once more takes possession of the ship and begins a frantic round-the-clock marathon to clean up the incredible mess left behind by the gangs. The goal is to restore the ship's interior to her former state of order and cleanliness, with everything spick and span and shiny bright. An incredible amount of elbow grease has to be expended, but the crew works willingly, if not always cheerfully, despite the long hours of (unpaid) overtime.

When the fast cruise begins, the crew operates all the equipment as though the ship were at sea. This phase normally terminates after three or four days, and if all is found satisfactory and any discrepancies can be termed minor, the crew is given a rest period of 24 hours. At the end of this time, the actual underway sea trials commence. These trials not only indicate the ship's diving ability, her speed, maneuvering and navigation capabilities, but also the state of her sonar gear. An extended period of sonar testing and alignment may take as long as nine days. It usually turns out to be one of the most difficult phases of the testing program on a submarine.

Following the underway trials, if no major problem has developed, the ship returns to the Yard and is then declared ready for her "shakedown" cruise. This is the normal sequence.

If, while at sea, the ship fails to perform according to specifications—if she doesn't meet the required standards—she is brought back to dockside and the necessary work carried out to bring her up to the desired condition. She then goes out on a "requalification" trial prior to the final shakedown cruise. That's the meaning of requalification. Something has been found amiss during the shakedown cruise and has to be done over again.

Our initial "fast cruise" aboard *Thresher,* which was also intended as training for the crew, began March 23, 1963. It was scheduled as a four-day test, but so many discrepancies were uncovered that the captain ordered the cruise aborted on March 26. No single problem was in itself a serious one, but collectively they took on very different proportions. This was a bitter disappointment for Wes Harvey, but he did the right thing and at once requested shipyard representatives to come aboard and correct the problems we had uncovered, before the "fast cruise" was resumed.

There was much discussion with the Yard people on which discrepancy should have priority of correction, but a schedule was finally worked out. This included all those problems which might impair the ship during her actual sea trials.

One of *Thresher*'s most serious discrepancies was in her low-pressure blow system. This is a system that blows low pressure air into the ballast tanks to discharge any remaining water that might be in there after surfacing. The valves for this system were electrohydraulically operated and the electrical connections on the entire system turned out to have been wired backward—exactly the opposite of what they should have been. For example, the valve-controlling switch indicator would show a "closed" position when in fact the valve was open. Had we gone to sea with this condition undetected, the result could have been very costly damage to the low pressure blow system itself—that is, the positive displacement blowers that pump the air into the tanks. Possibly even the venting of the main ballast tanks would have allowed water ballast to come aboard before it was called for or needed.

Another discrepancy which we did not care to live with was the misalignment of internal piping and equipment. This misalignment, it turned out, was actually absorbed by flexible hose connections that were not intended to do the job at all. As a result, a heavy strain was thrown on some of the piping in the ship, although this did not outwardly show because the flexible connections covered up the problem. The real reason for installing these flexible hoses was not to absorb misalignment of rigid piping to equipment, but solely to prevent sound vibrations generated within the ship from being transmitted into the surrounding waters and getting picked up by "enemy" sonar. These flexible hoses are actually called "sound isolating joints," and that is their prime and only function. The shipyard was therefore required to correctly align all the rigid piping with the equipment it served and take the strain off the flexible hoses.

As a matter of record, *Thresher* had (the year before) encountered still another piping problem with silver brazing. It was the subject of a memo from BuShips to the Commander, Portsmouth Naval Yard. A *Thresher* design feature was involved which contributed to silver-braze joint failures. It had to do with the inadequate support of piping and valves. Long, unsupported runs of piping (without brackets) put undue stress on these runs when subjected to shock. One result was the failure of a drain line in which a three-quarter-inch silver-brazed joint supported (unaided) the valves and piping associated with a vertical run of pipe 10 feet long!

Anyway, by the time this work had been satisfactorily completed, it was March 31 and we went into another "fast cruise," testing the components we had worked on. At this time an incident occurred that was, to say the least, not reassuring. During one of the drills involving a "flooding casualty" in the after-auxiliary sea water system, it took the detail in charge 20 minutes to "isolate a leak." True, some changes had been made to this system during *Thresher*'s long overhaul—but 20 minutes could become a critical lapse of time in a real emergency. Disaster would be likely to strike much faster.

The second "fast cruise" was satisfactorily concluded on April 1—April Fools' Day, ironically enough. At that point, in the captain's estimation at any rate, the ship was ready to sail. I don't mean to imply by this that Wes Harvey accepted anything substandard, but that he was champing at the bit after these endless delays which had involved 875 separate work requests, including hull repairs and stiffening, correction of access hatch problems, and fixing the periscope. The skipper was eager to go to sea—as indeed we all were. At that point, the cost overrun on *Thresher*'s PSA must have been enormous. The original estimate of 35,000 man-days to complete the overhaul had risen to 100,000 man-days.

On April 1—I recall that date well—we finally did get underway from Portsmouth Naval Shipyard and proceeded to the Sound Basin for a four-day sonar test in a back channel of the Piscataqua River. During this period, we cycled (opened and shut) the sea water valves throughout the ship. And at that stage we were not kidding any more. But once again we ran into trouble when the main sea water suction valve would not close. This was a big butterfly-type valve of about 36 inches in diameter and nothing would coax it into a closed position. We therefore had to return to the shipyard, April 4, and go directly into dry dock for another four days. To remove and replace a sea water valve of that size would have been impossible without tearing apart a lot of other equipment. As a matter of expediency, therefore, any other solution that would do the job was preferable. Someone in the shipyard finally hit on the idea of straightening the butterfly valve shaft by using hydraulic jacks. This was a pretty crude method, but it did solve the problem, at least for the time being. I use that qualifying term because sooner or later the job would have to be done properly. As it was, although the valve did close, the strain gauges in the hull indicated some distortion due to the excessive friction caused by the movement of the butterfly inside the piping. During that same period, repairs were also made to some malfunctioning torpedo door shutters. The crew, who by now were badly in need of a rest, got a four-day period of liberty.

But on that note, we received an operational order directing *Thresher* to proceed to sea, there to conduct her first trials following overhaul. On April 8, 1963, the day *Thresher* came out of dry dock and returned to her berth, I left home at about seven o'clock in the morning, telling my family that I would be back in a few days, as soon as we had completed our sea trials. I did not then know that in any event the skipper had no intention of staying at sea more than three days on that first outing. This was no doubt because of the numerous shipyard personnel who were going to make the trip as "observers."

As we have seen, *Thresher* was scheduled to sail on the following morning, but it was necessary for me to be there during the day prior to getting underway. It would give me time to prepare the reactor plant in readiness for next day's operations when the reactor would be brought to critical.

Then, although I was totally unaware of it, Fate

reached out and took a hand. At about 0200 on the morning of April 9, 1963, I received a phone call from my wife via the land line still connected to the ship.

"Ray!" she told me in a frantic and rather pained voice, "I can't see a thing. I've burned my eyes. Can you take me to a hospital?"

"You've done *what?*" I felt myself going cold all over. "Is it serious?"

"Please, Ray. Come and get me . . ."

Knowing Barbara was not a person of many words and would never have expressed herself in that manner unless she was in real trouble, I didn't even stop to ask her what had happened.

"Okay, honey. Hold on," I told her. "I'll be right there."

I turned the reactor over to Lieutenant Commander John Lyman, our Engineer Officer, and since he was my senior and the only other officer on board who outranked me at that moment, I requested permission to take Barbara to the hospital.

"Sure, Ray. Go ahead," John nodded.

I don't know how many traffic regulations I must have broken on my way home, but even so my mind raced ahead with all kinds of dire apprehensions and I must have set a record for the trip. I picked Barbara up at home, in obvious pain and quite unable to see, and as we raced to the hospital she told me what had happened.

"I was trying to open a bottle of liniment to rub into my shoulder muscle—you know how it gets a bit sore from carrying the baby around [Kerry was then eight months old]—and suddenly the stopper blew up in my face. It really hurts."

"I'll bet," I sympathized. "Did you use plenty of water?"

"That was the first thing I did," Barbara said. "Got my head under the cold tap and let the water run."

"Good girl." I didn't want to express too much concern so as not to alarm my wife, but she had certainly done the sensible thing. "Everything's going to be all right."

While Barbara was being treated at the hospital, I phoned my sister-in-law, Kay Brown, and asked her would she please go directly to our home and take care of the children. When Kay heard the news, she didn't even hesitate.

"I'm on my way. Take good care of Barbara."

During our drive to the hospital, I'd found out that Barbara's accident had occurred as the result of a pressure build-up in the bottle of liniment. It now remained for the eye specialist to make his diagnosis, which I prayed would not be serious.

I remained in the hospital with my wife for about three-quarters of an hour while the doctors determined the severity of her burns. Luckily, she would not suffer any permanent injury or loss of sight. So, while Barbara's eyes were being bandaged, I returned to the ship briefly. I was anxious to find out how *Thresher*'s primary system heat-up was going. I stayed only a few minutes before driving back to the hospital.

"With any luck," the doctor reassured me, "your wife can be out of bandages in a week to ten days. But during that time, of course, she'll be quite helpless and unable to take care of the children. You've five youngsters, I understand?"

"That's right," I said. "But I've already arranged for my sister-in-law to take care of them while I'm gone."

I left Barbara at the hospital, where she could get expert care, and with proper treatment, reassurance and pain sedation she felt much better. Anyway, she was never one to make a fuss about anything and the fact that her eyesight would not be impaired was an enormous relief to us both.

Kay assured me over the phone that all was well with the kids, and I therefore doubled back to *Thresher* at about 0400 on April 9—just a few minutes before John Lyman started a four-hour countdown which would result in a full head of "clean" steam. That's to say, uncontaminated by any radioactive material. The reactor was not due to start "cooking" until 0600, when permission would be requested to pull out the first uranium rods and begin a controlled nuclear reaction.

I knew that Barbara would probably be sent home the next day, and even though heavy bandages would totally deprive her of her sight for some time, I would be home long before the day came to remove the bandages. It had been a close call, but everything seemed to be working out okay.

Soon after I got back aboard ship, however, John Lyman appeared at my station in the Maneuvering Room, wearing rather a blank expression.

"The Exec would like to see you, Ray," he said. "I'll relieve you here while you go up and talk to him."

"Aye aye, sir."

When the Engineer Officer tells you that the Executive Officer wants to see you, it's not the time to ask questions, so I quickly made my way upstairs to the Control Center, where I dug out Pat Garner, who had taken over from John Cowhill hardly more than a month ago.

"You wanted to see me, sir?"

Garner, his face as ever betraying nothing, gave a slight shrug which I interpreted as one of regret.

"Ray, the Captain would like to have you remain with your wife until we get back. I'm having a yeoman type out a set of leave papers for two days. You can go home immediately."

For a moment I was stunned. I had a cold feeling in the pit of my stomach and things seemed to fall in on me. This was not only hard to take—it was almost impossible to believe.

"But everything's taken care of," I objected. "Barbara's going to remain in hospital until tomorrow. This isn't necessary. I really would like to see *Thresher* during her test operations."

"I'm sorry," Garner sympathized, "but the CO left me no room to make any decisions myself. That's an order. You're to stay with your family for that short period."

Knowing Wes Harvey extremely well because of our long and close association aboard *Nautilus*, I realized at once what had prompted his decision. It was a mixture of compassion and expediency. In his mind, my proper place was with Barbara, who, at that moment, was helpless. There was also the tremendous overcrowding problem on shipboard—21 non-crew members to berth, feed and accommodate, even for that short period of the initial sea trial. In the captain's ordered mind, everything dovetailed with impeccable logic, but I still wasn't ready to forego an experience I had been looking forward to for months. Logic, at that moment, had little to do with what was to me a bitter disappointment, order or no order.

"Have you any objection to my having a word with the Captain?" I asked Garner.

Pat shook his head "no," almost imperceptibly. "Go ahead, Ray. But I don't think it'll do you any good. You know the Captain. I'm only carrying out his order, so you're on your own."

"Thanks," I nodded, still hoping. Looking around the Control Center, however, I couldn't see Harvey anywhere. "Any idea—?"

"He just went to his cabin to write a message, I think," Garner said. "You'll catch him if you hurry. Maybe it's better if you talk to him in private."

"Thanks again, sir."

I scrambled down to the Commanding Officer's stateroom on the second level and knocked on the door.

"Come in," said a well-known voice.

Harvey was sitting on his bunk, scribbling something on a pad close at hand on a folding table. He looked up, not too pleased for a moment at this interruption, but the instant he saw me his expression changed to one of genuine concern.

"Ah, Ray. How's Barbara? Everything's going to be okay, I gather?"

"Yes, thank you, sir. She's doing fine and the kids are being taken care of by my sister-in-law. She's coming to stay for a couple of days. No problem at all—but the XO tells me you've ordered me off the ship?"

Harvey didn't smile. He seldom did, especially while on duty. But for an instant I spotted a gleam of amusement in his eye.

"Come now, Ray. I'm sure Pat Garner didn't put it in those words?"

"But it's an order, isn't it, sir?"

"That's right," the captain nodded. "The mess we're in leaves me no choice." I noticed for the first time that Wes Harvey's face looked drawn with fatigue. The tiredness in his eyes belied his firm tone. "I'm talking about all the overcrowding. Twenty-one extra bodies. It's lucky we're just going out and back."

"Captain," I pleaded, "that reactor means a lot to me. I've put in months of work on it. And not I alone, either. Couldn't you cancel your order just this once?"

"There's no way I can do that, Ray." Harvey took a deep breath. "Your bunk's already been allocated and, as you know, even the Torpedo Room's a dormitory!"

"I don't care where I bunk down, sir . . ."

"No," Harvey said. "The order stands, Ray. There'll be plenty more cruises for you. I shouldn't have to explain but I know what's on your mind. Let's just say that the engineering spaces are in good hands. And as for young Jim Henry, the extra bit of experience will make him all the more valuable to you later on."

And that was it. There was no way I could go beyond this point without deliberately disobeying an order from the ship's Commanding Officer. Harvey inclined his head slightly to indicate that our interview was over. "Tell Barbara we're all thinking of her," he concluded, "and wish her a speedy recovery. Take good care of her. We'll be back in a couple of days, I expect."

It was the last time I set eyes on Wes Harvey, though little did I dream it at the time.

I went back to Pat Garner in the Control Room, and as he looked up from a chart and read my expression, I played my last card.

"The Captain says no," I shrugged. "So no it is. Permission to remain with John Lyman until the reactor's critical?"

"Granted," Garner said briefly. "Don't take it too badly, Ray. You know the problem with all those extra types on board. Consider yourself lucky, rather . . ."

And with that I had to be content.

I was still aboard *Thresher* when, shortly after 0600, Harvey gave permission to pull out the first control rods in the reactor. These rods, which are made of absorbent materials, are interspersed between carefully spaced enriched uranium 235 rods in the reactor, which give off atom-splitting neutrons. The more control rods are withdrawn, the more neutrons become free to split the uranium atoms. Without a sound, or the need of oxygen, tremendous heat is generated as more and more neutrons become available to split more and more atoms and sustain a controlled nuclear reaction build-up.

Sea water, pumped around the reactor in a sealed system to cool it off, instantly turns to steam, but this steam is radioactive. A second water circulating system quickly builds up superheated steam by contact. This is "clean" steam, free from contamination, and after it has passed through the turbine, it is routed back to a condenser which turns it once more into water, ready for recycling. To speed up condensation, cold sea water is brought in from the outside through the submarine's pressure hull. It is admitted through sea valves and circulated along large pipes before being pumped out into the ocean again.

The fuel rods in a nuclear reactor are equal to about 40,000 gallons of diesel oil, and the clean water is reused again and again.

This is perhaps an oversimplified explanation of how

we have been able to return to steam power without using cumbersome fuel oil, but at this point it will have to do.

I hung around for another hour until the SSTG's (Ship's Service Turbine Generators) began producing electricity to supply the countless demands made by *Thresher*'s on-board equipment. Everything from running clocks and toasters to computing exact courses and even the angle of fire required for SubRoc missiles.

Finally, just before 0730, when the Engine Room notified the CO that *Thresher* was self-sustaining and her reactor ready to drive the main turbine, I stepped reluctantly ashore. I drove to the hospital and stayed with Barbara—who was very happy to have me back—until the following afternoon. Then I was allowed by the doctors to take her home.

During this period of the ninth of April, *Thresher* was, of course, at sea, and by schedule should already have conducted her surface trials and a few shallow dives. I remained home with my wife and children, acting as her eyes and with no foreboding whatever that anything had gone wrong with *Thresher* until the following afternoon. Suddenly, the quiet of our home was broken by the jingling of the phone. Having no idea who it might be, I picked up the receiver. Captain Louis Larcomb, of the diesel sub USS *Dogfish* (SS-350), was on the other end. At the time he was acting as SOPA (Senior Officer Present Afloat) in Portsmouth Naval Shipyard, and was chief of casualty control. He came straight to the point.

"Ray? This is Lou Larcomb."

"Yes, sir." For some reason I was instantly alert. "What seems to be the problem?"

"I guess you haven't heard?"

"No, Captain. This house has been pretty quiet. My wife—"

"Yes, I know. But *Thresher*'s overdue. We have reason to believe she's down."

"You can't mean that?" I said.

"Well—at least we haven't been able to communicate with her for several hours. Too long. I'd like to have you come over to the shipyard immediately."

"Right away," I said, but at that moment I still wasn't convinced or even seriously concerned. "It's probably another case of loss of communications. Has to be."

"Don't bank on it," Larcomb said, "though there's always the outside chance that you might be right."

As it turned out, I was tragically wrong.

When I reported to the shipyard, Captain Larcomb was standing by in the Communications Center, talking to *Skylark* and other units in the area, USS *Sunbird* (ASR-15), an Auxiliary Submarine Rescue ship, and the nuclear submarine *Seawolf* (SSN-575). Right away I could tell that something pretty serious had happened, and bit by bit the story of *Thresher*'s disappearance after a deep dive that morning came together. I remained with Captain Larcomb all that evening and the following day, by which time a massive search was in progress and more reports kept coming in from ships on station. But as the hours passed, it became evident that the very worst had happened and I was delegated the harrowing job of contacting the families of missing personnel.

The most difficult part was to inform them truthfully of what had happened without closing the door to all hope yet, but at the same time without raising false hopes which would only intensify their grief.

I still could not believe that a wonderful ship like

Thresher was really lost, and worse that she had taken with her so many fine human beings, including several to whom I was especially close. In fact, I did not reconcile myself to this tragic situation until some debris was delivered to the Communications Center. This consisted of calking that was once on the ship's interior bulkheads and hull. Also brought in, as I recall, were some rubber gloves normally used in the reactor compartment when handling radiologically contaminated waste, or when coming into contact with radioactive water and equipment related to the primary coolant system.

My wife also found it hard to believe that the ship was lost. She must have quietly worked herself up into a state bordering on shock, but there were no outward signs of emotion for days afterward. It was not until the shock began to wear off that she finally broke down. During this period her eyes were still bandaged and would remain so for another two or three days on one eye and perhaps two to three weeks on the other.

Each family of the *Thresher* crew was assigned a casualty assistance officer by the First Naval District, through Portsmouth Naval Shipyard. This was to assist them in their period of grief and ensure that they were all taken care of, financially and otherwise. I was assigned the job of overseeing all the families—129 of them —and this involved visiting first each one of the officers' wives with whom I was more familiar, then going on to each of the enlisted men's families, and of course those of the luckless civilian technicians and specialists who had been engulfed in the disaster.

Barbara accompanied me on these visits, but it was not until she came into direct contact with the inexpressible grief of the womenfolk, tempered in many cases by great

courage, that she finally broke down. This happened on
the first of these painful visits, I remember, when we
called on Edna Di Nola, Mike's wife, who was a close
friend of Barbara's. It was an experience that neither of
us would want to go through ever again, no matter what
the circumstances. The sum total of the sorrow, shocked
disbelief and pathetic but futile hope we encountered was
absolutely awesome and left us emotionally drained to
the last drop.

I remained attached to *Thresher* for the next few
months, even though she was by then officially declared
lost and "Stricken" from the Navy's basic available fleet.
This is the term applied to a ship that is beyond the
SUBMISS and SUBSUNK period and has totally disappeared as an entity. During that phase, while the most
intensive underwater search ever carried out by the Navy
continued around the clock in the area of *Thresher*'s last
dive, I was assigned to COMSUBLANT office, New
London, Connecticut. This was the time when I was
continuously heckled by newspapers, writers and radio
station reporters who dubbed me the Luckiest Man Alive.
At the time I had other things to think about, but even
this was bearable until the sick telephone calls started.
Perhaps Barbara is better qualified to tell this part of my
story because of an unbelievably cruel personal experience she had to endure.

"The phone never stopped ringing during those first
few days. Mostly they were well-wishers who marveled at
Ray's 'luck' and said he had me to thank. And of course
there was the press, looking for some new story angle
and asking endless questions. But then came the first—
and perhaps the last—'sick' call. I say the last because

after that experience I wouldn't answer the phone to anyone.

"Anyway, there was this man's cutting voice. He didn't identify himself or say where he was calling from, but when he had finished I didn't know whether to throw up or cry.

"'I'm a doctor,' he said, 'and I want to tell you that I don't believe a word of that story about spilling liniment in your eyes. It's much too pat and it doesn't fool me for a moment.'

"'What—what do you mean?' I stammered.

"'Well, it's quite obvious,' came the gloating tone. 'Your husband is the reactor control officer, isn't he?'

"'So, what does that have to do with it?' I asked.

"'Everything,' that loathsome voice went on. 'What *really* happened was that your husband sabotaged the ship. He knew she was going to sink—that's why he stayed home!'

"Something froze inside me. It was my first contact with what is known as a psychopathic character. All I could think to tell this man was that I didn't have to listen to his vile accusations, and that I didn't have any explanations to give to anyone like him. And on that I hung up—and for weeks after didn't answer the phone."

THE LUCKIEST MAN ALIVE
Aftermath

Looking back, now, I can readily understand the reason why the media gave me so much publicity as the Luckiest Man Alive that it was hard to live down.

The *Thresher* disaster not only was our first nuclear ship casualty but also the greatest submarine disaster of all time. My seemingly extraordinary survival—like backing a total outsider at impossible odds, which nevertheless comes through to win by a neck—was bound to create something of a sensation and at the very least arouse public curiosity.

Naturally, it also gave rise to many legitimate questions which I have never, so far, bothered to answer. To resolve the first of these questions once and for all, at no time did I have the slightest premonition that anything would happen to *Thresher,* much less that she would be totally destroyed by the sea, taking the entire ship's company with her. For one thing I had far too much confidence in the Commanding Officer and crew, even though this was Wes Harvey's first command and his first trip on *Thresher,* while the crew as a whole lacked the benefit of long teamwork. Nothing short of his being totally overwhelmed by some sudden and dreadful situation could have resulted in what happened.

I've heard of people canceling trip tickets or bookings because of a foreboding or a feeling of insecurity which in the end proved justified. I believe such a case occurred when a man got off the "unsinkable" *Titanic* at Cherbourg, her last port of call before New York, because it had been revealed to him in a dream that she would sink with a dreadful loss of life, including his own. There was also a passenger on the same ship who, though he was convinced she would go down, decided to take the trip anyway. However, he went to great trouble making a last-minute will and putting his personal affairs in order.

For my part, I was not in any sense bothered by such thoughts. In fact, I greatly looked forward to taking the ship to sea, and the only thing that really worried me was Barbara's painful last-minute accident.

Still, if the story has rightly been told, and it certainly appeared in print, the fact remains that one member of *Thresher*'s crew was greatly bothered by a premonition. He felt certain that something would go disastrously wrong during her trials and that he would lose his life.

So convinced was George J. Kiesecker, machinist's mate
2nd class, that he would die aboard *Thresher* on her
next trip he did not want to go at all. Kiesecker insisted
that the ship was still, at the end of her long overhaul, in
no condition to begin her sea trials. "*Thresher*'s a coffin.
I don't want to go on it . . . There was too much trouble
from the beginning," he allegedly said. To the best of my
knowledge, this unfortunate man was the only crew
member with such forebodings. That he proved right was
all the more tragic.

As to what happened after the loss of *Thresher*,
another question I have often been asked is whether I
felt apprehensive about going out to sea again. The answer to that one was definitely negative. In fact, not only
did I remain attached to *Thresher* for several months
after she was declared Stricken from the Navy annals, but
I was also attached to her sister ship, the USS *Tinosa*,
during her overhaul in Portsmouth. By then, the Navy's
SUB-SAFE program was already underway, and as
a result besides radiographing all *Tinosa*'s hull welds
when it was discovered that the X rays had either
been lost or never taken, other important work was done.
All silver-brazed piping joints were ultrasonic tested,
and as the result of computer studies the main ballast
tanks were provided with a much higher compressed air
blow rate. This enabled the ship to blow her main ballast
tanks at far deeper depths and increased recovery
capability from accidental flooding. Then the high-
pressure air cylinders were relocated *inside* the ballast
tanks to get rid of the icing problem caused by air reducers and all that extra piping.

One recurrent and aggravating problem I recall with

Thresher during her long overhaul was the reducers in the air system. They never seemed to function properly and were replaced I don't know how many times. At the end of almost every work day it seemed as though at least one reducer had to be replaced. *Tinosa* benefited by the knowledge we had gained with *Thresher* in this and many other areas. For example, dockside deballasting with the emergency blow system at simulated test depth—a maneuver which had never been tried out on *Thresher*—brought to light a variety of problems, including the freezing and jamming of screens and the inadequacy of the blow system for deep diving.

Now, after an overhaul, a sub could no longer get sailing clearance from the shipyard alone. It had to come directly from BuShips and the auditing system of the work done was tightened up considerably.

Two months after the loss of *Thresher,* in June 1963, the recently appointed Chief of BuShips, Rear Admiral William A. Brockett, established a Submarine Safety Steering Task Group which looked into and acted upon many other safety problems in deep-diving nuclear subs of the *Thresher* type.

Concurrent with my attachment to *Tinosa,* I acted as leg-man during the Navy's Court of Inquiry into the *Thresher* disaster. Following this, I was transferred to the diesel sub USS *Dogfish* (SS-350), where I had a chance to complete my qualification. This term may require a brief explanation, since it is highly important. In fact, an officer's qualification is a definite requirement of COMSUBLANT and COMSUBPAC. All officers must know and understand every aspect of their ship—its characteristics, the methods of firing weapons, and the potential weapons themselves. They must be familiar

with all the internals and externals—that is, the fighting
capability of the ship. Also included in qualification is
the ability to put a submarine totally through its paces.
The normal time period for the course is about a year,
and it is certainly a worthwhile experience—in fact a
must for any career submarine officer.

I was able to accomplish this during the ten-month
period between the loss of *Thresher* and the beginning of
1964, when I was also attached for a brief period to the
USS *Albacore* (SS-569), whose new teardrop hull made
her the fastest submarine in the world. Incidentally, the
predecessor of *Albacore,* which at the time of this writing is stationed in Portsmouth under the command of
COMSUBFLOT-2, is the USS *Dolphin* (SS-555), now
equipped with an experimental system called FRISCO
—Fast Reaction Integrated Submarine Control. This is
a computerized system for automatically locating and
isolating a potential casualty or leak. It can do so far
quicker and much more accurately than any human
brain, and this I well believe. For example, the "flooding
casualty" I mentioned earlier, which occurred during
Thresher's final "fast cruise," could have been isolated
about 60 times quicker. Regardless of changes made to
the valve system, FRISCO could today accomplish the
same job, unerringly, in about 20 seconds.

My next transfer was to Commander Submarine
Squadron 10 staff, as Electronics Matériel Officer, Sub-
Roc liaison Officer and Engineer for Commander Submarine Division 102. During this period, Commander
Submarine Forces Atlantic Fleet (COMSUBLANT)
gave me the opportunity to be aboard all the nuclear
attack class submarines which came after *Thresher* during their initial sea trials. With the loss of *Thresher,* by

the way, after whom her particular class of ASW/Attack submarines had been named, the class was renamed *Permit*, because that was the name of SSN-594, the ship that immediately followed *Thresher*.

Anyway, my experience soon broadened to include USS *Dace* (SSN-607), USS *Tinosa* (SSN-506), USS *Jack* (SSN-605), USS *Sturgeon* (SSN-637), USS *Skate* (SSN-578), USS *Gato* (SSN-615), USS *Greenling* (SSN-614), and USS *Nautilus* (SSN-571) after her big overhaul. All of these ships, not counting *Nautilus* and *Skate*, were similar to *Thresher*. As a matter of fact they were all direct or modified sister ships of the same class, with the exception of *Sturgeon*.

My duties aboard these subs were those of Safety Inspector and Representative COMSUBLANT during sea trials. That is, I was the direct representative on board of the Submarine Admiral of the Atlantic Fleet, and thereby had absolute authority in my field. However, I never found it necessary to exercise that authority. From the foregoing may be judged whether I felt any reluctance or uneasiness about going to sea again in a nuclear submarine.

To elaborate a little on those duties, although they followed much the same pattern, I found them interesting and challenging. Here is an example of the kind of schedule I had to meet in those days. Depart New London, Connecticut, my home, and proceed to Portsmouth, New Hampshire, to embark on, say, USS *Tinosa* for a three-month underway period. Leave *Tinosa* someplace in the Caribbean, proceed to the nearest air station for a flight back to my home base in New London for perhaps a weekend. Then jump on a flight to Norfolk, Virginia, or maybe Charleston, South Carolina, to catch the USS *Skate* for her sea trials. Disembark once more in the Caribbean, two or three months later, jump on an airplane and fly to Quincy, Massachusetts, there to report to USS *Greenling*. Take her to sea and again leave her in the Caribbean. Fly home for a few days, then pack up to go aboard the USS *Gato*. Ride that ship for a few months through her sea trials and return to Connecticut. And so on.

This continued until 1969, at which time I took command of the diesel sub USS *Carp* (SS-338) for a short period (I had by then made Lieutenant Commander), following which I was transferred to the Farho Building in Boston for processing prior to retirement. In June 1970, I retired aboard the USS *Constitution*.

Since I spent so much time in the Reactor School at Arco, Idaho, it has been rightly assumed that I came into fairly frequent contact with the controversial Rear Admiral Hyman G. Rickover, Assistant Chief, Bureau of Ships (Nuclear Propulsion) and Chief of the Atomic Energy Commission's Naval Reactors Branch. Such was indeed the case, and the next question I have been asked for years and am still being asked today is, What kind of a man is he?

That's a fair question and it deserves more than a passing answer, since one can only describe Rickover as an absolutely unique individual and a law unto himself. In a sense, Rickover is to the Navy's atomic submarine fleet what J. Edgar Hoover was to the Federal Bureau of Investigation, although a very different person. He is slender-built, gray-haired, lynx-eyed, peppery and abrasive, and his determination once he sets himself a goal is an awesome thing to behold. Nothing—but nothing—can prevent him from reaching his objective. Where other men would pause and perhaps quail, Rickover wades in with a two-fisted verbal attack that is guaranteed to overwhelm the opposition. It invariably does, not only because of his iron will and tremendous intelligence, but because right is on his side. Above anything else, Rickover is a man who understands perfectly the relationship between cause and effect, and knows only one way to do anything—the right way. He can, on occasions, be extremely foxy if that will best suit his purpose, but of one thing you may be absolutely sure—he will get where he wants to go and accomplish what he starts out to do.

My initial encounter with Admiral Rickover was some time prior to his making Admiral, and it is not too easy for an Engineering Duty Captain to make Admiral. The odds are against him because he has never actually commanded a ship and he is liable to be passed over in favor of career men with command experience.

At the time I first came under Rickover's command, in the early 1950's, he was a Captain and I was only an enlisted man selected for nuclear power training in Schenectady, New York. The training consisted of the Union College courses for which Rickover personally filled the curriculum, and then going on to a S1G prototype reactor, of which at that time there were only two. Besides the Idaho plant, there was this particular prototype designed and built by General Electric and located at Balston Spa, New York. It was initially scheduled for installation aboard USS *Seawolf*, sister ship of *Nautilus*. In those days, anyway, Rickover was not spread as thin as he has been in recent years. Consequently, he spent a lot of time with us and we got to know him quite well.

The then Captain Rickover was by far the most demanding and downright tough Naval officer I have ever met, but this toughness must in fairness be weighed against the stupendous job he set out to do. Not the least part of it was bucking The System—the slow, ponderous welter of paperwork that clings like glue to every action initiated by the Naval bureaucracy. Commander William R. Anderson (later Captain, U. S. Navy, then Senator after his retirement), who was my commanding officer aboard *Nautilus,* has quoted Admiral Rickover perhaps better than anyone else.

"A military organization is set up to do routine, not imaginative work. If anyone comes along with a new idea, the people in the organization naturally tend to make him conform. The first thing a man has to do is make up his mind he is going to get his head chopped off ultimately. If he has that feeling, perhaps he can accomplish something."

And again, "Super efficient administrators are the curse of the country. Their main function seems to be to harass brainworkers with trivia and waste as much time as possible."

The problems that Rickover faced when he conceived his original idea of fitting an industrial atomic reactor which occupied two city blocks (as at Oak Ridge) inside a submarine hull were staggering. And they were not the only ones. No matter how ingeniously designed, the reactor would need heavy, foolproof shielding to protect the ship's crew from radioactivity. There was more. The water that was pumped through to cool the Oak Ridge reactor did turn into steam pretty quickly, but that also was radioactive. There was no way of getting it to drive an accessible steam turbine in a normal engine room without the instant danger of contamination. This meant

providing some means of transferring valuable heat
energy from radioactive water to a secondary circulation
system that would generate "clean" propulsion steam for
use in the turbine.

No wonder, perhaps, that Rickover was ridiculed and
at times openly laughed at—by those senior to him, of
course. Yet the advantages of adapting (nuclear-
generated) steam propulsion to submarines was incal-
culable. No longer would a sub have to carry huge quantities of diesel oil for surface running and an endless
array of batteries for running submerged. Electric underwater propulsion required so many batteries that everything else in a sub's hull had to be crowded into a minimal space while crew accommodation was merely an
afterthought. Even so, the ship's performance beneath
the surface was severely limited, for the batteries soon
ran down and the ship was then forced back up to re-
charge them. At best and for short periods only, she
might sustain 10 or 12 knots—which also put a crimp
on her evasive capabilities.

For three years (1946–49) Captain Rickover battled
The System singlehanded. The Navy did give him an
office in a converted ladies' powder room, but his letters
went into pending trays, there to remain for months
while the logic of his verbal appeals blunted itself on deaf
ears. Many a lesser mortal would have given up in de-
spair, but not this obsessively dedicated man who
pursued his goal with a kind of tigerish ferocity that
nothing could daunt.

Finally, after countless losing spins of the wheel, the
ball fell into a winning number. Rickover wrote directly
to the then Chief of Naval Operations, Admiral Chester
K. Nimitz, outlining his proposal for a nuclear-powered

submarine. He wrote so convincingly that the idea intrigued Nimitz, and soon afterward Rickover was appointed head of a newly formed activity in BuShips, called the Nuclear Power Section.

Sometimes, at roulette, the ball drops into the same slot twice running. It's a rare occasion but it does happen and Rickover played his winning streak to the hilt. He knew that, to get anywhere without endless bureaucratic delays in the Navy's chain of command, he would have to wear two hats. So, with the help of a sympathetic Admiral, he talked the Atomic Energy Commission (which kept a tight hold on uranium supplies) into forming a Naval Reactors Branch with himself at the head. It was a shrewd move, since the AEC couldn't very well stand by and allow the Navy to encroach on its preserves. And—who knew?—there just might be something to this harebrained scheme of Rickover's.

At all events, from that moment on when Rickover wanted something done, he simply wrote himself a memo —a brief one—approved the request immediately and got on with the job. The "Super efficient administrators" were out of the loop and, in so far as Rickover was concerned, were left with nothing to channel through their bureaucratic maze but thin air.

The writer who described this move as "a classic maneuver in anti-bureaucracy" probably coined the understatement of the year. Rickover and a handful of dedicated men were now on their way. This little caucus included some highly skilled civilian physicists, engineers, technicians and Naval architects, augmented by counterparts in the Navy itself and fired with the same enthusiasm. But these men were far too few. To translate Rickover's "Jules Verne" dream of a steam-powered submarine into reality, he needed a vast array of talent. It was not readily available, more so as Rickover was a perfectionist without peer who knew exactly what he wanted. He had spent World War II in BuShips, turning out improved electrical equipment for the Navy, and he also had behind him a year's intensive study in reactor physics at the AEC's Oak Ridge plant.

Rickover interviewed literally hundreds of engineers without finding the level of skills he sought. He therefore set up his own nuclear engineering school and even funded a crusade to seek out and educate talented youngsters. This was to pay off handsomely, but meantime he accomplished a tour de force without precedent. In less than a year, using the AEC's desert test center at Arco, Idaho, plumb in the middle of nowhere, he managed to squeeze the working prototype of a nuclear reactor into an existing submarine hull.

Here, it is worthwhile pausing for a moment to examine the parallel between the automobile and the submarine. For half a century, car designers clung to the outdated notion that an automobile was a horseless carriage, and so built and styled it, using the same antiquated suspension, high center of gravity and boxlike body.

Hypnotized by "tradition," Naval architects persisted for about 50 years in building submarines that were little more than modified and waterproofed surface vessels, equipped with ballast tanks which enabled them to dive. Handicapped further by inadequate and unsuitable power units, these old-fashioned "undersea boats" had performance limitations that, by present-day standards, were laughable. The advent of nuclear-generated steam

power and, in fact, totally new hull configurations reversed their characteristics and put things in their right
order. From that time on, a submerged submarine was
in its true element and able to perform in a manner far
superior to what was possible on the surface. They
could dive, rise and maneuver in a state of "neutral"
buoyancy comparable with a "weightless" spacecraft.
With power available in abundance, air became the only
limiting factor in keeping a ship submerged. The internal combustion engine of a diesel sub requires so
much air that it can consume the entire atmosphere
within the hull in a matter of minutes. Therefore means
had to be provided of ventilating the Engine Room, and
this in turn restricted diving. Yesterday's sub was uncomfortable in the deep. Today's sub is uncomfortable
on the surface, which is no longer its natural element.

Anyway, my first encounter with Admiral Rickover
after I became a commissioned officer took place much
later than the spectacular events just related. He remembered me, of course, but it was just a formal interview
for selection to remain on the Navy's nuclear program.
Furthermore, if the Admiral approved, I would be given
a specific job. He was still as tough as nails, but my
tremendous respect for him had, if anything, increased.
Beyond that, I would be lying if I said we liked him. Yet,
according to Captain William Anderson, my former
skipper, "In private, I found Rickover, after I came to
know him, one of the most gentle, warmhearted and unselfish men I have ever met. And one with a keen sense of
humor, too."

So you can take your pick. Admiral Rickover, who
dislikes wearing uniforms and is nearly always attired in

civilian clothes, somehow gets across the ancient adage, "Don't do as I do. Do as I say." Yet I am the first to admit that his gift for inspiring blind loyalty surpassed anything I ever encountered during my fairly long Navy career.

Naturally, I have often been asked since the *Thresher* disaster what Admiral Rickover's views were, unofficially. I mean by this, outside his Congressional testimony, which in itself was pretty acid. The fact is that he never spoke to me directly about it, yet I got the clear impression that he had warned the Navy repeatedly. Unless they mended their ways and undertook a much higher degree of quality control for the rest of the ship, as opposed to the reactor compartment, sooner or later we were bound to have serious trouble. This, unfortunately, turned out to be terrifyingly correct.

Until *Thresher* went down, the Navy had apparently reconciled itself to accepting two standards of quality control. And that which was deemed adequate for the hull, piping system, and deballasting equipment consistently remained far inferior to what the truculent (but farseeing) Admiral Rickover would tolerate in his reactor compartment. Instead of taking heed, however, the Navy almost seemed to hold this against Rickover— as though he were too finicky.

To answer a couple of other questions, first the term "Conn," which appears in every submarine's Deck Log, seems to confuse many people outside the Navy, and especially those outside the submarine service. Sometimes the captain is at the Conn, or has the Conn, sometimes the Navigator and at other times the OOD (Officer of the Day) when in port. If the ship is underway, OOD

signifies Officer of the Deck. Conn is derived from Conning, which in Naval parlance means controlling the
ship. (The older diesel subs all had conning towers
from which the ship was controlled. Nowadays, in a
nuke, the equivalent area is known as a sail.) The Conn
does not necessarily have to be in any given part of a
submarine. For example, when the ship is on the surface, she will be Conned most likely from the bridge—
that is the space atop the sail. When submerged, the
Conn will probably be in the periscope area, which
in turn is at the Control Center.

To be at the Conn, or have the Conn, therefore, is to
have control of the ship, regardless of the area whence
the orders are issued.

Then in a nuclear sub you may hear that rather
ominous word "scram." When the reactor scrams, this
means it shuts down prematurely and unexpectedly and
propulsion power is lost (as almost certainly happened
with *Thresher*) except for the backup battery-driven
electric motor. What is interesting, and certainly amus-
ing, is the origin of the term "scram." The first nuclear
reactor, built in Chicago, was a crude enough affair, but
it did prove out the principle of a sustained and controlled reaction, as opposed to an uncontrolled one—an
atomic explosion.

This reactor consisted of a block of uranium 238 ore
—not the enriched 235 variety used today. And at that
time the operators did not know just when a chain reaction would be reached. They therefore hung a chunk
of boron carbide above the reactor, suspended by a rope.
A man was stationed with an ax in hand, ready to cut the
rope when the self-sustaining reaction was reached.
"Scram!" simply meant "Run for it!" the moment the

safety shutdown signal was given and the rope cut.

Finally, I think it might be appropriate to give a word of explanation about Watches—or the manner in which duty spells are rotated for the crew of a ship. On a nuclear sub such as *Thresher,* there are normally six Watches in each 24-hour spell. Thus the crew is rotated every four hours, but still puts in eight working hours during that time interval.

The first Watch starts at midnight (2400 or 0000) and ends at four A.M. (0400). This is called the Dog Watch. Men coming off duty at that time often help themselves to a steak or some other edible which they call "Midrat," a contraction for Midnight Rations.

The second Watch runs from four to eight A.M. (0400–0800) and is called the Swing Watch because it is halfway between the Dog Watch and the Blue Watch which begins at eight A.M. and ends at noon (0800–1200). It is then that crewmen who had the Dog Watch go back on duty. This gives them four hours on and eight hours off. We are now at the end of the Day Watch (1200–1600), which terminates at four P.M. To be consistent, this is really the second Dog Watch, but nobody calls it that.

The next Watch, from four to eight P.M. (1600–2000), doesn't actually have a name, either, although logically it should be called the second Swing Watch. Nor does the sixth Watch, eight P.M. to midnight (2000–2400), which is really the second Blue Watch.

The name Dog Watch apparently arose from the fact that the crew can "Dog" that particular Watch or cut it in half, reducing it to a two-hour span. This enables the men to get more sleep. For that reason, on an extended cruise a crewman allocated the Dog Watch would remain on it only for perhaps a week before being rotated to another Watch.

Fortunate is the man who draws the second Blue Watch, from eight P.M. till midnight (2000–2400 or 0000), for in that case he can get a full eight hours' sleep at a normal time (midnight till eight A.M.).

In conclusion, my wife was often asked after *Thresher* went down whether she was bothered or apprehensive about my going to sea again in so many different submarines. I have never known her to do otherwise than steadfastly shake her head.

"It's Ray's career," she would say, "and if he wishes to pursue it, then it is his privilege and duty. I have nothing to say about it and I am no more apprehensive than I was on that terrible day before we heard the news that *Thresher* was down."

Until my retirement, seven years later, this remained her philosophy.

14

TASK GROUP 89.7
April 13—May 26, 1963

The Deputy Commander, Submarine Force, U. S. Atlantic Fleet (Rear Admiral L. P. Ramage, USN) on his way back to New London, Connecticut, from Key West, Florida, had scarcely touched down at Trumbull Airport, Groton, Connecticut, when a message was handed to him. The time was 1830 and the message gave such details as were then known in New London concerning *Thresher*'s SUBMISS status. A radio message intercept from the pilot had already alerted the Admiral of serious trouble, though of course without going into specifics.

Oddly enough, the original public awareness that something was seriously amiss appeared to have begun in Newport. The place was agog with rumors that "a submarine is on the bottom and unable to rise."

Ramage at once switched to a helicopter and proceeded to Newport, Rhode Island, where he embarked aboard the destroyer *Blandy* (DD-943) and at 2030 headed full speed for the scene where the search was already in progress. The Auxiliary Repair Ship USS *Recovery* (ARS-43) had joined *Skylark* in her futile attempts to locate *Thresher* earlier that afternoon, and an hour before Rear Admiral Ramage landed at Groton, she had spotted an oil slick about seven miles southeast of *Skylark*'s 0917 position (the point from which *Skylark* had received *Thresher*'s last message), or 41° 44' north and 64° 59' west. Recovery also found some floating debris which were rushed back to Portsmouth Naval Shipyard for examination by laboratory personnel.

The debris consisted mainly of pieces of white plastic, but samples of the oil slick also were taken. The verdict was that both the plastic and oil "could have come from *Thresher*."

By then, however, more than six hours had elapsed since *Thresher*'s last garbled message and no one needed to spell out her almost certain fate to the grim-faced officers and crew aboard Admiral Ramage's destroyer. Much had already happened that pointed inescapably to *Thresher*'s total loss, and as the USS *Blandy* clove her way "full ahead" through rising seas toward *Thresher*'s datum, there were already 15 ships either on their way to the search or making ready to sail.

Commander Submarine Flotilla Two, New London, (Captain Frank Andrews), who was also *Thresher*'s squadron commander, had been handed *Skylark*'s message at 1245 that afternoon and had acted immediately. Naval commands up and down the coast of Maine had been ordered to move forces into position to assist the search (there was little talk of "rescue"). Commander Submarine Force, U. S. Atlantic Fleet, Vice Admiral E. W. Grenfell, received from the Atlantic Fleet Movement Report Center a list of all ships within 100 miles of the *Thresher* area, approximately 220 miles east of Boston. Messages requesting *Thresher* to report were routinely placed on the submarine fleet broadcast, which is copied by all submarines at sea. Naval Air Station, Quonset Point, Rhode Island, immediately sent a helicopter to transport Captain Andrews to the Destroyer Leader USS *Norfolk* (DL-1). Andrews boarded the *Norfolk* at about 1700 and also raced toward the search area.

There was still no sign of *Thresher,* and somewhat earlier, at 1830, well over nine hours since the sub's last garbled message, Vice Admiral Grenfell had alerted Mrs. Irene Harvey, wife of *Thresher*'s commanding officer. He had also begun notifying other next of kin that *Thresher* must be presumed missing and was officially so declared.

By approximately 2100, it became tragically apparent that COMSUBLANT had not anticipated the bad news and *Thresher* was indeed down in some 1,300 fathoms of water. Darkness had set in, the sea was getting angry and any further search operations had to be postponed till first light, April 11. In the meantime, however, Admiral H. Page Smith, Commander-in-Chief Atlantic

Fleet based on *Norfolk*, had established a special Task Group, designated 89.7 (an odd combination of numbers derived from Operational and Administrative Groups), charged with the responsibility of organizing and co-ordinating a thorough search for the missing *Thresher* and utilizing a virtual armada that grew during the night and into next morning from 15 to 28 warships of all types imaginable. In addition, five oceanographic or surface vessels joined the fray. It was a formidable rescue force, had there been the slightest hope in that direction; but as the likelihood grew into a certainty that *Thresher* had gone to the bottom with everyone aboard, the emphasis quickly shifted from rescue to oceanographic search.

Next morning, further debris began to show up and was swiftly retrieved and rushed back by destroyer to the New London laboratories. USS *Blandy* spotted several pairs of rubber gloves and some pieces of yellow plastic material. One fragment of this material was sent back for quick analysis. USS *Skylark* fished out more yellow plastic, a small tube of "Baker's Flavor" squashed and bent at the bottom end, and several pieces of cork. The Submarine Rescue Ship USS *Sunbird* (ASR-15) contributed several more pieces of plastic and two rubber gloves which were not, however, a pair. The destroyer *Warrington* (DD-843) picked up an additional rubber glove.

Radio reports indicated that while any or all of these items could have come from *Thresher*, and most probably did, there was nothing which could *positively* and beyond doubt be identified as having come from the lost sub.

By then, Task Group 89.7 was faced with an almost superhuman challenge—that of locating the presumably broken remains of a submarine now resting at least 8,000 feet below the turbulent waves. By comparison, a search for the proverbial needle in the haystack would have appeared simple. The restless sea, once it has engulfed an object—even a sizable one like *Thresher*—wipes the slate clean of any point of reference from which to begin a search. Yet, to obviate an enormous waste of time and effort in scouring the ocean bed—with no promise whatever of success—*some* point of reference or datum was required.

It was therefore decided to use the co-ordinates in which *Skylark* had established the position of *Thresher* in very deep water at 0917, April 10. That was when she had last been heard from by underwater phone, and even though she had undoubtedly moved from there, perhaps before losing control and certainly afterward, it would have to do. Having marked this datum with a buoy anchored to the sea bed, the search could begin on the basis of an area of 10 square miles, covering four million square yards. That was a generous arbitrary figure and in the end it turned out to be so.

On April 11, the fleet oiler USS *Waccamaw* (AO-109) sailed out of Newport to meet and refuel the search units already at the scene. However, within 20 search hours following the disappearance of *Thresher* (0517, April 11), which included recovery of nothing more than minor debris (probably) released from the lost ship, the whole project, as we have seen, changed character. From being a random search it turned into an oceanographic expedition of great complexity.

By 0217, April 12, 39 hours after that garbled message from the deep ("900 R") which was the last ever heard from SSN-593, the destroyer *Blandy,* carrying Rear Admiral Ramage, reached the search area. At about the same time, five other destroyers, two submarine rescue vessels, one salvage ship, two submarines, and the famous and brand new research ship *Atlantis II,* whose skipper, Captain Hiller, was diverted by Navy request from an oceanographic cruise aimed at making biological and chemical observations in the Gulf of Maine, arrived on scene. At early light, a fresh patrol of aircraft from two Navy squadrons also appeared overhead. Aircraft had already been scanning the bleak, cruel and unyielding ocean most of the previous day, without success, it may be added, despite the use of radar.

On their way to *Thresher*'s unmarked graveyard at this time were also the USS *Rockville* (EPCER-581), a radar patrol craft carrying a special high-precision Fathometer, the USS *Redfin* (SS-272), a specially equipped diesel submarine, and the USS *Hazelwood* (DD-531), a destroyer loaded with deep-mooring buoys, specialized personnel and a vast array of instruments from Woods Hole Oceanographic Institute, which were transferred to *Atlantis II.* The last-mentioned ship, as soon as the datum was fixed, set about taking water and bottom samples from the vicinity. These were tested for radioactivity, but not a drop of water or a speck of silt revealed any trace of it above totally normal background radiation.

The nuclear submarine *Seawolf* (SSN-575) had already been on station, crisscrossing the area for the best part of two days, using her sonar and UQC in between keeping a sharp lookout on the surface for any more likely debris.

At this time it may be interesting to anticipate for a moment the climactic point of the greatest Naval search in history—the day when the exact location of *Thresher*'s torn hulk was finally pinpointed, even before the Bathyscaphe *Trieste* went down, made visual observations, and retrieved some debris that ended months of painstaking and doggedly determined effort.

The point of interest was the datum originally chosen and fixed by a marker buoy—a point of reference which turned out to be surprisingly accurate—if only the searchers had known it. As we have seen, the dead center point of the search was that from which *Thresher*'s last message had been received—41° 44' north and 64° 59' west, taking into account her last known course of 090°, or due east of the Eastern Channel between George's Bank and Brown's Bank (Fig. 39). Her wreckage, when finally located on the sea bed, was 41° 45' north and 64° 56' west. Thus she was resting only one minute north latitude and three minutes west longitude away from the co-ordinates originally decided upon as the datum of the search.

This in turn made it possible to arrive at a reasonable assumption of *Thresher*'s angle of descent from the time she was doomed until she hit the sea bed, and possibly to estimate what her impact speed may have been. During the Joint Committee Hearing held June 27, 1963, *before Thresher* was located, Rear Admiral Edward C. Stephan, Oceanographer of the Navy, pointed up some interesting facts.

When asked by Representative Bates, "In view of your

knowledge of oceanography and currents and that type of thing, how far could Thresher be now from where she actually went down?" (How far from the established datum co-ordinates could she have struck ocean floor?)

Admiral Stephan cautiously replied, "In looking at this —first of all in considering the oil slick, and where it should be, due to currents from where it [first] appeared, we felt that the resultant current from the 8500-foot depth to the surface was insignificant in terms of navigational error. In other words, we calculated some 10 minutes for this to rise from the bottom. The currents don't all flow in the same direction. It is the resultant current that affects it. We felt that this was insignificant.

"There are estimates as to the velocity of Thresher, from the time she was . . . sinking out of control . . . that are engineeringly sound. [They] indicate she could have been going as fast as 160 knots [about 184 mph] when she hit the bottom. This is an extreme and the lowest estimate is about 15 knots." (An estimate of 114 knots from another source fits more credibly into the ultimate picture.)

Secretary Korth: "Going straight down?"

Admiral Stephan: "Yes sir. This means in any event there would not have been much time for her to have been affected by the currents . . ."

In his final estimate from calculations, Admiral Stephan put it this way: "If she is at a 30° angle from the vertical and she drops 8000 ft, she will be 4000 ft [about 1,300 yards] from you . . . I think they have very good information that the submarine is, in fact, in the area they are covering."

This "information" turned out to be an actual set of spare "0" rings or gaskets used in submarine hydraulic piping. Each ring had been enclosed in a neatly typed envelope, giving the stock number and manufacturer. There were three different sizes (see Fig. 24), and while two of these were common to certain destroyers, the third was suitable only for *Thresher*. Captain Charles Bishop, Office of the Chief of Naval Operations, in charge of the technical information group, search effort, stated that these "0" rings were known to have been in the spare parts kit aboard *Thresher*. There was no positive proof that this particular find came from the lost sub, but in cautious technical jargon it was described as "a very high confidence level."

Another "piece of evidence" too fragile to be brought into court was the greater part of a badly damaged submarine battery grid or plate, measured and examined by an Exide battery representative and identified by him as coming from *Thresher*.

The neoprene rings were recovered May 28 and the battery plate on June 24, only three days before Admiral Stephan gave evidence at the Hearings. However, the point of this early sea bed debris was not merely that it fixed the location of *Thresher*. It also determined (because she came to rest so close to the datum) that she had plummeted, almost certainly stern first, at a very sharp angle and consequently a very high speed. Enormous craters, seen from the Bathyscaphe *Trieste* at a later date, tend to add substance to this theory. They are referred to in the next chapter.

It was indeed an ironical turn of events that the original 10-square-mile area shrank in less than five months to two miles by two, and eventually to 700 by 200 yards. But there is another delaying factor to take into account. Even assuming that the datum or "hub" of the search is reasonably accurate, you have to cover every one of 360° in a theoretical circle, and the odds are heavily against heading in the right direction first time off.

At this point, though, since the original search area ended just beyond the 1,000-fathom curve of the Continental Shelf, the search team correctly deduced that *Thresher* had "fallen off" the edge of the shelf into a chasm several thousand feet deep.

As the hunt for *Thresher* quickly took shape, it was divided into three distinct elements, the first of which was already well underway. This was the "seagoing" element, or Search Group—the vessels, hardware and personnel that were going to do the actual searching. The second element was a shore-based team consisting of 11 men who formed a "brains trust" called the CNO Technical Advisory Group. Its job was to provide the necessary technical guidance for the activities of the seagoing vessels. In fact, this second element went far beyond making suggestions and proposing plans. It not only procured exactly the kind of ships and hardware required, but on many occasions sent various members out to sea to help in the search.

The chairman of this advisory group was Dr. Arthur E. Maxwell, Senior Oceanographer, Geophysics Branch of the Office of Naval Research. Captain Bishop became co-chairman and CNO liaison officer. The committee membership included some of the finest brains in the science of oceanography. There were senior representatives from the Naval Oceanographic Office, the Bureau of Ships, the Lamont Geological Observatory, the Hudson Laboratories, the Woods Hole Oceanographic Institution, the Naval Research Laboratory, the Oceanographic Department of Rhode Island University, the Naval Reactors Branch of the Atomic Energy Commission, and even the Oceanographic Group from the University of Miami.

The third element set up operations at the Woods Hole Oceanographic Institution, Woods Hole, Massachusetts. This group soon acquired a logical if strange name which resulted from the phonetic pronunciation of its acronym—TAG WHOI (*Thresher* Advisory Group, Woods Hole Oceanographic Institution). And from there to "Tag Hooey" was just a step. The group was led by Mr. Arthur Molloy, of the Navy's Oceanographic Office in Suitland, Maryland. Tag Hooey's complement was a variable one, but at least 15 different civilians or Naval officers were a part of it for periods ranging up to three weeks or even longer. These men represented the all-important Submarine Development Group (SUBDEVGRU), normally based on New London, although they belonged to different parent organizations.

The mission entrusted to Tag Hooey was a critical one. It was to receive and analyze all data obtained at sea and prepare search charts based on the location of clues turned in by the search group. Beyond this, TAG WHOI became the main briefing source for Naval officers or chief scientists aboard oceanographic vessels prior to their sea trips. It also did a big job of expediting demands for equipment and help made by the search group. Moreover, since Tag Hooey was working out of Woods Hole, it could open up rapid radio communication as needed with the search group, which, by then, was centered on a point 220 miles east of Cape Cod—*Thresher*'s datum.

So much for the three elements involved in the staggering hunt for a minuscule broken object lying somewhere
just off the Continental Shelf, at the foot of a gigantic
undersea cliff, several thousand feet high (see Fig. 39).

The plan for locating *Thresher* was developed aboard
the Woods Hole Oceanographic ship, *Atlantis II,* on a
date that could hardly be called auspicious—Friday,
April 13, three days after *Thresher* disappeared forever
and was put on the Navy's "Stricken" list. However, while
very rough seas almost totally inhibited the physical
search for any more floating objects which might have
come from the lost submarine, the time was not wasted.

Through April 13, a conference hosted by *Atlantis II*
went on with hardly a break. Presiding was Captain
Frank Andrews, USN, then Commander Submarine
Development Group 2. His right-hand man was Mr.
Sidney Scott, Jr., senior WHOI scientist of the *Atlantis II*
and a sonar expert, but the proceedings included a long
radio-telephone conversation with Dr. Brackett Hersey,
Chief Physical Oceanographer at Woods Hole. Dr.
Hersey approved the plan evolved that day and said it
reflected the thinking of the oceanographic community
of scientists who, for the past 36 hours, had been racking
their brains about the best way to locate *Thresher.*

Later that evening, a message was sent to Vice Admiral E. W. Grenfell, then Commander Submarine
Force, U. S. Atlantic Fleet (COMSUBLANT), outlining
the plan. It would consist of four phases. The first was
to organize the assembly and use of all ships, personnel,
and equipment then converging on the scene, define the
search area, and do some experimental dredging and
echo-sounding in selected places. This phase lasted from
April 13 to May 1, a period of 18 days.

The second phase would include a "bathymetric survey," conducted by *Atlantis II*. This is a term used by oceanographers to describe a sonic depth-finding study in a given area (see Fig. 38). For this a Fathometer would be employed. Simply explained, a Fathometer (or precision echo sounder) is an instrument used to bounce echoes off the sea bed or off any object encountered in its scanning path. The same type of instrument, looking upward, is used by submarines travelling under the ice, to obtain a very precise delineation of the underside of an ice pack. Also as part of the Phase Two equipment were some stereographic underwater cameras, a towed TV camera, a towed radioactive decector, Loran "C" electromagnetic navigator, a Decca Receiver and Plotter and a deep-towed magnetometer. The estimated time span was May 2 through 15, or 13 days.

In Phase Three, all such Fathometer echoes as were classified "possibles" would be investigated by deep-towed Geiger counter, a side-looking echo sounder and a magnetometer where required. In the event, this phase lasted from May 16 through 26, some 11 days.

During Phase Four, any contacts passing Phases Two and Three would come under the scrutiny of a camera —either the still kind or a deep TV camera. If a logical pattern developed, *Thresher*'s hull, or parts of it, would show up in the photos. The lapsed time, here, was 19 days—May 27 to June 14 inclusive.

The fifth and final phase, which was added to the over-all plan as the days wore on, called for a close examination and study of *Thresher*'s hull. This could be done only by using the Bathyscaphe *Triest* under the right conditions. It would really be a visual confirmation, enabling the crew to make a close study of the wreck. For reasons which will become apparent, it was to be an extremely difficult venture. This phase is described in a later chapter.

The Navy, meantime, got busy. On April 11, just 24 hours after *Thresher*'s loss, the Bathyscaphe *Trieste* had been ordered made ready for *Thresher* search operations. This deep sea research vehicle (described elsewhere), which holds the world's record for deep submergence, was then located at the Navy Electronics Laboratory, San Diego, California. She was quickly prepared for the move and brought directly to Boston aboard the USS *Point Defiance* (LSD-31), passing through the Panama Canal. Even so, several factors needed careful consideration before committing *Trieste* to the search. One was her operational limitations, which included a very slow submerged speed of less than two knots. Another was her maximum endurance on the bottom of approximately four hours, and a third was the restricted search view of only about 100 feet. Then there was the need of careful checkup and overhaul after each dive. Therefore, even though *Trieste* got underway as quickly as possible, it was decided that the journey would be based on the expectation of pinpointing *Thresher*'s wreck with great accuracy. *Trieste* was a search vehicle only in a very limited sense. Having come close to her objective, however, she could, by means of extremely delicate maneuvers, probably obtain some marvelous photographs. And with luck, the mechanical arm designed for the gondola might be able to pick up something by way of light debris.

Phase One produced the greatest concentration of search vessels and the most formidable array of equipment and oceanographic talent in maritime history. At the start of the operation, the 10-square-mile area of search was quartered, and one ship was assigned to each sector. The four vessels were the *Allegheny* (ATA-179), an auxiliary ocean tug; the *Mission Capistrano* (AO/T-112), a sonar research ship; the *Prevail* (AGS-20), a surveying ship; and the *Rockville,* a Fathometer-equipped radar patrol craft already mentioned.

Early in the search, the navigational problem was solved by an excellent Loran "C" electromagnetic system. Loran "C" receivers were not easy to obtain, but top priority soon got them on station. Used in connection with the Decca navigation system, they produced good results. Far better, certainly, than the downward-looking beam of the so-called "precision echo sounder" first tried. This was found to work well only on portions of the sea floor that were relatively smooth. Otherwise, a degree of navigational capability was required which the research ships simply did not possess. To these four vessels, the oceanographic ships *Robert Conrad* (Lamont Geological Observatory), *Gillis,* and *Atlantis II* added their deep-sea search expertise, so that seven vessels in all were at hand. Allowing roughly 250 yards between tracks, investigation was pursued of every possible contact that might have any significance. This systematic survey took two weeks and started with 90 sonar echoes, any one of which could have been *Thresher*'s hull. The number was soon reduced to 12 possibles which were named ALFA, BRAVO, CHARLIE, DELTA, etc. This was less than one-eighth the original total, but by then there was little doubt, even among the conservative scientists, that "the hounds had picked up the scent."

Still, it was hard work. Random surface currents and substandard navigation at first gave the searching vessels a rough time. So did the weather. There was another problem, too. In the search area, with the Labrador Current flowing southwest, parallel to the Gulf Stream, which generally moved northeast, surface currents were chaotic and confusing since they might come from any direction of the compass. Here, Loran "A" proved to be the best navigation tool. But even this, under the most favorable conditions, couldn't be counted on for accuracy closer than 2,000 yards.

With the ending of Phase One, which took 18 days, as we have seen, Phase Two began at once. This was called a "fine grain" survey. Till then nothing further had shown up than the pathetic floating remnants (rubber gloves, torn insulation, etc.) picked up within the first 24 hours. In order to narrow down the search to a reasonable area it was necessary to determine some focal point that would justify photographing and dredging operations. All Fathometer echoes that might be classified as "possible" were carefully studied. Then another run was made over each, to confirm or deny the original contact. Every time a survey ship passed over an echo, this would be carefully plotted, after which two or three more vessels would make the same run and the plotting began all over again. Successive charts with echoes plotted at about the same sea bed position now showed up as a constant picture or "cluster."

Up on the surface the weather was vile, with poor visibility, heavy seas and a low cloud ceiling, but 1,300 fathoms below, not a ripple disturbed the delicate minuet of the listening and "bouncing" equipment. Where enough echoes confirmed a "cluster," this was put down as a possible *Thresher* hull position. It looked as though the Fathometers, with their narrow (300-yard) sweep, were adequate for the intended operations, which would be an overlapping photo-mosaic of the area where the echoes were encountered.

Phase Two, completed by May 15, 1963, involved a 10-mile sweep and a dozen "possible" Fathometer sweep contacts, accurately charted. A detailed account of the dogged determination with which these seven ships tackled their job would alone fill a good part of a book. Several long articles at different levels of technicality have already covered this episode, but the nontechnical reader would get little out of them. Sufficient that a stupendous job was accomplished in just under two weeks.

Now came Phase Three, which, though different, presented as many difficulties as the previous phase. It was the shortest of the four phases, but by May 26, when the oceanographic vessels called a halt to the "sweep," the charted contacts were no longer a dream or a hope. Since their exact co-ordinates were known, it would now be the turn of the underwater cameras to make every attempt to identify them.

TASK GROUP 89.7
May 27—June 14, 1963

Among the question marks that loomed before the oceanographers and scientists engaged in the most difficult undersea hunt of all time were three that would have given pause to many less determined individuals.

First, there was no certainty that *Thresher* could even return an echo by means of a Fathometer. The potential for echoes was there all right, but they might come from a dozen other objects than the broken hulk of a nuclear submarine. A large enough mound of rock on the sea bed, of about the right shape, could do it. Some long-forgotten wreck of a ship might produce an authentic-sounding echo. A pile of debris dumped in the vicinity anything from a year to a century earlier would certainly upset the applecart. There were many scientists, in fact, who held firmly to the view that even if *Thresher was* somewhere within reach, her very steep, fantastically rapid dive had probably buried her deep, if not completely, in the silt.

Then again, no one felt certain that the navigation of the surface ships in the disaster area had been so accurate as to ensure a 100 per cent Fathometer coverage of the ocean floor without the risk of duplication—perhaps too much of it. Trying to "sweep" four million square yards of ocean bottom with a "broom" only 300 yards wide was quite an undertaking.

Last but not least, there was no one around with any real operational experience in towing a magnetometer, Geiger counter, TV camera, or even a side-looking echo sounder between 15 and 200 feet off the bottom at depths of 8,500 feet. The only "ready" equipment to implement Phase Three (or anticipate Phase Four) was the deep-sea cameras and their lighting. Every other type of sensor remained, during April, nothing more than the focal point of a debate. The most advanced oceanographic labs in the U.S. were barely at the "parts purchasing" stage of their complex plans.

Even the accumulated experience with undersea cameras had little bearing on the stringent Phase Four requirements of the *Thresher* search. At the time, no one had tried towing a camera—still or TV—in water a mile and a half deep with a surface current of three knots. Faced with almost unpredictable conditions and never knowing the precise location of the trailing sensor down below, on the end of a 9,000-foot wire, even the Phase

Three requirements of a so-called "fine grain" survey were like trying to fly a kite blind in gusty weather and hoping to get pictures of neighboring clouds.

Then someone had a great idea. Why not check out the degree of precision of a Fathometer as a search tool? And what better "target" to employ than an old, disused World War II diesel sub which could be sunk on the spot, at about the same depth as *Thresher* under "controlled conditions"?

The Navy didn't have to look very far. The USS *Toro,* decommissioned a month before *Thresher*'s loss and destined for target practice, was just the right kind of ship. She was quite a bit longer than *Thresher*—311 feet 8 inches, even though her beam was much narrower and she displaced about half *Thresher*'s tonnage. She could certainly be turned into a suitable "object," especially when fitted with a sonar reflector. The old *Toro,* in fact, was not without some interesting facets of her own. She had been built and launched in 1944 at Portsmouth Naval Yard, primarily for surface cruising, but the remarkable thing was the speed of her construction. Round-the-clock gangs of shipyard workers had put her together in less than 200 assembly-line days, ready for her trials. Underwater, *Toro* had a maximum endurance of about 15 minutes at full speed on her batteries, but now she wasn't going anywhere. The plan was to tow her to the search area, open the sea valves, and fill her ballast tanks. The event was scheduled for some time late in May, but at the last moment the idea was shelved. *Conrad*'s lucky dredge of the "0" ring packages increased her ambitions. She decided to "leapfrog" into Phase Four by using her deep sea cameras on a large, unidentified object which, by a stroke of luck, might turn out to be *Thresher*'s hull.

May 30, *Conrad* developed eight photos which were so clear that they left little doubt of a sensational find. The sail, diving planes, and a large part of the lost sub's ruptured hull had been located. *Conrad* sped back to New London with her find, and May 31 the photos were flown to Washington for expert examination by the Navy's Photographic Interpretation Center. The Navy was at first so gung-ho about those pictures that Secretary of the Navy Fred Korth actually told an eager gathering of newsmen, ". . . a submarine determined to be the *Thresher* [has been] located on the ocean floor with a rupture in the hull."

Unfortunately, by the following morning NPIC had punctured that bubble. The series of pictures brought up were, in fact, part of the camera rig itself. None could in any way be identified as a part of *Thresher*. Even Dr. Joseph Lamar Worzel, assistant director of Lamont Geological Laboratory, Columbia University, New York, and chief scientist aboard *Conrad,* had been fooled. And that, considering his long experience in underwater photography, including that of submarines, was saying quite a lot.

Since June 10 had been forecast as probably a good day, the Bathyscaphe *Trieste* was being held in readiness to go down—until *Conrad*'s photos proved worthless. At that point things relaxed just a bit. The search plan reverted pretty much to the original "blueprint" but did not yield any tangible benefits until *after* the completion of Phase Four, which kept the so-called "classifier ships" busy. These were *Atlantis II, Conrad*, and *Gillis,* all three of them oceanographic vessels which pursued their spell of programmed activity. The dates and time span in days of each of the four phases preceding the *Trieste* dives are given in the previous chapter.

By then, the intensive search area had been reduced to two square miles with point DELTA as the exact center. The dredging by *Conrad* of 15 packages of neoprene "0" rings, which almost certainly came from *Thresher*, was the first of the fringe benefits, since it occurred on May 28, two days after the oceanographic vessels completed their part of the job. For this purpose, *Conrad* used a scallop ridge for a dredge, which had as its normal purpose the retrieval of sea bed rocks and pebbles.

Atlantis II now took off at a gallop. Basing herself on the assumption that *Thresher*'s last known bearing, due east, was part of a clockwise turn during her deep dive, *Atlantis II* concentrated on a bisecting north-south path. The idea certainly paid off. Her trailing cameras picked out a whole series of debris from man-made materials covering an area about 1,000 yards wide and 4,000 yards long. Included was a close-up of a book, lying wide open on the sea bed, its ghostly printed pages indecipherable. Nothing in fact could be definitely identified as belonging solely to *Thresher*, but, taken all together, they were a clear indication of where to look further. Taking advantage of the lifting of an earlier restriction on dredging, *Atlantis II* also attached a dredge to her sea bed sweeping camera. By its very crudity—it was made up of bailing wire and coat hangers neatly shaped like a dustpan—this dredge indicated that the *Atlantis II* crewmen were not too hopeful about picking up anything but at least wanted to go through the motions.

The date was June 24, with the ocean surface quite moderate, when the 9,000-foot line suddenly encountered a mild resistance which could well have been due to some long-sunk debris tossed overboard by a ship.

They began hauling, and when the "dredge" finally

came into view, none of the crewmen and scientists involved in this effort had any immediate idea of what they were looking at. For besides the usual small sea bed rocks and pebbles was a latticed rectangle of broken metal, about six inches by five, framed by angular and straight members.

"My God!" someone exclaimed. "Know what that is?"

There were no immediate takers.

"That's the inside of a battery. A grid or plate . . . all broken up."

"You're probably right," one of the others said after a closer look. "See those bits on the edges—they're part of the framework that held the thing together."

"Yeah, but there's nothing to identify it as coming from any particular ship . . ."

It only required the expertise of an Exide representative, however, to settle any doubts. His company had built *Thresher*'s huge banks of batteries and he confirmed that it was indeed one of the numerous plates.

Incidentally, the "Rube Goldberg" dredge used by the magnificently equipped *Atlantis II*, was something of a paradox. At the time, not only was she a new vessel and the pride of WHOI, but probably the most up-to-date ship of her kind in the world. She was 210 feet long, displaced 2,300 tons, and her twin screws powered by a 1,400 hp diesel enabled her to cruise at 12 knots. Her range was 8,000 miles and she carried 25 scientists besides a crew of 28. *Atlantis II*'s underwater equipment included two 35 mm stereoscopic cameras in separate watertight cylinders, for simultaneous focusing. She also had electronic flashlights, a powerful bank of batteries, and an acoustic device called a sonar "pinger." This pinger was designed to emit signals which helped position the camera rack just above sea bottom while on a visual search. The cameras and xenon lights were triggered by a bottom-sensing switch, then operated automatically.

Since it was the skill and persistence of the so-called "classifier" ships which had really started the whole *Thresher* project swinging, a brief chronology of the (released) underwater photos (or objects) secured by these vessels may be of interest. Nothing subsequently photographed (or rephotographed from clues) by the Bathyscaphe *Trieste* is included. The year was of course 1963.

Vessel	Date	Findings
Robert Conrad	May 28	Three sizes of neoprene "0" rings dredged-up in 15 packages. At least one of these three types could only have come from *Thresher*. (Object.)
Robert Conrad	June 14	Compressed air bottle upright on sea bed. No definite identification but found in "ground zero" area. (Photo.)
Robert Conrad	June 14	Broken piping on sea floor. Similar to type used in *Thresher*. (Photo.)
Robert Conrad	June 14	Metal plate, approximately 8 by 9 feet with perforated metal and some insulation attached, used in submarine construction. Located at 8,400 feet, *Thresher*'s bottoming depth. (Photo.)
Atlantis II	June 24	Badly damaged battery plate dredged up from ocean bed. Identified as belonging to *Thresher*'s battery bank. (Object.)

Many more underwater photos were taken, developed, printed and in some cases identified as showing parts of *Thresher*, but an unspecified number of these was suppressed by the Navy. It was *Conrad*, however, which did the trick. Her three photos taken June 14 (after the "false alarm" picture of *Thresher*'s "hull," taken May 30) decided the Navy to go ahead and use the Bathyscaphe *Trieste* without further delay.

And that craft, in itself, was so unique that it deserves some description. On April 26, barely 16 days after *Thresher*'s fatal dive, the USS *Point Defiance* (LSD-31) had steamed into Boston, carrying aboard the famous Bathyscaphe *Trieste*, holder of the world's diving record (the Pacific Ocean's 35,800-foot Mariana Trench, off Guam, deepest body of water yet known to man). *Point Defiance* had come through the Panama Canal, and on May 5 *Trieste* made a brief test dive to just under 700 feet, some 60 miles off Boston. That was to make sure everything was set. At the controls was Lieutenant Commander Don Keach, officer in charge, who had dived into the Mariana Trench with Professor Jacques Piccard, son of *Trieste*'s inventor, and who was to take *Trieste* down several times in her outstandingly successful search and identification of the lost *Thresher*.

Trieste was, to say the least, an odd craft (she underwent extensive refit in 1964), though entirely logical in her basic design and capable of descending with ease to submarine depths where the emphasis is no longer on "rescue" but "search and find." Or just "survey and report."

In effect, the 50-ton *Trieste*, originally designed and built by the French scientist, Professor Auguste Piccard, was purchased by the U. S. Navy back in 1958. It consists of two separate units—a large floating gas tank, 60 feet long, and a steel gondola (built by Krupp) seven feet in diameter, slung amidships, directly underneath. These units, though totally different in character, operate as one and are called a Bathyscaphe. The name *Trieste* is simply one of identification. However, the gondola depends entirely (for safe return to the surface) on the huge, hull-like cylinder above it. This holds some 35,000 gallons of gasoline, and has at each end a sea water ballast tank which is flooded to reduce the craft's natural (positive) buoyancy. In addition, two large vented ballast hoppers (containers for bags of steel pellets) are located forward and astern.

The Bathyscaphe's gondola is certainly no place for anyone even remotely afflicted by claustrophobia. It is a perfect (or almost perfect) sphere because no other shape can withstand anything approaching the enormous pressures generated by deep-sea diving. (In the Mariana Trench, this gondola withstood a pressure of 16,940 pounds per square inch, based on an increase of 44 psi per 100 feet.) Its internal diameter is six feet six inches and is so crammed with electrical, electronic, mechanical and photographic equipment that if three men want to squeeze into the remaining space they must all be contortionists of extremely delicate touch. They are literally sardine-packed to a point where one false move can trip a switch with disastrous results (it actually happened during one of the *Thresher* dives).

For viewing, the gondola has two small portholes, one 18 inches above the other, relative to the horizontal axis of the sphere. These portholes are fabricated of special plastic material at least three inches thick and 39.37 inches (one meter) in diameter. Several immensely powerful lights operated in various directions from the gondola can turn the stygian darkness of the deep into an area of fantastic brightness. The intensity of the lights is controllable and the gondola is equipped with a pair of deep-sea, high-speed 35-mm cameras of a type similar to those used by WHOI's *Atlantis II*. They can take up to 2,000 pictures each.

At all events, before her second series of dives, that year, *Trieste* was fitted with a mechanical arm operated from the interior. It was this arm which eventually enabled Lieutenant Commander Keach to retrieve actual physical evidence proving that *Thresher* had been located.

As to how Professor Piccard's invention works, it is, like so many dependable and successful ideas, a simple one. In preparation for a dive, the sea water ballast tanks are filled. This deprives the *Trieste* of positive buoyancy and makes it neutrally buoyant—that is, it then weighs almost exactly as much as the water it displaces and has just enough floatability to keep it from going down. Now you start filling the fore and aft ballast hoppers with steel pellets packed in 22-pound "bean bags." Slowly at first, the Bathyscaphe begins to sink. As it goes down the water pressure increases and two things happen. The gasoline is compressed so that its mass is reduced and its weight increased, and at the same time the drop in ambient temperature due to the cold water makes the gasoline contract still further. This again reduces the mass and increases the weight. The more the Bathyscaphe sinks, the more pronounced this whole cycle becomes and the more it *wants* to go down. The whole thing is mathematically calculated, however, so that the

Bathyscaphe reaches a controlled rate of descent of one meter per second—that's a little over three feet.

Coming back up, the reverse holds good. First you jettison the steel pellets (in equal amounts to keep the vessel level). Then, as it rises, the ambient temperature also rises while the water pressure decreases. Both these factors help the *Trieste* regain buoyancy. After a while, no longer exposed to the enormous outside pressures and subzero temperatures, the gasoline expands and regains its volatility. Specific gravity in relation to the sea water is greatly reduced. More positive buoyancy is generated. Then, when the vessel regains the surface, the sea water ballast tanks are pumped out and it once more becomes a floating vessel.

The idea certainly should not be gained from the foregoing that the Bathyscaphe *Trieste* is some kind of foolproof contraption, always responsive to the basic laws it was designed to obey in its aquatic environment. In deep water it is not easy to manipulate and has limited performance capabilities. When you start jamming a mass of sophisticated, microminiaturized equipment in a space so small that living accommodations are an afterthought, while outside the sea is exerting terrible pressures on you, these are fertile conditions for gremlins.

Besides what *might* happen, *Trieste*—as already noted —suffers from serious operational drawbacks. One is her extremely slow ocean bottom speed. Another is the restricted visibility from inside the gondola. Close up, your downward visual range is very small, and if you peep out of the high porthole you can't see far sideways, either. The 100-foot scanning radius (search width) is a combined effort from both portholes or by overlapping cameras. Photo coverage is only 30 feet wide, so it is necessary to navigate the gondola to within a 10-yard radius in order to get to a desired spot. This kind of navigation requires not only outstanding scientific skill but also seamanship of a very high order. It is no game for kids, with the ever-present danger of becoming trapped in debris.

At *Thresher*'s final resting depth, the sea pressure of 3,600 psi on the gondola would mean very little. It would be the least thing to worry about.

Even so, when *Trieste* began the first of her 10 dives, on the morning of June 24, 1963, a number of earlier precautions had been taken. For example, the ever-busy oceanographic ship *Conrad* had secured a doughnut-shaped buoy, replacing the marker over *Thresher*'s original datum. The new buoy was extremely important. Its purpose was to serve as a float for a number of sensors which would enable *Trieste* to maintain a point of reference even when she got down to the ocean floor. This would give the Bathyscaphe considerable help during sea bed maneuvers which were bound to be very slow—about 1.3 knots on an even keel, 32 feet from the bottom. She did have sonar equipment, but of very limited range—only about 400 yards. Her sole vocal means of communication with the surface was through the UQC telephone system in the gondola. There were no cables. Voice transmission depended (as it did on *Thresher*) upon a system of sound waves or impulses.

Trieste, therefore, is best described as a strange paradox, with some areas of fantastic strength and others of extreme fragility. Maneuvering her is perhaps like riding a bicycle on a tightrope with a full jug of water balanced on your head.

"8,400 FEET BELOW"

Trieste's 10 Dives, June 24—September 5, 1963

The tentative date of June 10, originally set for *Trieste*'s first deep dive, was canceled when the research ship *Conrad*'s famous photos of *Thresher*'s "hull" laid an egg. Nine days later, however, the Navy announced that the Bathyscaphe would begin a series of exploratory dives "in an attempt to locate the nuclear submarine USS Thresher."

That same day, the salvage ship USS *Preserver* (ARS-8) took *Trieste* in tow and headed for the search area. The USS *Fort Snelling* (LSD-30), a dock landing ship, went along to provide logistic support for the Bathyscaphe and her gondola. The three vessels, making a steady four knots, arrived at the search area, June 23 at 1045. During the afternoon, *Fort Snelling* launched a 50-foot landing craft known as a "mike boat," which was to keep in direct communication with the Bathyscaphe's gondola during deep submergence.

Early next morning, in a slightly choppy sea, two men went aboard the Bathyscaphe and down into the gondola to make sure all was well. They were Lieutenant George Martin, assistant officer in charge of *Trieste*, and Giuseppe Buono, the strange vessel's engineer, who was a whiz at trouble-shooting. Several Navy frogmen stood by, just in case. When they gave the sign, a small boat carrying two other men sped toward *Trieste*, which looked rather small, bobbing gently up and down in a hostile and apparently endless sea. The newcomers were the ones who were going to guide the Bathyscaphe on her initial dive into the Atlantic. So far she had explored the Pacific Ocean and Mediterranean only. First to skip aboard was Lieutenant Commander Keach, officer in charge, followed by a brilliant civilian scientist, Kenneth V. MacKenzie, from the Navy Electronics Laboratory in San Diego. MacKenzie was also chief scientist for the Bathyscaphe and had come with her all the way from California. He was not going to miss this dive.

At 1000, Martin and Buono came up on deck, allowing Don Keach and MacKenzie to go down the access tube into the cramped gondola and secure the hatch. Minutes later, Martin and Buono were taken off by an outboard-powered boat and the ballast tanks of *Trieste* were flooded with sea water. Normally, this would have been enough to start her down, but the unsettled sea state gave the Bathyscaphe an unexpected lift. By UQC, Keach requested Martin and Buono, who were then aboard the "mike boat," for some added bags of steel pellets to increase the ballast. The outboard was ready for such an eventuality. She headed back for *Trieste* and began dropping 22-pound "bean bags" into the hoppers. She had to make two trips before *Trieste* really started down. Meantime, inside the gondola, Lieutenant Commander Keach spotted some loose rubber tubing hanging from the Bathyscaphe's "hull" and requested that it be fixed. Two scuba divers quickly swam out, clambered aboard *Trieste*'s deck and took care of the problem. Coincidentally, it seemed, *Trieste* decided to begin her dive to the ocean floor, 8,400 feet below. The time was exactly 1035. The downward trip was going to take her an hour at her normal rate of descent, which was about three feet per second.

To help *Trieste* navigate, far down below, the surface ships planned some very systematic homework. Following a carefully prepared grid pattern in the search area, 1,441 colored markers were to be placed methodically in long, evenly spaced, parallel (north-south) rows, which, it was hoped, would guide the Bathyscaphe between clearly defined paths. Each marker consisted of a window-sash weight which served as an anchor, and a colored (and numbered) circular plastic sheet secured to the anchor by three feet of nylon cord. Yellow, white, orange and red each had a different meaning and indicated *Trieste*'s exact position in the grid, as seen from the gondola. These markers, which were known as "fortune cookies," were to be carefully checked out for placement by Decca navigation on board USS *Alle-*

gheny (auxiliary ocean tug ATA-179). Nowhere along the grid was a deviation expected of more than 300 yards from the parallel. Unfortunately, this job was not completed until the interval that followed the Bathyscaphe's first five dives.

Anyway, *Trieste* began her dive a little too far east of the datum, and unpredictable underwater currents, though slow, did the rest. She went down to 8,700 feet without seeing any debris. To make matters worse, the prearranged electronic signal from the mushroom buoy failed to come through, so that the Bathyscaphe was navigating under a handicap. She halted her dive about 30 feet from the sea bed and very slowly, propelled by her main electric motor, explored what turned out to be bleak and barren territory for about two square miles. Meantime, *Gillis,* another oceanographic vessel on station, offered valuable navigational help. The 3D tracking system used by *Gillis* largely made up for the loss of the mushroom buoy's electronic signal. This system transmitted a sonar blip to a transponder located on the Bathyscaphe. In turn, the signal was retransmitted to three hydrophones on *Gillis's* hull. By measuring the time differences it took for the signal to be bounced back by the transponder, *Gillis* was able to compute very accurately both the range and bearing of the *Trieste,* relative to herself.

Gillis's scientists had gone even further. Simultaneously, she could locate another transponder secured to the ocean bed. This gave her an exact range and bearing on *Trieste* from a fixed geographic point. The dual system, designed by the Applied Physics Laboratory at Washington University, seemed to offer the greatest promise as a location and navigational aid on future

Bathyscaphe dives. As luck would have it, during that first trip it didn't work as expected. By the time they got the kinks ironed out, the ceaseless attrition of the sea so corroded the equipment on *Trieste* that the APL system never really showed its potential during the 10 dives of 1963.

By 1430, after nearly three hours on the bottom, which was stretching things a bit, *Trieste* signaled that she was starting back up. One hour 35 minutes later she broke surface. For once, the Navy, so adept at juggling with words and making unfortunate facts disappear, was struck dumb. An official announcement, released soon after the dive, simply stated that "nothing of significance was noted." For all the work, discomfort and nervous tension involved, that first dive had the (official) earmarks of a flop.

However, Captain Frank Andrews, COMSUBDEV-GRU-2, the on-scene commander and a veteran submariner of great experience who had spent much time aboard *Thresher,* took a more optimistic view. "From an operational standpoint," he noted, "it was an extremely satisfactory dive." They had logged the electronic signal failure from the buoy which hampered the Bathyscaphe's ability to navigate, and were working on it. Scientist Kenneth V. MacKenzie, who was observer on that first dive, wrote an account of it which came much closer to the unofficial statement made by Captain Andrews.

That first dive in the Thresher area [MacKenzie recalled in an account published by Chilton Books, 1965] was a little too far east and we sighted no debris. We did, however, make many interesting observations of marine life on the bottom. We saw myriad starfish and sea urchins. Codfish abounded and there were forms of life we didn't immediately identify. But the most striking feature we noted was the makeup of the bottom itself. Stretching away as far as our lights would let us see was a flat, monotonous gray silt-and-gravel bottom, studded here and there with large angular rocks. These outcroppings ran generally north and south. Occasionally, the almost flat bottom was interrupted by a slope, sometimes as much as 15 degrees . . .

A second dive was scheduled for next morning, with Lieutenant George Martin at the controls and MacKenzie assisting him and again acting as observer. However, at 1100 on June 25, it was decided to postpone operations for another 24 hours. The reasons for this change of plan were sound. The defective electronic signal from the mushroom buoy still had not been properly fixed. *Trieste*'s batteries needed further recharging and Lieutenant Martin himself was a casualty. The previous evening he had sprained an ankle while transferring from a small boat to *Trieste*. To confine him in the Bathyscaphe for six hours under cramped conditions was inviting trouble. Don Keach was willing and eager to go down again, but the other problems presented too many difficulties. After all, the complex teamwork involved in these dives, to say nothing of the ever-present danger element, was not part of an attempt to test out the Bathyscaphe. The sole objective was to locate *Thresher*'s hulk, or what remained of it.

Accordingly, *Trieste* started her second dive early on June 26. The gondola was manned by the scheduled crew—Martin and MacKenzie, and the submerged period was to extend to the limit of *Trieste*'s endurance. An hour for the slow dive. Four hours on the ocean bed, searching, and another hour to come up.

Again, MacKenzie's dramatic written report of that second dive is worth quoting in full.

Underwater snow appeared to rain upward as we plummeted toward the bottom of the North Atlantic in the Bathyscaphe Trieste. We were 220 miles east of Boston, searching for the lost nuclear submarine Thresher. We started our descent to the bottom, 8,200 ft down, cautiously. It may have been currents, temperature changes or some other factor that caused us to gain speed. When we finally picked up the bottom on our echo-sounder, we were only 250 ft away and were heading downward at an alarming rate of about three knots . . .

My chief concern was that when we smashed into the ocean floor, we might hit one of the jagged automobile-sized boulders Lieutenant Commander Don Keach and I had seen on our previous dive in the same general area. If we hit one, there was no telling what might happen to us in the spherical gondola we were crammed into.

To check our downward speed, Lieutenant Martin began dropping iron shot, the ballast of our craft. Anxiously, I peeked over his shoulder from the . . . observation window as we fought vainly to check our descent. Fifty feet from the bottom we could see the silty sea floor clearly. It seemed to be rushing up toward us. I crossed my fingers. It was all I could do as Lieutenant Martin expertly manipulated the controls.

The next moment I could see nothing outside the porthole. As quickly as the limited quarters allowed, I turned to the other port to determine what our position was and what had happened to us. That porthole was higher than the other . . . What a relief to see clear water beyond the thick plastic glass!

We had hit the bottom in an area of soft mud. The gondola with us in it was half imbedded in the ocean floor. We still had a problem—getting out of the mud.

We thought about aborting the dive. We could do this by dropping the big hoppers that held the iron shot ballast. That would return us to the top like a cork bobbing to the surface.

But it would mean an end to the operations until we could return to Boston, replace the hoppers and fill them with iron shot.

Instead, we decided to drop our ballast from both shot tubs, a little at a time, and free ourselves by alternating the drive of our two propellors so our craft would twist back and forth in the mud . . .

For the next 45-minutes we twisted the Trieste back and forth, wallowing in the soft ocean floor mud. We watched the bottom of the aft shot tub push through a large cone of dropped shot as we twisted. Normally, we drop a ton of shot for every 3,000 ft of depth. Before we tore loose from that gummy bottom, however, we had dropped a total of 10 tons. But we did, at least, break loose and rocket surfaceward.

Lieutenant Martin then valved off 1,000 gallons of gasoline from the maneuvering tank in the large float over us, to reduce our buoyancy and prevent us from going right on to the top. We ceased our upward motion 500 feet above the bottom. Then, as the remaining 34,000 gallons of gasoline continued to be cooled by seawater, we settled back down—gently this time to the bottom at a depth of 8,200 feet. This new descent took 35 minutes . . .

After the initial surprise of being stuck and freeing ourselves, I turned to my various scientific instruments. It wasn't long before I got such a beautiful, extended and sharp sonar contact that I photographed the sonar display. We measured the bottom current's speed and direction after we had settled back to the bottom when the gasoline cooled. (When the bottom of the sphere is just kissing the seabed, enough to stop lateral movement, Trieste orients itself at right angles to the current because it is essentially a large cylinder. Its true heading is given by an aircraft gyro-compass. A 99-degree correction then gives the current direction. The current meter aboard was not operative, but the reliable method of timing a particular piece of the ever-present snow across a fixed path was used. The observation was made by eye and stopwatch.)

We navigated back on the reciprocal (opposite direction) of the current but we never regained the excellent sonar contact. This undoubtedly was due to the limited sonar range and the fact that we had drifted differently while 500 feet above the bottom than the measurement back at the bottom indicated.

I'm sure that somewhere within 200 yards of the main body of Thresher wreckage, which we didn't find until later, is our little monument—a hemispherical incident (on the sea bed) with two five-ton cones of iron shot piled up on either side.

On June 27, just as *Trieste* was starting her third dive, another Soviet "trawler" passed through the area. This was the third snooping Russian vessel to steam through the search location in five days, despite U.S. requests that all shipping avoid that sea space while search operations were being conducted. There was not only the possibility that garbage or other debris tossed overboard by a passing ship might damage the submerged *Trieste,* but in the event that she were forced to bob suddenly to the surface and happened to collide with such a vessel, the consequences might be disastrous. This is what Ken MacKenzie wrote about June 27:

Lieutenant Commander Keach and I made the third Trieste dive. The operation went along routinely and uneventfully until near the end of our stay on the bottom. Then we began seeing many pieces of paper and a little metal debris. Finally, we spotted one of the orange plastic boots that are pulled over the shoes of anyone entering the reactor room of a nuclear-powered submarine.

With considerable anticipation and skill, Keach maneuvered to the boot and lined it up directly in front of our observation port. It lay there, just three feet away from us through the thick plastic porthole glass. We could clearly read "SSN 5," but that was all. The boot was folded so we couldn't read the rest of the number. Thresher's number was SSN-593.

Two days later, June 29, *Trieste* made her fourth dive. This time she carried three men in her gondola. Besides Lieutenant George W. Martin, the assistant officer in charge, and MacKenzie, there was Lieutenant Commander Gene J. Cash, an observer assigned to Captain Andrews' search operations staff.

MacKenzie's narrative continues:

The space was so limited . . . in the cramped gondola . . . we had to position ourselves carefully so as not to disturb the instrument switches and settings. My station at one time was at the observation port. As I watched, we moved slowly along the bottom. Then we passed over an area of considerable light paper debris, then light metal pieces and frayed electrical wires.

Suddenly, in front of us, I saw a ridge about two feet high and about eight feet across. I was afraid at first that we might scrape the bottom of the sphere into it and I wondered if I should ask Martin to drop some shot to bring us higher. I decided we could clear it and said nothing. As we skimmed over the ridge with about three inches to spare (this was much closer to the bottom than the gondola normally ventured) I could see that the ridge was really the rim of a large crater.

As we passed over the crater I sized it up. It appeared to be about 80 to 100 feet in diameter and seemed to shelve downward to a depth of 12 to 15 feet. It had the raised rim typical of an impact crater. The edges appeared to be a slag-like material with some starfish. Their presence led me to believe it was possibly an old crater, perhaps caused by some ancient meteor. But since the debris trail led directly to it, with the density of the material increasing as we drew nearer, we knew it was near the site of the Thresher. Inside the rim I spotted a piece of metallic debris which we photographed.

Another 300 feet along the bottom from this small crater, I saw another apparently large one with a flattened rim, and then beyond it black water. The slope from the edge into the black water dropped at an angle of 70 degrees. It seemed odd to have the bottom disappear so suddenly. A slump was visible on one side, about 15 feet below us. Our echo sounder probed into the darkness as we passed over the second crater and we measured its depth as about 30 to 50 feet. The second bottom break might be a natural escarpment on the ocean floor. However, there was still the very real possibility that these craters and depressions were caused by the impact of the heavy water-filled Thresher. More research must be done to determine whether this was true or whether they are natural geological formations.

The Bathyscaphe's fifth dive, carried out next day, June 30, though of shorter duration due to an accidental malfunction, had a special significance. Once again the gondola carried three men, but this time the third, besides Keach and MacKenzie, was Captain Andrews himself, celebrating his forty-second birthday.

The dive lasted only 4 hours 30 minutes, of which 2 hours 10 minutes were spent on the ocean bed. A gyro-compass failure made navigation almost impossible. Then one of the vessel's electric propulsion motors quit, greatly reducing her mobility and progress. The "failure" of the gyro occurred, it seemed, when one of the crew in the cramped gondola accidentally pushed against a switch that turned off the device. The problem was soon discovered, but the gyro-compass could be of no further use in providing accurate readings until it was reset. This meant returning to the surface and aligning the gyro with the operating compass of one of the ships. This dive was described as "disappointing," but not by MacKenzie, who always found something new and fascinating to record in his log.

We . . . observed many varieties of sea life. The deep-sea sharks were as spectacular as anything we saw in the way of (ocean) floor fauna. We utilized the bottom current of almost $\frac{1}{4}$ knot to move us for a search as we drifted west, about 600 yards north of the debris.

With the fifth dive the initial series was finished. We had searched a sizeable area and taken many photographs. But it was time to install new batteries and make other adjustments to improve our search operation.

The following day, July 1, USS *Preserver* started towing *Trieste* back to Boston for a general overhaul. The majority of the small task force that supported the Bathyscaphe also headed back for port. Only the research ship *Gibbs* remained on station, to pursue a bottom sweep of the area with her sonar and underwater cameras and do other work.

During *Trieste*'s overhaul period, which lasted nearly eight weeks (including travel time), the observations made on the fifth dive were sifted over and over again, but the craters led to only two possible conclusions. One was that *Thresher*, after flooding, had indeed gone down stern first at a tremendous speed and hit the ocean floor so hard that she was buried well below the silt. She could thus have dug a hole into the soft sediment deep enough to absorb nearly twice her 278-foot length. This, it was argued, might well explain the big crater seen by *Trieste*'s crew, while the adjacent smaller crater could have been caused by some part of the submarine breaking away just before she hit bottom.

Another group of oceanographic experts who were

studying the *Thresher* disaster argued that this theory was nonsense. They simply did not buy Rear Admiral Stephan's velocity estimates and the numbers he had put forward when questioned by the Secretary of the Navy. There was no doubt as to the validity of the speed, but they argued that for *Thresher* to bury herself that deep she must have not only maintained her steepness of descent at a mere 30° from the vertical, but have done so without breaking up.

In fact, the mass of small debris seen from *Trieste*'s gondola, which apparently came from *Thresher,* appeared to indicate strongly that the submarine *had* broken up during descent, and that the resultant drag had slowed her down greatly and lessened her impact with the sea bed. When the mass of *Thresher*'s broken hulk finally was located and photographed, it could be deduced that the truth lay somewhere between these two theories. It still seems reasonable to suppose that the submarine tore open and imploded at some point way below crush depth, and that a subsequent explosion before she hit bottom broke her up so that she landed on the ocean floor in large pieces. These, in turn, were further mangled on impact.

During the long interval occupied by *Trieste*'s overhaul, USS *Allegheny* duly dropped 1,441 markers in the precise positions called for by the prepared grid covering the search area. While this went on, the research vessel *Gibbs* also had a busy time of it. During 21 days on station, she not only continued her sonar tests and underwater photography, but also planted on the surface a line of buoys which would serve as electronic landmarks for *Trieste* in her next series of dives. These markers, though less frequent, followed the pattern laid down on the ocean floor.

Back in Boston, *Trieste* and her gondola were given a thorough going-over. Sea water had played havoc with a lot of the wiring and exposed parts, all of which had to be renewed. Every piece of equipment in the gondola was carefully checked out, and one vital addition was made to the Bathyscaphe. This was a remote-control prosthetic (or mechanical) arm, operable from inside the gondola. The arm was secured to the forward ballast hopper on the "hull," but the reason why the whole thing could not be sooner hooked up was that every opening in the gondola itself had been occupied by a strain gauge. Now that the strains imposed by the enormous sea pressure had been determined, at least one opening became available for the pickup control wires leading to the outside arm.

All the welds of the big hull-shaped gas tank were carefully gone over and six weeks elapsed before *Trieste* was ready to return to the search location. During the afternoon of August 15, USS *Preserver* once again headed for the operations area with *Trieste* in tow. She was followed two hours later by the much faster USS *Fort Snelling,* while the *Gillis* was back on station by August 17.

Ship by ship, the scientific armada (Task Group 89.7) began to reassemble, ready for another go at the toughest undersea search ever tackled by man.

The first dive of the second series was tentatively scheduled for Monday, August 19, but how many dives would be involved during this phase remained to be seen. The number generally assumed was at least six, with a possibility of 10, depending on the weather and a lot of other things. It did not turn out that way. The Atlantic was to yield up its secret much sooner.

On August 19, however, Lieutenant Commander Keach and his crew fretted in vain. *Trieste* remained surfaced. A navigation buoy had broken loose, then the electronic navigation devices on some of the ships went sour. Added to that, the August weather, instead of remaining stable, chose to attain rarely seen extremes of violence. It was as though the greedy and secretive ocean were conspiring against all efforts to wrest from its depths further knowledge as to *Thresher*'s fate.

At last, on August 23 (late afternoon because of a fog), Keach and MacKenzie started down again. They ran into trouble penetrating a cold water layer at about 200 feet and took one hour to reach their depth. As *Trieste* moved cautiously along the sea bed, her crew located one of the plastic markers laid down by *Allegheny*. It bore the number 45 on a white disc. After an hour and 15 minutes on the bottom, the Bathyscaphe began her return to the surface, which took another hour. Supposedly nothing new was located, and in fact, of the second series of five dives made by *Trieste*, MacKenzie has put very little on record. There is no reference to the excellent photos obtained that day, which included a manhole cover from one of *Thresher*'s steam generators and an external portion of her sonar dome. Nor is there mention of some rock-wool thermal insulation and a junction box.

MacKenzie concludes:

Later in the summer we continued our search. We photographed more debris and were able to determine that it came from the submarine's bow section. One distorted length of pipe from the galley had engraved on it the ship's number, the part number and the job number. With Trieste's mechanical arm, Keach picked it up and brought it to the surface.

In later dives (of this series) we had the additional advantage of plastic markers dropped to the sea bed in a grid pattern. But weather and the wear and tear on equipment sharply reduced our operating ability.

The skimpy closing paragraphs of this otherwise fascinating account do have a valid explanation. Kenneth MacKenzie knew the exact dates of each of the final five dives in 1963, but he missed the last three altogether and so had no firsthand feeling for many of the dramatic things that occurred.

However, despite the Navy's tight-lipped policy, the record is there. During the next three days (August 24 through 26) poor weather repeatedly thwarted any further dives. An attempt was even made to provide a sheltered diving area for *Trieste* by placing USS *Fort Snelling* on the windward side of the Bathyscaphe, but to no avail. Then word came through that Hurricane Beulah was headed that way. This resulted in an immediate order for USS *Preserver,* still towing *Trieste,* and USS *Fort Snelling* to head for Shelburne, Nova Scotia, where they would find shelter from the storm. When it became obvious that the storm would not endanger the ships in the search area, the order was countermanded and *Trieste* towed back to her diving point.

On August 27, the second dive of the new series finally got underway. Nothing significant was found, although *Trieste* spent 3 hours 23 minutes on the ocean floor. She did, however, sight another plastic marker, this time a red one bearing No. 32. The gondola carried a crew of three, with Lieutenant Martin as pilot, Ken MacKenzie in his usual place, and Lieutenant Commander A. H. Gilmore as additional observer. Gilmore was Operations Officer on the staff of the Search Commander.

The third dive of the new series took place within 24 hours, and August 28 proved to be a date to remember. *Trieste*'s crew included Keach and Gilmore and a newcomer observer, Commander J. W. Davies, of the Navy Electronics Laboratory in San Diego. It seems as though MacKenzie lost his place to Davies on what turned out to be the most exciting and momentous dive of all, the one that definitely clinched the location and identity of the lost *Thresher*.

Trieste spent 3 hours 40 minutes on the bottom and shortly after "touchdown" found herself in what Keach later described as "an area like a large automobile junkyard. There were dozens of pieces lying around on the ocean bed, some up to 20 feet long."

He decided there and then to use the mechanical arm to bring up something that could be identified beyond any doubt as a part of *Thresher*. But the question was what?

"It was difficult to decide what to bring up," Keach said. "I considered trying to loop the pickup arm through a large piece of debris but decided not to try it after all."

The size of a submerged object is hard to determine, and there was always the chance that the Bathyscaphe might strike some debris or become entangled in it and stick to the sea bed.

Suddenly Keach spotted just the thing—a section of twisted and battered brass piping long enough to have some meaning (it turned out to be 57 inches long) but not so unwieldy or heavy that it would prove too much for the mechanical arm.

"I chose it," the Bathyscaphe's officer in charge later said, "because there were appendages hanging from it, lagging insulation and connections, and it was bent. I thought that if the arm's grip lost it on the way up, some of the appendages might catch on the arm and hold it."

Keach went through 15 minutes of delicate manipulation with the remote control pickup arm to hook onto the pipe, but he got such a good grip on it and came back up so slowly—the ascent took just under two hours—that his trophy finally saw the light of day. This operation stretched *Trieste*'s endurance to just about the limit, but now there was no longer any doubt. The nuclear submarine experts on COMSUBDEVGRU-2's staff promptly identified the pipe as having come from a hot water flushing line inside *Thresher*'s galley. They didn't even have to bother with that. Stamped on the pipe with a vibrator-type drill were various job order and serial numbers and clearly, if not very artistically, the legend "593 boat." The weight of this object was a modest 10 pounds, even though it came from a vessel which had displaced over 3,500 tons on the surface, but the Submarine Type Desk at BuShips and the Navy hierarchy concerned had a high old time of it—in complete secrecy, of course.

Trieste had two more dives to make for the even 10 finally decided upon, and by golly, nothing was going to violate the secrecy of that program. On August 29, down went the Bathyscaphe again for her fourth try of the second series. This time, besides Lieutenant Martin and Commander Davies, she carried yet another new observer, Lieutenant Commander A. D. James, a submarine medical officer. She stayed on the bottom four hours and was again at maximum endurance when she finally surfaced. Obviously, the "vast automobile junk-yard" was quite an attraction and fertile ground for some excellent photography.

Three days later, on September 1, the Bathyscaphe made her 10th and last dive of the series. As was fitting, Lieutenant Commander Don Keach piloted the craft, while the medical officer, A. D. James, signed on for another trip. The third man, this time, was Lieutenant E. E. Henifin of the search force staff. *Trieste* stayed down for 1 hour 40 minutes, but the dive was cut short by a partial battery failure.

Trieste and her two escort ships, USS *Preserver* and USS *Fort Snelling,* at once returned to Boston. But despite repeated inquiries by the Press, the U. S. Navy had nothing to say about the vessel's third, fourth and fifth (second series) dives.

On September 4, 1963, with *Trieste* safely back in port and already being prepared for return shipment to San Diego, Captain Andrews and Lieutenant Commander Keach caught an evening plane to Washington, D.C. The curtain was about to rise on the last act of the most dramatic search-and-find operation in the history of any navy. It was a saga of unrivaled technical skill, tremendous ingenuity, unshakable determination and selfless courage that will probably never be beaten for a first-time effort. The tragedy overshadowing it all was that, if the Navy had taken heed of some good advice and set aside its selfish, lazy, myopic, and outdated approach to modern technology; if it had tried to translate great ideas into safe reality instead of gambling against fearful odds, this awesome disaster need never have occurred.

At all events, early on the morning of September 5,

1963, the Press got wind that something big was about to break and converged on the Pentagon. It was not mistaken, since the whole thing was the result of a cautious leak. Precisely at noon, the doors opened on a press conference hosted by the SECNAV office. A release with the familiar blue DOD letterhead was handed out, fresh from the duplicating machine, in the form of a statement by Secretary of the Navy Fred Korth. The first paragraph told it all.

The location of structural parts of the Thresher on the ocean floor having been positively confirmed by the Bathyscaphe Trieste during her latest series of successful dives, I have today directed that the associated operational aspects of the search for the nuclear submarine Thresher be terminated . . .

The nine paragraphs which followed were merely an elaboration of the simple statement: "It's all over."

Standing beside a table on which his latest find was displayed, Lieutenant Commander Don Keach, a trim, dark-haired young man with a somber gaze and a pleasant smile which he used sparingly, stood before a mike answering questions.

Besides the Honorable Fred Korth, Vice Admiral L. P. Ramage (who had led the early phase of the *Thresher* search but by then had been promoted Deputy Chief of Naval Operations for Fleet Operations and Readiness) also was present. At his side stood Captain Frank Andrews, the dynamic on-scene commander of Task Group 89.7, and Dr. Arthur E. Maxwell, Chairman of the Advisory Group, facing a battery of TV cameras, more mikes and reporters.

In the event, Captain Andrews and Lieutenant Com-

mander Keach were awarded Navy Commendation
Medals for their outstanding leadership in the search
operations. Dr. Maxwell received the Superior Civilian
Achievement Award for his able direction of the
Scientific Committee. These men certainly deserved rec-
ognition and they were not alone.

Yet there was a sad postscript to this gallant episode.
A flyleaf ("The Lesson of the Thresher") issued by the
Connecticut Mutual Life Insurance Company revealed
some startling Navy facts about the negligence of those
aboard *Thresher* in regard to their personal affairs. Only
55 per cent of the officers with dependents had drawn
up any kind of will and only 44 per cent of those wills
were valid. It would be well to remember, however, that
the average age of *Thresher*'s 12 officers was only 29.
In the case of enlisted men with dependents a mere one
per cent had wills. Further, only 11 per cent of the
officers and 22 per cent of enlisted men with dependents
left any life insurance.

The Navy survey concluded: "It is manifest that the
deceased sailors did not wish to deprive their loved ones
of financial security in the difficult period ahead. Rather,
the failure to provide for them was due to a lack of understanding of the importance and nature of estate
planning. Further, procrastination and negligence, as always, played a role in these matters . . ."

While undoubtedly correct, this warning was conveyed in terms that were less than tactful and the whole
thing was in bad taste. There were many other ways for
the Navy to convey these thoughts to its personnel.

If it comes to that, The System didn't turn out to be so
provident, either. Excluding figures from the NRL
(Naval Research Labs) and NOL (Naval Ordnance

Labs), which were unavailable, the search for *Thresher* cost $863,000. To this can be added the cost of improvements and retrofits required by the submarine safety program on all nuclear ships built prior to *Thresher*. These ran up the bill another $180 million during fiscal years 1964 through 1966. The grand total probably reached a quarter of a billion dollars, but there is no way of estimating the value of even one of the 129 lost lives.

THE PASSING OF THE BUCK
Congressional Hearings

Once upon a time there was a President of the United States who thought words were intended to convey ideas, and not to be used in a political parlor game where their meaning could be distorted to suit the occasion. The President's name was Harry S. Truman, and upon his desk was a simple little sign made up of exactly four words: THE BUCK STOPS HERE.

One would think that sign was abundantly clear, but so far as the military hierarchy is concerned it was a nonsign. It didn't exist.

Leafing through 190 pages of "evidence" and "testimony" which make up the greater part of the Hearings before the Joint Committee on Atomic Energy, Eighty-eighth Congress of the United States, on the loss of USS *Thresher* is an education in reading. Hiding behind contradictions, evasions and murky answers to simple questions, the U. S. Navy brass seemed determined to baffle and confuse the committee of seven senators and eight representatives.

The Hearings began Wednesday, June 26, 1963, in room AE-1 at the Capitol, and witnesses who testified for the Navy included three vice admirals, five rear admirals and several captains, in addition to the Secretary and Assistant Secretary of the Navy.

The man with the least enviable job, though luckily the most forthright and unequivocal, was Vice Admiral Hyman G. Rickover, "father" of the nuclear reactor in atomic submarines. He spoke both for the Atomic Energy Commission and the Department of the Navy, but he never minced words nor attempted to hide behind meaningless phrases and futile evasions. Nor did he try to lead the Joint Committee members down blind alleys which were skillfully routed under torrents of empty verbiage. There are instances where the elaborate circumlocution of Navy witnesses bears a striking resemblance to one of those mind-boggling monologues by Lily Tomlin in the late lamented TV show "Laugh-In." Elsewhere, one might be reading straight out of the pages of fourth-grade whimsey such as "The Cat and the Hat," or "The Lorax," by Dr. Seuss.

Let's turn the spotlight on the leading witnesses for the Department of the Navy as they strutted on stage in full panoply.

First came Vice Admiral Bernard L. Austin, president of the Naval War College and of the Navy's original Court of Inquiry into the *Thresher* disaster. Austin served as "an expert source of information for all matters pertaining to events leading to and possibly causing the loss of Thresher." This would be quite a tag to stick on anybody. His opposite was Senator John O. Pastore, Rhode Island, Chairman of the Joint Committee on Atomic Energy.

"Admiral Austin, will you oblige us by coming forward, please?"

The Admiral graciously obliged.

"Mr. Chairman, I appreciate this opportunity of appearing before you and giving you some of the background of this court [the Navy Court of Inquiry] of whose report you have been furnished a copy . . . I would like to say on behalf of the members of the court how much we appreciated your sending us as observers such fine gentlemen who made it easier for us to cooperate with them . . ."

Dale Carnegie could have done no better.

In deep, resonant tones, the Admiral then uttered the classical understatement of all time. "We had a difficult problem to inquire into . . ."

The sound track was suddenly cut off because it turned out that the "problem" was "classified" and therefore had to be deleted.

When the sound came on again, the Admiral was explaining, "And so we had to explore the complete spectrum of possible causes. I think this was a blessing in disguise. It . . . caused us to look into things that probably would never have been looked into for some time to come had it not been under the impetus of this investigation."

This was a magnificent piece of sophistry, intended to cover up every conceivable error for which the Navy might be found accountable.

". . . things that probably would never have been looked into for some time to come . . ."

Apparently, nothing short of the terrible fate which overtook *Thresher* was enough to awaken a sense of responsibility in all those who made her ready for sea and indeed ordered her to sail.

"We looked first into the design of this ship," Admiral Austin boomed on. "We looked into the construction of the ship, into the materials of which it was constructed, the processes by which these materials were fabricated . . ." and so on, *ad nauseam*. Nothing new there. It had long ago been done by Rickover, whose conclusions appear in the next chapter.

Now, carried away perhaps by the hypnotic effect of his own words, Admiral Austin permitted himself a flight of fancy.

"We found that the shock tests, for example, were no greater than those which had been given to other submarine hulls . . ."

Once again the sound track is switched off while the eager audience is denied some more "classified" material.

Had no one taken the trouble to inform Admiral Austin of a fact that was common knowledge throughout *Thresher*'s crew? That in at least one of those shock tests carried out off Key West, which *Thresher* had to endure in the form of depth charges, a navigational error somehow sneaked in. This might there and then have had tragic consequences. Whereas *Thresher*'s hull, in conformity with those of other nuclear submarines of this type, was supposed to be subjected to a predetermined maximum stress factor, the ship had actually withstood a force 20 per cent greater, luckily without serious damage to herself or injury to her crew.

If this was a sample of "the many things we pointed out in our 166 facts, 54 opinions and 20 recommendations," it was an unfortunate one.

Early in the Hearings, Representative Chet Holifield, California, vice chairman of the Joint Committee, took on two admirals almost simultaneously. One was Rear Admiral Wm. A. Brockett, Chief, Bureau of Ships. The other was Vice Admiral Bernard L. Austin. The question had been raised sometime earlier: why, over his strongest objections, had Commander Axene, *Thresher*'s commanding officer, been detached from his ship and assigned other duties while *Thresher* was still in dry dock after an overhaul of six months—let alone afloat.

Brockett had just given Representative Craig Hosmer, California, a politely patronizing explanation of the Navy chain of command assigned to superintend the overhaul of a ship.

"But occasionally there are things that upset the applecart. There are resignations and just distributions of shortages, as it were, and although I don't have the details in this case—"

Holifield hastened to refresh the Admiral's memory.

"May I give them to you? There was a change in Thresher's assistant ship's superintendent in November 1962 and a change in her chief superintendent in December 1962. And in January 1963 there was a change of Thresher's executive officer, and in the same month there was a change of Thresher's commanding officer.

"So there, in a period of less than 90 days, four of your top people on this job were removed and it was during the time, as we understand it, when the submarine was in overhaul and where it would seem to me the continuity of superintendents should have remained in the same [Navy] people."

Admiral Brockett looked far from happy.

". . . Let us assume there is a death or resignation . . ." he answered in part. "The latter is our biggest problem at the moment."

Representative Holifield was unimpressed.

"On the face of it, if I were doing a complicated job of construction, I wouldn't want the four top men to be pulled out of it and four strangers come into it to take on a job without a complete transfer of the background of experience and knowledge of these four men. It just looks to me . . . as if this is a weak point."

Admiral Brockett reluctantly nodded agreement. So did Secretary of the Navy Korth. Chairman John O. Pastore then dropped his bombshell.

"May I ask Admiral Austin, did the [Navy] Court [of Inquiry] place any emphasis upon this incident that we are discussing now, with relation to what the causes [for all these changes] might have been?"

Vice Admiral Austin looked shocked.

"Mr. Chairman, we placed sufficient emphasis on it to pull it out of 1,700 pages of testimony and make it one of the 166 facts. We did not feel that it warranted an opinion on our part . . ."

Representative Holifield: "I don't quite follow you on that, Admiral. It is either important enough, it seems to me, to require a recommendation of change, or it is unimportant . . ."

Here, Secretary Korth interposed, "It is important enough for me to now look into this sufficiently."

Representative Holifield took careful aim.

"Maybe I am in error," he told his listeners, "but in opinion 53 of the [Navy] court record, it says that:

"'A substantially contemporaneous transfer of Thresher's commanding officer, executive officer, ship's superintendent, and assistant ship's superintendent in the final stages, was not conducive to optimum completion of the work undertaken.'

"So apparently you have rendered an opinion on that."

Admiral Austin: "I stand corrected."

While the admirals and captains made (frequently inadequate) attempts to field questions thrown at them by the Joint Committee on Atomic Energy, certain facts emerged beyond argument. It was agreed, for example, that an attack ship of the *Thresher* class relied on at least 3,000 pipe joints, both of a nuclear type (for the reactor section) and a non-nuclear type for the rest of the ship. All the reactor pipe joints (by special order of Admiral Rickover) had to be welded and then checked for integrity with radiographs or X-ray photos which were kept on record for seven years. In other parts of the ship, where limited space precluded welding pipe joints, a silver-brazing process was used. Silver-brazed joints (totaling several hundred) were tested for integrity by a hydrostatic system. Each joint was subjected to fluid pressures of 150 per cent, or half as much again as they were supposed to withstand. This is known as destructive testing, but for years nothing better was available.

However, while *Thresher* was undergoing her final overhaul, a new method of testing silver-brazed joints was adopted by the Bureau of Ships. It was referred to as Ultrasonic Testing (U-T). The operating principle of U-T not only is nondestructive but simple and practically foolproof. Sound energy passes through the pipe joint and the reflected sound waves are measured on an oscilloscope. These can give a trained operator an unfailing picture of a dependable or faulty joint. As a safety check for U-T a joint must indicate an average of 40 per cent continuous bond, or a minimum of at least 25 per cent on either land (each flange). If it falls below this standard, the joint is considered defective.

Representative Holifield was not easily intimidated, sidetracked or confused by the coruscating effect of gold braid or the impressive rows of "fruit salad" facing him. He was there to help conduct a vital inquiry into the apparently needless deaths of 129 men and to get as many complete answers as possible to his questions. And Representative Holifield was a persistent man. He kept coming back to inadequate piping inspection—a subject which to the Navy was beginning to feel like a third degree burn.

"I notice . . ." Holifield carefully enunciated each word, "that the Portsmouth Naval Shipyard did not aggressively pursue the ultransonic inspection of silver-brazed joints as required by the Bureau of Ships letter of August 28, 1962. The deputy commander of the submarine force [Rear Admiral Lawson P. Ramage] did not aggressively pursue the ultrasonic inspection, nor did the commanding officer of Thresher. [Further] that the management of the Portsmouth Naval Shipyard did not exercise good judgment in determining not to unlag [dismantle] the pipes in order to continue the ultrasonic tests as directed, after November 1962. That the Bureau of Ships improvement and corrective action regarding the silver-brazed problem were not applied at the Bureau level or in the field with sufficient vigor . . .

"I refer back to the [BuShips] letter of August 28 which required ultrasonic inspections, and I am still unclear in my mind as to why the requirement was not continued after the first of December or thereabouts, and if this *was* a Bureau of Ships letter, what was the final determination, the response to that letter. Was a report required or not?"

Admiral Brockett: "There was a report required."

Representative Holifield: "And the report was presented to the Bureau of Ships?"

Admiral Brockett: "The report was presented."

Representative Holifield: "*After* the termination of the inspections?"

Admiral Brockett: "It was in process and it was received after the 11th of April." (The day following *Thresher*'s loss.)

Representative Holifield: "*After the 11th of April?*"

Admiral Brockett: "Yes sir."

Representative Holifield: "They terminated it [the U-T work] the first of December and you did not receive it at the Bureau of Ships until April?"

Admiral Brockett: "That is right."

Representative Holifield: "Do you have any explanation for that?"

Admiral Brockett: "No sir, *except that I don't believe it was considered a matter of priority* . . . "

Here was a rear admiral, Chief of the Bureau of Ships, admitting that on August 28, 1962, his office had sent the Commanding Officer, Portsmouth Naval Shipyard, a detailed letter laying down specific criteria concerning the ultrasonic testing of silver-brazed joints on deep-diving submarines. Further, that BuShips had requested a reply concerning the progress of U-T and had received no reply whatever until *the day after Thresher's loss*. And on top of that he was asking Representative Holifield to believe that the matter was not one of priority!

Since the entire Joint Committee on Atomic Energy already knew that 145 of *Thresher*'s silver-brazed joints in the salt water system had been ultrasonically tested, and that 14 per cent of this total had been rejected as unsound, the Navy in leaving some 2,855 joints untested, three months before *Thresher* took to the water, showed a lack of responsibility that was almost beyond belief. A simple projection of this casualty rate over the ship's 3,000 joints would result in a probable expectancy of 412 danger areas.

The whole thing was a bit too much to swallow, even for the reasonable and urbane Chairman Pastore of the Joint Committee.

"Could I ask a question at this point?" he wanted to know. "Did this question of 14 percent below standard on the examination that was made of the 145 joints come to your attention, or come to the Bureau's attention?"

Admiral Brockett: "Not to my knowledge, Senator. I read the record here to the effect that the report was not made to the Bureau of Ships." (This, it should be remembered, was Brockett's own bureau.)

Chairman Pastore: "Did the [Navy] Court [of Inquiry] in its actual findings determine that this situation had come to the attention of any one of the agencies of the Navy?"

Here, Admiral Austin hastened to Admiral Brockett's aid: "It was known to the commanding officer of the ship, Mr. Chairman. It was not reported higher in the operational chain of command than the commanding officer *of the ship*, and it was not reported to the Chief of the Bureau of Ships."

Chairman Pastore: "Was the determination made by him that this 14 percent below standard was safe?"

Admiral Austin: "By whom, sir? By the commanding officer?"

Chairman Pastore: "By the commanding officer [of *Thresher*]. I mean, as I understand it, there were 3,000 joints and only 145 were examined and out of that 145 there were found to be 14 percent under standard. Now, who assumed the responsibility to say, 'This is safe,' or 'This is not safe,' or do nothing about it and let it be the way it was?"

This time there was no verbal escape—no way of ducking the question or beclouding the issue. No possible means of dumping the responsibility on nebulous shoulders. Senator Pastore had asked a question and he was waiting for an answer. It was Admiral Austin who replied.

"The Shipyard Commander, in effect assumed the responsibility, sir [author's italics]."

Chairman Pastore (his tone clearly skeptical): "Did the [Navy] Court in its findings determine that he was right in that assumption?"

Admiral Austin (pianissimo): "No sir. We determined that he had used poor judgment."

Since the (Navy) court had concluded that "a flooding casualty in the engineroom" was the most probable cause of *Thresher*'s sinking, and that it was "most likely that a piping system failure had occurred in one of the . . . salt water systems . . . that in all probability affected electrical circuits and caused loss of power," it is not surprising that we find the Joint Committee coming back to this particular problem like a dog with a bone. The welds and workmanship in Admiral Rickover's reactor part of the ship were in no way suspect. His formidable reputation as a perfectionist was a guarantee of reliability that amounted virtually to a certainty, whereas not all the obfuscations and verbal minuets of BuShips and the Portsmouth Yard succeeded in covering up errors and omissions that nurtured the seeds of a catastrophe.

At the opening of the Navy Court of Inquiry (the "hush-hush" one), Rear Admiral Palmer, Commander Portsmouth Naval Shipyard, asked to be made "an interested party to the proceedings." He was thus entitled to counsel and to give evidence on his own behalf. It also meant, of course, that he could be cross-examined by the Navy Judge Advocate's office. This did, in fact, occur, but mainly because the Navy had little choice in the matter. It could not very well totally ignore Palmer.

Yet his name crops up only once among the list of witnesses, and whatever he had to say was never made public. At the Joint Committee Hearings, Palmer did not on any occasion appear as a witness, but his utterances before the Navy court leaked out anyway.

Palmer indicated that there were indeed specific instructions from BuShips to the effect that U-T should proceed during the entire availability period (of the ship) if they found what might be considered a hazardous condition of these silver-brazed joints. And none but an imbecile would attempt to argue that such a condition did not exist on *Thresher*.

(At a later press conference, some three and one half months after he took over from Palmer as commander of the Portsmouth Naval Shipyard, a Captain Hushing, former supervisor of shipbuilding at Groton, Connecticut, made an ingenious attempt to throw a smoke screen to divert public curiosity—and in many cases indignation—away from the almost incredibly careless manner in which Portsmouth and BuShips handled the matter of *Thresher*'s ultrasonic testing.) Hushing said that U-T "was not a prescribed part of the [overhaul] specifications at the time." He added that ultrasonic testing was "clearly defined as a pilot or an experimental operation," and that "all of the tests which were required at that time for this kind of piping system were carried out."

Foisted on a technically disinterested public, such a statement can be dangerously misleading since it is compounded of half-truths. And that, to an agile mind, is sufficient to make a point which, in intent, is totally false.

It is true that ultrasonic testing of silver-brazed joints on submarines was not "a prescribed part of the [overhaul] specifications" at the time. It is also true that *Thresher* was subjected "to all of the tests which then were required." But these were nothing more than water pressure tests and hammer tests of a destructive kind, and were used only because the Navy had nothing better to work with until U-T was developed. The fact that

BuShips pressed hard for ultrasonic tests to be continued during the entire availability period of the ship if a hazardous condition was found is what proclaims the truth.

To downgrade U-T to the status of a "pilot or a so-called test" was again to misuse words. And for Hushing to compare the "poor judgment" exercised by Palmer in suspending these tests with "poor judgment" exercised by some of that press audience who smoked "although medical reports clearly indicate that smoking can cause lung cancer," was arrant nonsense.

During that interview, however, one newsman managed to extract from Hushing a straight answer to a vital question—an answer which underscored Navy admissions at a higher level.

"Captain Hushing, who finally determines when the ship is ready to go? Who has that responsibility?"

There was no ducking that one. "The Shipyard Commander has the basic responsibility," came the answer. "He is in command of the yard. He has all aspects of the operation within his control as regards the technical completion of the ship . . ."

Mr. John T. Conway, Executive Director, Joint Committee, was one of the many investigators who showed a marked reluctance toward swallowing some of the Navy's amnesia pills.

"If I may interpose here, my recollection is that the court *did* inquire *and the commandant of the Yard indicated that there were specific instructions* from the Bureau of Ships that it should proceed during the *entire availability period* [author's italics], if they found what might be considered a hazardous condition in these silver-brazed joints."

December 1962 was not the "entire availability period" of *Thresher*, since she did not sail until April, due to several other problems which surfaced in the meantime and, in fact, into and beyond the "fast cruise" period.

"I think," Mr. Conway continued, "the Bureau of Ships also asked for comments and recommendations and the results of this preliminary limited testing. Somewhere around November there was a decision made at the Yard not to go further, and I think they knocked off in December. And as I recall the testimony, *no decision or recommendation was sent to the Bureau of Ships* [author's italics] and the decision was made locally, in the Yard."

At this point, Vice Admiral Austin made another attempt to take the pressure off his colleague.

"Yes," he added with immense fortitude, "and the court determined that this decision was made with the knowledge of the shipyard commander. It was not made by him but it was made with his knowledge, and the court found that the shipyard [it is now no longer the shipyard *commander*] did use poor judgment in not continuing those tests."

Since Rear Admiral Palmer was the Portsmouth Naval Shipyard Commander, the final decision to discontinue tests on *Thresher* rested with him and with nobody else.

On the first day of the Joint Committee Hearings, Rear Admiral William A. Brockett condescendingly explained to Representative Craig Hosmer the chain of command in the subordinate organization entrusted with the overhaul of submarines such as *Thresher*, working from the bottom. First there is a ship superintendent aided by an assistant. The immediate boss of the superintendent is the repair superintendent, who, in turn, reports to the production officer. These were all Navy officers, but none was an admiral. Had Palmer decided to go ahead with the ultrasonic testing and unlag every last silver-brazed joint on *Thresher* that showed substandard workmanship, no one (other than perhaps BuShips itself) could have overridden him. Therefore, to shift the responsibility to the shipyard as a sort of vague generality is merely to play with words.

And yet, so deep-rooted is the chauvinism of the Navy when taken to task by outsiders (particularly civilians) that in spite of his "poor judgment" (a euphemism if ever one was coined) BuShips was almost apologetic in its treatment of Palmer.

For example, during the second session of the Joint Committee, 13 months after the *Thresher* disaster, we find Rear Admiral C. A. Curtze, Deputy Chief, Bureau of Ships, discoursing on the question of "the permanency of personnel." And we hear him saying with easy assurance, "Speaking of shipyard commanders, you probably are already aware that Admiral Palmer is retiring . . . He has a very active case of glaucoma and finds it very difficult to carry on with the medication that is required."

Let's backtrack for a moment in this "Cat and the Hat" thing. The reader will recall that during the first session of the Hearings, Vice Admiral Bernard Austin specifically told the Joint Committee that the percentage of defective silver brazings in *Thresher* was not reported higher up the chain of command than the commanding officer of the ship—the commanding officer of *Thresher*.

Representative Jack Westland, Washington: "You are

speaking of Harvey when you say the Commanding Officer?"

Admiral Austin: "No sir. This was Axene, then at the time the 'quality assurance' memo was written. Now, whether Harvey actually saw that memo or not, I don't know sir . . ."

Representative Westland: "I would like to pursue a matter one step further. On page 10 of the [Navy] summary of events, you say that all work undertaken by the shipyard during Thresher's post-shakedown availability was reported as having been completed satisfactorily, and the commanding officer expressed his concurrence that the work was completed. I would expect that to be the case.

"Now, how did the commanding officer express his concurrence? Was it in writing when he accepted the ship as ready for sea?"

Admiral Austin: "It was in a letter to his immediate superior in the chain of command, stating that he was ready for sea, that everything tested out all right."

Representative Westland: "And is this Commander Harvey?"

Admiral Austin: "That is correct, sir . . . We thought we ought to look into that a little bit, and we inquired into the type of man that Harvey was, and every indication was that he was the type of man who would not have hesitated to say a ship wasn't ready to go if it had not in his opinion been ready to go."

Representative Craig Hosmer: "A nagging doubt about whether some silver brazing was the right way to put these joints together, wouldn't have prevented him from signing that letter, would it?"

Admiral Austin: "Well, of course, he might have had

doubts about the process itself, but certainly I don't think he felt he was taking an unsafe ship to sea."

Representative Hosmer: "The report went to the previous commanding officer, Axene, and do you know whether Harvey in fact was aware of this problem with reference to the silver brazing?"

Admiral Austin now stated that he thought Axene would have turned over "something like that" to Harvey, but could not answer this definitely.

The worst form of myopia is probably 20/20 hindsight, but for nine days (January 9 to 18, 1963) Harvey and Axene virtually shared command of the ship. It is therefore extremely unlikely that Axene failed to inform him of the shipyard's decision to cease U-T tests, and in any case Harvey would have had to know before signing the letter of release.

No one will ever know what he thought or what he concluded. There are, moreover, other speculative factors that can never be resolved. This was Harvey's first command—his first chance to make good with a splendid ship like *Thresher*. He was therefore caught in a squeeze. If he refused to sail *Thresher* (and the defects developed during her fast cruise had obviously told him a lot), he might be putting his career on the line. If he signed and played it very very carefully, the chances were that he would be able to cope with an unexpected problem.

As for Admiral Austin, this was an issue on which he could afford to feel safe. John Wesley Harvey, deceased, could no longer speak for himself.

Thus, when during that same session, Representative Westland again asked Admiral Austin, "So you do not know whether or not Harvey knew that there was this 14 percent deficiency as the result of Shipyard tests?"

Austin again replied, "It is difficult to determine what he did know, sir."

But Austin had not counted on Representative Holifield, who quoted verbatim from Commander Axene's evaluation letter No. 16 to BuShips, regarding *Thresher*'s weaknesses:

In my opinion, the most dangerous condition that exists in Thresher is the danger of salt water flooding at or near test depth.

"Now," Holifield continued, "Axene gave this report as he was leaving, and as Harvey was his replacement, Harvey must have known about this, did he not?"

Admiral Austin thought about that one for a moment. "It would be presumed, Mr. Chairman, that he did know about it, but of course we can't be certain."

Representative Holifield's patience, at this point, may have been wearing a bit thin. "You cannot be sure. [But] in the Bureau of Ships August letter as to the instructions, you said that the intent of the Bureau is that the inspection directed by this letter shall serve as a pilot test of silver-brazed piping inspection . . . The letter went on to the effect that Portsmouth Naval Shipyard was requested to forward comments, suggestions and recommendations based upon their experience as a result of this pilot test. This was signed by Rear Admiral Robert L. Moore, Jr., Deputy Chief of the Bureau, [yet] as far as the record shows then, you had no response to this request for comments, suggestions and recommendations based upon their experience . . ."

Admiral Brockett: "That is right, sir."

Holifield was not the only Joint Committee member

who felt uneasy. A question put by Representative William H. Bates (Massachusetts) suggests that he could hardly believe some of the stuff the Navy had been dishing out, that he needed a playback to convince himself.

Representative Bates: "We have no record of who called off this [ultrasonic] inspection?"

Admiral Brockett: "The shipyard commander knew about it and it was a question of.going only so far. They were trying to get the ship finished and at that time I am sure the philosophy was, 'This is as good as any other ship . . .'"

Representative Bates: "Was this a Bureau of Ships team or a shipyard team?"

Admiral Brockett: "A shipyard team."

Representative Bates: "They were still there, at the Yard, but they went on to something else?"

Admiral Brockett: "They put them on something else."

Lieutenant Commander Stanley W. Hecker, skipper of *Thresher*'s escort ship, *Skylark,* because he delayed by several hours transmitting to New London the stunning information that *Thresher* had disappeared, got his knuckles verbally rapped by the Navy. Worse still, he was made a "party to the proceedings" and put in a position of legal involvement. However, since the Navy Court of Inquiry determined that Hecker's delay in getting the news through to New London had nothing to do with the loss of the ship and absolutely nothing to do with the loss of more than a hundred and twenty lives, there was little the Navy brass could do at the time, other than look grimly displeased. What a marvelous patsy Hecker would have made if only there had been something— some remote thread of evidence connecting him with the disaster. The episode itself, however, got a lot of publicity and it came up again during the Joint Committee Hearings.

During the second session of the Hearings (June 27, 1963), Secretary of the Navy Fred Korth was questioned about it by Senator Hickenlooper (Iowa). Korth's reply was, "I suppose more than anything else, Senator, is the fact that there was a failure to disclose something, even though it was not material. It was irritating. It was irritating to me to learn that this fellow had the information and I didn't know about it."

Senator Hickenlooper: "That was put in the press release. I understand he [Hecker] was not even consulted for a couple of days out there. He was just kind of given a good letting alone."

To which Representative Holifield added, "The log was not even called for by his immediate superiors until the court of inquiry requested it."

The subject of the Commanding Officer of *Skylark*, his treatment immediately following the tragedy and the possibility of what might next happen to him evoked a strong reaction from Senator Hickenlooper. He said in part, "The thing that has been intriguing me throughout the hearing is that *I have not seen one word of criticism of any higher authority, or commanding officer or anybody else who failed to explain why, when they discovered 14 percent deficiency in the silver braze joints on that ship . . . [they] did not test the rest of them . . . No criticism of anyone who failed to see whether this blow system would work at depths, even though it was equipped to work at such depths* [author's italics]."

He was of course referring to Representative Holifield's query of the day before as to why 2,855 of 3,000 silver-brazed joints on *Thresher* were simply ignored, even after test sampling had revealed such poor workmanship. It is clear that Representative Holifield was highly sensitive (and rightly so) to an earlier verbal skirmish between Admiral Brockett and Chairman Pastore. This concerned the *Barbel* flooding incident, which (due to a silver-brazing failure of the salt water system during a dive) placed the ship in serious jeopardy. *Barbel* (SS-580) was one of three high-speed diesel attack submarines. She was commissioned January 7, 1959. At the time this matter was aired, Chairman Pastore asked Admiral Brockett, "Had you ever had an incident in any other of the submarines whereby a brazed joint had become loose?"

Admiral Brockett: "Yes, sir; the best known would be the Barbel."

Chairman Pastore: "Had that happened before the Thresher went to sea?"

Admiral Brockett: "Yes, sir."

Chairman Pastore: "Had this matter been called to the attention of the commanding officer?"

Admiral Brockett: "It was common knowledge throughout the Navy; yes, sir."

Chairman Pastore: "You mean to tell me this commanding officer who passed on the 14 percent below standard [on *Thresher*], had known before this that one of the brazed joints had gone loose on one of the other submarines?"

Admiral Brockett: "I am sure that Barbel was common knowledge throughout the submarine force."

Adroitly, Admiral Austin now stepped in. ". . . The commanding officer of the Thresher who accepted this condition and took his ship to sea was not available for questioning, sir, and we could not ask him whether or not he considered this a dangerous thing."

Chairman Pastore was not to be deflected from the true intent of his questions, however. At this point he clearly did not have in mind the skipper of the lost *Thresher*.

"I am talking about the commandant *of the yard* [author's italics] who passed upon this."

Admiral Austin now had no choice but to make the best of a bad job. "We did question him, sir, and he, in retrospect, *admitted that he thought he should have looked into this more thoroughly* [author's italics], but at the time he did not consider it a dangerous situation. They were trying to meet a deadline date for the completion of the ship's availability, and to have gone further with the testing would have required unlagging [dismantling] of piping and delaying the ship and running up the cost of the overhaul . . ."

Running up the cost of the overhaul? With 129 human lives on the opposite side of the scale?

Chairman Pastore: "Are the procedures of the Navy such that this man could make the final determination, and he could pass on the final judgment without consulting the Bureau of Ships? Is that the procedure, and could he make that final determination?"

Admiral Brockett caught that ball in outfield, but he caught it nonetheless. "In the normal course of events we expect our people in the field to make decisions affecting the work that is in progress in their shipyards. Again, the 20-20 hindsight on this is that it probably should not have been done and it should have been reported up the line."

Representative Holifield: "Was not this known at the Bureau of Ships?"

Admiral Brockett: "It was not known—"

Representative Holifield: "Were there any telephone conversations?"

Admiral Brockett parried that he didn't know, or at least the matter had not come to his attention. In a somewhat ambiguous explanation, he was, he said, in a position not as Chief of the Bureau of Ships, but "one notch further down the line, in the chain in which this information would have come." (This was a roundabout way of saying that at the time Brockett's appointment as Bureau Chief had not yet come through, although it was imminent.)

In the Admiral's judgment, however, "the 14 percent deficiencies below standard do not mean that these were bad joints *in the normal sense* [author's italics]. They were tight joints and they held 150 percent of the normal working pressure . . . These hydrostatic tests were made."

The sophistry of this rejoinder seems so absurdly transparent that it is hard to believe the Admiral himself was deceived by it. If the archaic system of (destructive) hydrostatic testing for submarine piping systems was so great, why did BuShips insist that the Navy go to ultrasonic testing, and why did it bother to write a very detailed instruction covering the whole matter?

As the Joint Committee on Atomic Energy continued its hearing on June 27, 1963, another matter came into the open which was obviously bothering the senators and representatives conducting the Inquiry.

This followed on the heels of some rather embarrassing questions put by Joint Committee members to Navy witnesses, as to why no submarine had, until that time, been subjected to a full-scale deballasting against the pressure of test depth? After a brief verbal pass with Representative Holifield, Admiral John H. Maurer (Director, Submarine Warfare Division, Naval Operations) admitted that the point was "very well taken" and assured the committee that it would be done.

Holifield was not disarmed quite so easily. "I know it will be done, but why hasn't it been?"

Admiral Brockett intervened and quickly changed course.

"We are in the phase of starting alongside the dock [fast cruise]. This part is being done. We start on the surface, as you suggested."

When Representative Holifield discovered that the Admiral was not merely talking about *Thresher* but about other submarines, too, it was as much as he could take.

"You are further than that on those others," he pointed out. "Nuclear submarines have been running since 1955 and going at depths lower than conventional depths since that time. *That is eight years.* Yet you tell me that you have not made these [deballasting] tests. I can't understand why you have not made them during the eight years."

Admiral Maurer then stated that "to his knowledge" submarines had been blown "at depth."

Representative Holifield still was not satisfied.

The Navy's attempt to gloss over the difference between the terms "depth" and "deep depth" was not lost on him.

"You have never gotten around to the point of testing them at *deep depth?*"

This drew from Admiral Maurer a truly startling admission.

"May I say, sir, that I accept your thesis completely. Let us accept this as being something that we have learned from this disaster, and we will do it." He added, "In other words, this is one of the many lessons we have learned, sir. The fact that we did not blow those tanks on the first [nuclear] ship that came out and make a definitive test at test depth was an error. We should have done it; yes sir."

But even then Chairman Pastore was not mollified. "Which is also an error, too, Admiral, that since we have had the Thresher [disaster] that we have not done it yet. You are now promising that you will do it. The thing that amazes me is that since you have had the experience with Thresher . . . why shouldn't you have done it up to now since the Thresher. That is the thing that surprises me."

Secretary of the Navy Korth now intervened, turning the question over to Captain Bishop, technical liaison from the Office of the Assistant Chief of Naval Operations for Development. The latter, while admitting that Chairman Pastore's surprise was "certainly true as far as the desirability to test deballasting capacity . . ." pointed out there were other factors involved in recovering a submarine from emergency. "Our basic training when we get into trouble," he explained, "is first speed, then angle, then deballasting."

Mr. John T. Conway, executive director of the Joint Committee, blew that one all to hell.

"The ballast system is the most critical emergency system?" he wanted to know. "If it is that much of an emergency system, the question would be, Why hasn't it been tested? It is the most important emergency system you apparently have."

Not even Captain Bishop, it seems, was aware of the bitter irony of his statement; for by all accounts what he advocated was exactly what Captain Harvey had tried to do to save *Thresher*. First, power; then up-angle, and finally deballasting. He could not use power because his reactor had almost certainly shut down. He got the up-angle, but of what use was this when he was unable to blow tanks and give his ship the vital buoyancy that might have saved her?

Shortly after these startling revelations, painstakingly wrung out of the Navy, Senator Hickenlooper came up with another point that was obviously bugging him. What was the fate of the Commanding Officer of *Skylark?*

". . . I have not seen any criticism of the failures that occurred in the Portsmouth Navy Yard. I wonder why this young fellow [Hecker] is being singled out for criticism . . . Is he being made a patsy?"

Secretary Korth: "Certainly not."

Senator Hickenlooper: "I think there is evidence from which one might argue that he is. I am not saying that he is. *But it is rather significant that higher authority is not being condemned or criticized in any way* [author's italics] . . ."

To which Secretary Korth had to admit: "No action has yet been taken. You are absolutely correct." (There is no record that any action ever was taken.)

Senator Hickenlooper: "It is rather interesting, but a great deal has been made of this fellow commanding the Skylark, and I understand the evidence shows he didn't even have working sonar equipment on this thing that could enable him to receive and identify locations. I wonder what is happening to this fellow?"

Secretary Korth: "I can't answer that."

> What was the Lorax
> And why was it there?
> And why was it lifted and taken somewhere
> from the far end of town where the Grickle-grass grows?
> The old Once-ler still lives there.
> Ask him. *He* knows.

These lines, lifted straight out of *The Lorax,* by Dr. Seuss, make just as much sense as the dialogue that developed between the Navy and the Joint Committee over the *Tinosa*'s hull radiographs and how their strange disappearance related to *Thresher.* This particular episode occurred on the third day of the hearings (July 23, 1963), and it was Mr. John Conway who started the ball rolling.

Mr. Conway: "Admiral, [Rickover] the committee has been informed the Tinosa has not gone to sea as scheduled. That is the sistership of the lost Thresher. We understand the reason is because the radiographs have been lost. No one can find them."

Admiral Rickover: "I believe that is correct. They are being done over again."

Mr. Conway: "Have they lost any of the radiographs of the reactor plant?"

Admiral Rickover: "No sir."

Mr. Conway: "Yours have not been lost?"

Admiral Rickover: "No sir. Not mine."

Mr. Conway: "But the others are lost."

Admiral Rickover: "I believe that is correct, but since

Admiral Brockett is here, I think he probably has the answer to that."

Admiral Brockett: "Yes sir. They are missing and that is why we have docked the ship. These are hull welds of the HY80 structure and they are being retaken."

Senator Clinton P. Anderson (New Mexico): "When were these radiographs made of the Tinosa?"

Admiral Brockett: "They were made some months ago."

Senator Anderson: "Before the loss of Thresher?"

Admiral Brockett: "Yes sir."

Senator Anderson: "After the loss of Thresher they became lost?"

Admiral Brockett: "They were found missing after the Thresher."

Senator Anderson: "Good. The point is they were made prior to the loss of Thresher and then they turned up missing."

Senator Bates: *"How do you know they were ever made?* [author's italics]"

Admiral Brockett: "We don't."

Senator Anderson: "You just finished saying they were lost."

Admiral Brockett: "I said they were missing, not lost."

Senator Anderson: *"I asked you whether they were made before the Thresher incident and you said they were* [author's italics]."

Admiral Brockett: "The general radiographing of the hull would have occurred over this period . . ."

Senator Anderson: "Do you have any for the Thresher?"

Admiral Brockett: "Yes sir."

Senator Anderson: "Are there any missing?"

Admiral Brockett: "Not that I know of, sir."

Senator Anderson: "Have you looked?"

Admiral Brockett: "No sir. I have not."

Senator Anderson: *"Wouldn't it be almost time to check?* [author's italics]"

Admiral Brockett: "I assume they are but I accept the suggestion."

Senator Anderson: "Mr. Chairman [John O. Pastore], at this point could we put in the record another inquiry which was addressed to this same subject? Mr. Conway wrote . . . to the Navy, trying to find out about Tinosa. He received in reply what might be called 'gobbledegook.'"

Senator Wallace F. Bennett (Utah): "A brushoff."

Senator Anderson: "Yes. I ask that the letters he wrote and the replies he received be made part of this record."

Representative Holifield: "Without objection that will be done."

Senator Anderson: "Thank you."

It later was determined that the loss of *Tinosa*'s original radiographs was the result of "the breakdown of an out-dated accountability system."

Was this (quoting Vice Admiral Bernard L. Austin) one of the "things that probably would never have been looked into for some time to come . . . ?"

It was not until the final session of the Joint Committee Hearings (July 1, 1964) that Representative Holifield got some straight answers to questions that had long bothered him as well as Senator Hickenlooper.

"I hope," said Holifield, "that the Committee will bear with me while I go through as quickly as possible certain pickup questions from our previous Hearings . . . In our earlier Hearings it was stated that no action had yet been taken with reference to the commanding officer, USS Skylark and commanding officer, Portsmouth Shipyard. Is this still the case?"

Vice Admiral L. P. Ramage (Deputy Chief, Naval Operations): "No disciplinary action has been taken. Is that what you were referring to?"

Representative Holifield: "Yes."

Admiral Ramage: "No sir. The commanding officer, Skylark, has since been transferred to the command of a submarine—an advancement in his career."

Representative Holifield: "And the commanding officer of the Portsmouth Naval Shipyard?"

Admiral Ramage: "He is retiring."

ADMIRAL RICKOVER ON
RESPONSIBILITY

Beyond doubt, in many respects the most controversial
figure in the U. S. Navy is Admiral Hyman G. Rickover,
the genius who "dehydrated" a block-long commercial
atomic reactor plant, squeezed it into a submarine hull
and made it work with awe-inspiring reliability. He, indeed, it was who gave submarines an entirely new
dimension and endowed them with capabilities that
hitherto had existed only in the fertile mind of Jules
Verne. And, oddly enough, it was Rickover who restored
steam to its rightful place in maritime propulsion—at one

stroke outdating all known fuels used to produce heat energy.

It would be fair to say that Admiral Rickover is not exactly a popular figure in the U. S. Navy or shipyards and that in terms of personality his detractors have enough material to work with. Lynx-eyed and sarcastic, abrupt and abrasive—a contemptuous enemy of the endless weaknesses of The System and "the proper channels," utterly intolerant of anything short of perfectionism— the least of Rickover's problems has been making enemies. And the most galling thing to his critics has been the monotonous way he has forced them to eat their words—the countless times when he has proved himself absolutely right and his opponents absolutely wrong.

For years prior to the *Thresher* catastrophe Rickover repeatedly warned the Navy that, unless it took drastic steps to uprate quality assurance in submarine building, it was headed for certain disaster.

No one could have spelled it out more clearly, yet that was the signal for some idiot to start circulating the famous "joke" about the Navy using two standards of quality assurance for its submarines—Rickover's nit-picking requirements for the reactor units and the "regular" standards for the rest of the ship.

Before we go any further, I want to identify myself unequivocally with views expressed by former Commander (later Captain) William R. Anderson, skipper of *Nautilus*, who instinctively understood Rickover's intolerance for mediocrity and viewed him as he really is— a warmhearted, unselfish and considerate man with a keen sense of humor.

In his famous book *Nautilus, 90 North*, a copy of which he generously inscribed to me, Captain Anderson

injected perfect balance into his pen sketch of Admiral
Rickover with the evaluation, "[He] is frequently pic-
tured as a . . . tough-minded intellectual who believes
that the shortest distance between two points is a line
that bisects six Admirals."

Marvelous!

It was at the Hearings before the Joint Committee on
Atomic Energy that Rickover's devastating sincerity—his
uncompromising honesty of purpose—became apparent
to all right-thinking people, whether technically oriented
or not, whether civilian or service personnel. Admiral
Rickover's position was a particularly delicate one at
that time, since he was forced to wear two hats while
giving evidence. He appeared, as we have already seen,
as a witness both for the Atomic Energy Commission
(which was trying to get at the truth about *Thresher*)
and for the Department of the Navy, which seemed
equally determined to confuse every possible issue by
using filibuster tactics and verbal smoke screens. And of
course Rickover's position was complicated still further
because of his leadership of the Naval Reactors Branch.

Some idea can be gained of what Rickover really felt
and thought about many of the Navy's practices if we
analyze an address he made at the 44th Annual National
Metal Congress, New York, October 29, 1962, less than
five months before *Thresher* was lost forever. Although
this speech was published in its entirety in the government publication entitled "Hearings Before the Joint
Committee on Atomic Energy, Congress of the United
States," nevertheless it carried a U. S. Navy disclaimer:
"This speech reflects the views of the author and does not

necessarily reflect the views of the Secretary of the Navy or the Department of the Navy."

The reader may bet his boots that it didn't, even though this is just one passage taken out of Admiral Rickover's timely presentation. The inertia of a century or more of lethargic progress by the U. S. Navy and its many contractors cannot be halted and reversed in a week or a month, but you have to start *somewhere— sometime*. Ironically, the speech is entitled "The Never-ending Challenge."

". . . Too often," Rickover reminded his audience, "management is satisfied to sit in plush offices, far removed physically and mentally from the design and manufacturing areas, relying on paper reports for information about the status of design and production in the plant itself—the real center of the enterprise. This lack of firsthand evaluation results in poorly designed and manufactured equipment, late delivery, or both. During the past few years, hundreds of major conventional components, such as pressure vessels and steam generators, have been procured for naval nuclear propulsion plants. Less than 10 percent have been delivered on time. Thirty percent were delivered 6 months to a year or more later than promised. Even so, reinspection of these components after delivery showed that over 50 percent of them had to be further reworked in order to meet contract specification requirements.

"We have tried to improve matters by sending representatives of the naval reactors group to manufacturers' plants to make on-the-spot checks of engineering and production progress. Often our men discover extremely unsatisfactory conditions of which the management is unaware. The usual management reaction is to disbelieve the facts submitted to them. Corrective action is therefore often taken too late. *The most prevalent inadequacy found in our audits is the failure to recognize that timely production of high quality components requires almost infinite capacity for painstaking care and attention to detail by all elements of the organization, both management and non-management* [author's italics]. This is as true for a so-called conventional 'old-line' product as for a new one . . ."

One facet of Rickover's genius is perhaps best described by Carlyle, who wrote of this great gift that it "means a transcendent capacity of taking trouble, first of all." This comes very close to the Admiral's words, but it still falls short of doing him justice.

There are those who have tried to ridicule Rickover by applying to him that quotation, "Don't do as I do—do as I say," because of his dislike of uniforms and ceremony conflicting with a total devotion to discipline. What these people have never understood is that the most abiding and efficient form of discipline is *self*-discipline, which springs from the mind—from ordered, logical and far-seeing mental processes, and from a clear realization of the direct, immutable relationship between cause and effect. Not from stomping up and down a parade ground and certainly not from fear.

Elsewhere in that same speech, Vice Admiral Rickover, pointing out the too frequent errors made in welding together parts of submarine piping systems made of different (and therefore incompatible) materials, remarked:

"I feel rather strongly about this problem. On more than one occasion I have been in a deeply submerged submarine when a failure occurred in a sea-water system because a fitting was of the wrong material. But for the prompt action of the crew, the consequences might have been disastrous. In fact I might not be here today."

Rickover pointed out a specific case where a stainless steel fitting had been welded into a nickel-copper alloy piping system. The fitting had been "certified by the manufacturer as nickel-copper and had all the certification data including chemistry and inspection results. Yet it was the wrong material . . . The manufacturer simply had no effective quality control organization."

There was a great deal more in this vein, but perhaps the Admiral's key remark came toward the end of his speech.

"I only wish I could tell you that the somber situation I have described no longer exists; that our efforts over the past 15 years have been successful in eliminating these problems. But I can't. As the naval reactors program grows in scope and more companies engage in manufacturing components for it, our difficulties with conventional components multiply. They get worse rather than better. I have no sweeping solution for this never-ending problem, but several things can be done . . ." He went on to outline several things that could be done but it is worth repeating that his speech was delivered while *Thresher* was well into her final overhaul and several other nuclear submarines were in varying stages of construction on the slipways.

During the Joint Committee Hearings (Eighty-eighth Congress), Vice Admiral Rickover gave a great deal of valuable—if at times startling—evidence. That part of it which is given in this book does not necessarily appear in chronological order (the first hearing took place on Wednesday, June 26, 1963 and the last on Wednesday, July 1, 1964), but rather in the order in which it produces the strongest impact.

For example, at the third Hearing when Rickover was asked a blunt question by Representative Thomas G. Morris, his reply came back, equally blunt.

"You state [that] defective welds, poor radiography and incomplete inspection records are typical. Does that mean they are the rule, rather than the exception?"

Admiral Rickover: "Yes, they were the rule . . ."

At the last Hearing, Rickover said (after a disagreement with Rear Admiral C. A. Curtze over the quality of the steel used for *Thresher*'s hull): "In my opinion, the Thresher is a warning made at a great sacrifice of life, that we must change our way of doing business to meet the requirements of modern technology. Our management concepts must be changed if we are to keep pace with technology requirements of our high-performance ships. We must correct the conditions that permitted the inadequate design, poor fabrication methods and incomplete inspection to exist, if we are not to have another Thresher."

Rickover then offered some invaluable advice, much of which was standard practice in his own particular sphere of authority—submarine atomic reactors.

"I have made a few notes. First there is written procedures for the construction of ships. I have always had written procedures for the nuclear part. They are now going to have written procedures for the rest of the ship.

"They are now having audits. I have always had

audits. The Bureau [of Ships] is now going to have the Yard keep audits. We have always kept our records. We have all our radiographs. At the beginning we required them to be kept for three years. Now we require that they be kept for seven years. The Bureau is now requiring that these records be kept.

"Next is nondeviation. Right now the shipyards are permitted to have deviations on nonnuclear items in a submarine. But not on nuclear items. But the yards are still fighting it. It is only recently, the Bureau has stated, that the yards cannot deviate from specifications without their permission. We have always required this for the nuclear plant. In fact, if anyone wants to change from our nuclear specifications, he has to write an official letter which we call a 'degradation of specifications.' That is an expression I have instituted. If a manufacturer wants to change anything, he must write an official letter requesting a degradation of specifications."

Representative Thomas G. Morris: "Supposing he wants to upgrade specifications?"

Admiral Rickover: *"That has never occurred* [author's italics]."

There were some significant intakes of breath through the audience, and Rickover allowed just enough of a pause for this to register. His timing was superb.

"The Bureau is doing a great deal," he now conceded. "The most significant thing is adding more blow capacity to the ships [the ability to deballast more rapidly and safely under greater pressures].

"But they are now [also] doing many other things. However, we have been doing these things all the time."

Representative Morris: "Wouldn't it be a more simplified procedure if you were to put those together?"

Admiral Rickover: "You believe in a certain religion so you think it would be a good idea for all the others because you know it is the best one. [But] you can't legislate it.

"We have used these procedures all the time. The Bureau of Ships has known about these procedures, *but they thought they weren't necessary* [author's italics] . . ."

Representative Holifield: "Admiral Rickover, I understand that before the Thresher incident at least, there was quite a bit of pressure to get you to reduce some of your rather strict requirements in the selection of operators and the training of those operators. What is the status of that situation?"

Admiral Rickover: "The attempts toward 'degradation of specifications' on personnel—I will use that simple expression—still go on. However, I have had fine cooperation from Vice Admiral Semmes, who is Chief of Naval Personnel. He has stopped a lot of the attempts at degradation. We have had the cooperation of Vice Admiral Ramage [Deputy Chief of Naval Operations—Fleet Operations and Readiness] and Rear Admiral E. P. Wilkinson [Director, Submarine Warfare, Office of the Chief of Naval Operations] and from the very top staff.

"Our problem is in the submarine staffs where nearly all of the people are nonnuclear people, some of whom have a deep resentment against the nuclear navy because it has put them out of business . . . They are constantly trying to get personnel degraded. It takes a lot of fighting to keep it going. *In accordance with the request of this Committee previously made of me, I will advise you if the problem starts getting to the point where I need help* [author's italics] . . ."

A classical example of the Navy's urgent need for more stringent nonnuclear tests, which must have hit the anti-Rickover people like a rock between the eyes, occurred after the loss of *Thresher*. Dockside tests were being conducted of an identical high pressure air system aboard *Tinosa,* sister ship of *Thresher*. *Tinosa* was nearing completion at the Portsmouth Naval Shipyard. The purpose of the high pressure air system is to expel the water from the ship's ballast tanks, so increasing her buoyancy. During these tests, ice formed on the screen-type wire strainers in the air piping system, cutting off air flow to the ballast tanks. Even in a later "fast cruise," after the strainers were removed, compressed air lasted long enough to blow half the tanks, which was under what the specifications called for. This inability to de-ballast against great water pressures at deep depths undoubtedly deprived *Thresher* of her last hope of regaining the surface.

Back-tracking to the Joint Committee's Hearing of July 23, 1963 (the second one), Vice Admiral Rickover explained why he came to the inexorable decision to scrap all the silver-brazed joints in the reactor compartment and replace them with welded joints. When it came to his notice that *Thresher,* during her builder's trials in May 1961, had suffered a serious incident when a one-inch trim system line let go at test depth, Rickover decided, "I could no longer depend on silver brazings for high-pressure systems. I therefore took the following action for systems under my cognizance:

"(1.) All systems exposed to salt water would be fully welded, regardless of pipe size. Welding and its inspection would be in accordance with established reactor plant welding and nondestructive testing standards [radiographs].

"(2.) Salt water systems would be fabricated to the same standards and quality control as the rest of the reactor plant.

"(3.) In addition, I required that joints and sea water piping passing through the reactor plant also be welded, even though this piping was not under my cognizance.

"In the Thresher, this work was all completed before she last went to sea."

Clearly, Rickover wanted to make the point that the "flooding casualty" which most probably led to *Thresher*'s loss was in no way connected with any piping problem in the reactor. All the welding had been done and the radiographs were available to show that it had been done properly—according to the Admiral's standards and the specifications laid down by Naval Reactors Branch.

Shortly after, that same day, Vice Admiral Rickover, while running through a list of written recommendations which would eliminate a repetition of the *Thresher* disaster, or at least minimize it to a point far lower than that which was being currently accepted by the Navy, made a startling disclosure.

"I have been out on all first trials of all nuclear-powered submarines except two, when I was in hospital, and some things have occurred to me. I will try to relate them to the Thresher as closely as possible. Prior to Thresher's trials in April 1961, in connection with some casualty studies I had run with a new reactor plant design, I became aware that the blow capacity of Thresher was small. I pointed this out to the officer in charge of the Bureau of Ships, Submarine Desk at that time. During Thresher's trials I also pointed it out to the Navy

Yard, to the Bureau of Ships, the Board of Inspection and Survey, and Commander of Submarine Forces Atlantic Fleet representatives who were on board. I think this is a point which should go on record.

"Another incident in connection with Thresher was about two weeks before her first sea trials. As I was to be in charge of these trials, I asked my people to look into the measurements and tests and the proposed method of conducting this first dive. I found little thought had been given to the details of how this dive was to be conducted . . .

"I arrived at Portsmouth the evening before the trials. I met the following: the Deputy Chief of the Bureau of Ships, the head of the Bureau of Ships Submarine Type Desk, the shipyard commander, the shipyard planning officer, the shipyard design superintendent, the commanding officer of Thresher, and others. I requested them on a crash basis to detail in writing the whole sequence to insure safety during the dive. Of course, all this was done during the night. The plan, as finally evolved, which I approved, provided for a slow, deliberate descent at given stages; at each stage there was to be a cycling of all sea valves, flapper valves and other items affected by pressures. At each valve station a man was present to observe and to act if necessary. I did this to ensure that as the ship went deeper, our damage control devices were instantly operable. I also did this because of my concern at the lack of blowing [deballasting] margin. Also, I considered all this would be necessary since this was the first time one of our submarines was to go to so great a depth . . .

"The lack of planning for this dive was indicative to me of what I considered the casual way in which the

Navy was going to those great depths. An index of this casualness can be obtained by reading the minutes of the meeting held by the Ship's Characteristics Board and the Bureau of Ships in early 1959, at which Thresher's depth was discussed.

"I did the best I could to bring the HY-80 [pressure hull steel] situation to the highest level in the Navy. I took the matter up with the Chief of the Bureau of Ships and the Chief of Naval Operations early in 1959. Later that year, cracks were discovered in the submarine at Mare Island. I again took it up with the Chief of Naval Operations . . . who appointed the President of the Board of Inspection and Survey to conduct a study. He recommended to the Chief of Naval Operations that the Navy proceed as planned." Nothing was changed.

What Vice Admiral Rickover was referring to was that, in the matter of welding versus silver-brazing, COMSUBLANT had merely recommended that an economic assessment be made of this.

But where Rickover really tossed some depth charges overboard was in his conclusions to the lengthy evidence he had given and the many recommendations he had made that day.

"I consider that the most important step to be taken by the Navy is to eliminate transient technical management. No industrial organization that operates on a profit and loss basis would ever dream of continually shifting its top people. An industrial organization so operated would soon go out of business . . .

"Another factor I believe to be responsible for many of the Navy's technical difficulties *is the lack of individual responsibility* [author's italics] . . . It is significant to me how few of the senior people in the responsible man-

agement positions at the time of Thresher's loss had anything to do with her basic design . . . For example,
during the five to six years encompassed in the design,
construction and evaluation of Thresher, some of the key
job changes were approximately as follows: The Portsmouth Naval Shipyard, which was assigned the detail
design responsibility for the Thresher, had three shipyard
commanders, three production officers, five planning
officers and three design superintendents. The Bureau of
Ships during this period had two Chiefs of Bureau, six or
so heads of the Design Division, and three heads of the
Submarine Type Desk. Some of the individual Bureau
technical codes concerned with Thresher had about four
to six changes of management during the same period.
Of course, these figures do not include the numerous
changes in the subordinate ranks which were made during this period. How can you have individual responsibility on this basis?

"Much of the effort of the court," Rickover reminded
his listeners, "was directed to finding out who was responsible for the design of Thresher; who made funda-
mental technical decisions; who authorized deviations
from plans; who authorized deviations from specifications. The inadequate ballast tank blowing system is a
case in point. Who is responsible? With the present Navy
system, this is an almost impossible question to answer.
The nearest you can come is to say 'The Navy is responsible.' In other words, all you can do is point to a
collectivity. In my own area, for example, when the
adequacy of a scram procedure is questioned—'It is
Rickover's procedure.' *And this is as it should be* [au-
thor's italics].

"In this connection, I believe you will be interested in

the following testimony I gave this committee on June 15, 1961:

"Responsibility is a unique concept. It can only reside and inhere in a single individual. You may share it with others, but your portion is not diminished. You may delegate it, but it is still with you. You may disclaim it, but you cannot divest yourself of it. Even if you do not recognize it or admit its presence, you cannot escape it. If responsibility is rightfully yours, no evasion or ignorance, or passing the blame can shift the burden on someone else. Unless you can point your finger at the man who is responsible when something goes wrong, then you never had anyone really responsible."

Representative Bates: "Did you say that 'off the cuff'?"

Admiral Rickover: "Most of it, yes."

Representative Bates: "That is pretty well said."

Addressing himself to Rickover, Representative Holifield agreed, "Of course . . . you do have these large [private enterprise] organizations with responsibility placed in specialized compartments. However, with the military, it seems to me, to a great extent you have to make every member of the Armed Forces a generalist rather than a specialist."

Admiral Rickover, who had just finished implying a great deal more than he had said, was not looking for qualified agreement. It quickly became obvious that he was concerned with a principle.

"Mr. Chairman, this is a subject on which I hope the Armed Services Committee of the House or Senate might call on me to testify. *Essentially, it gets down to personnel* [author's italics]. It gets down to the kind of people you bring into the organization, how you educate and train them and what ideas you inculcate in them.

"Whenever something goes wrong, do you say: 'Read another book on leadership . . .'? Sometimes I feel all we do is talk about leadership and principles and define them by rules of conduct. What are those rules? You are not supposed to have a soup spot on your blouse. Abraham Lincoln had soup spots. You are not supposed to drink. Ulysses S. Grant drank."

Representative Holifield: "Let's not take this too far." (Laughter.)

Admiral Rickover: "I was only talking about military people. You are not supposed to run around with women. Napoleon ran around with women.

"Such rules are not the basic essentials of leadership. There is more to it than that. I think perhaps we lose sight of this with our nice, easy rules and the idea that all we have to do is follow rules and we are great leaders. I have never been a great leader, but then I have never read the rules."

Representative Holifield: "You had better continue."

Admiral Rickover: "The present-day technical complexity is beyond the point where you can count on 'the system' to do the job well . . . On the other hand, if you eliminate transient technical management and assign *individual responsibility* [author's italics], other benefits logically follow. Only then can the necessary detailed technical control, the establishment and enforcement of proper standards and the selection and training of personnel be done at the level commensurate with the degree of technical excellence required by modern-day weaponry . . ."

There was no doubt but that on Tuesday, July 23, 1963, Admiral Rickover stole the whole show and impressed his listeners in a way no other witness had been able to do or was able to duplicate. At the end of a long day, Rickover summed up his views in masterly fashion:

(a) "There is insufficient information to pin down what really happened to Thresher. I do not know. We therefore have to look at *everything* [author's italics] that may have contributed to her loss.

(b) "I do know there were weaknesses in her design, fabrication *and inspection* that must be corrected. These are symptomatic of the basic problems facing the Navy today in the conduct of its technical work.

(c) "Significant upgrading must be effected in our Bureaus *and shipyards* in design, fabrication and inspection.

(d) "This upgrading cannot be done until there is a permanence in technical management *and an assignment of individual responsibility.*

(e) "There must be a change in the philosophy that the Navy exists for its people and that the career of its people takes precedence. Promotion should be on the basis of results and contributions to the Navy, not on the multiplicity of jobs a man has had.

(f) "Outdated concepts of the officer-civilian relationship should be abandoned—the best man should get the job.

"Mr. Chairman, this concludes my prepared testimony."

DEEP SUBMERGENCE
SYSTEMS REVIEW GROUP
April 24, 1963

Fourteen days after USS *Thresher* vanished with 129 men aboard, the U. S. Navy pushed the panic button. Or rather, SECNAV did, with Notice 3100. Not only did the greatest undersea search ever organized get underway, but a five-year submarine rescue program was launched. For those who didn't bother to think too deeply, or let themselves be carried away by their emotions, it seemed like the answer to all dangers associated with deep-sea diving. It was not, and although its objectives were clearly stated, by the time it became operational, some 60 nuclear subs, both missile-firing and attack, had long since completely outdated them.

On June 27, 1963, testifying before the Joint Committee on Atomic Energy about the *Thresher* disaster, Rear Admiral Edward C. Stephan told Senator John O. Pastore, the presiding chairman:

"I am Admiral E. C. Stephan. On the 24th of April I was relieved of duties of Oceanographer of the Navy and Commander U. S. Naval Oceanographic Office, and assigned to be Chairman of the Deep Submergence Systems Review Group [DSSRG].

"The objectives of this group, and my responsibilities, are to review the current plans for location, identification, rescue and recovery of large objects from the deep ocean floor. To recommend changes to these plans for expeditious improvement. To recommend changes for a longer term improvement, and to develop a five-year program to improve toward a maximum capability our ability to locate, identify, rescue and recover large objects from the ocean floor.

"I am also responsible for recommending the means and the organization required to implement this program. I am specifically directed to not become involved in the current operations in the location of the Thresher."

There was a good deal more in the same vein, and unless Admiral Stephan had a total recall memory, he must have been reading from a prepared statement. Save for the part about not becoming involved in the *Thresher* search, none of this other stuff made any real sense, even though it sounded great.

Ten years ago, exactly as they do today, nuclear-powered submarines had a theoretical "test depth" at which they were supposed to be able to cruise for as long as was necessary in comparative safety. And a "crush depth" where the sea pressures were so enormous that no human being had the slightest hope of surviving the collapse of the hull and the flooding of the ship.

And for the decade prior to that—from the time *Nautilus* (the U. S. Navy's first nuclear-powered sub) went to sea—ships of her ilk had been diving to "test depth" (about 1,000 feet) almost daily. Many of them encountered flooding situations from which they extricated themselves only by the greatest good luck. But *all* of them knew one thing for sure: if they ever found themselves in such trouble at that depth that they could not surface unaided, then no power on earth could help them. There was no known salvaging equipment capable of reaching a distressed sub that deep. Existing rescue chambers and diving bells were useless. The few miniature submarines available, assuming they could go to these depths, were designed for an entirely different purpose.

To this day, the most daring and successful submarine rescue of all time took place on May 23, 1939, when 33 crewmen were snatched alive from the forward torpedo room of the partly flooded diesel boat *Squalus*. The rescue took 40 hours, and four separate trips down to the escape hatch of the distressed ship were required. Even so, 29 men trapped in the afterpart were drowned. Oddly enough, *Squalus* sank off Portsmouth, New Hampshire, though on a very shallow part of the Continental Shelf, at a depth of only about 240 feet. The McCann rescue chamber used was located in New London, and although this happened more than 34 years ago, the U. S. Navy still has no handy rescue device any better than the McCann chamber. More sophisticated, yes, but more efficient, no. It holds eight survivors and two operators at one time and is 10 feet high and eight feet in diameter at its widest. It weighs 10 tons but has been sufficiently improved to operate at a maximum depth of 800 to 850 feet, given ideal surface conditions. These ideal conditions, aside from the weather, presuppose that the distressed submarine is settled only at a slight angle to port or starboard, or lengthwise, since otherwise the rubber-gasketed skirt at the bottom of the chamber would be unable to mate with the standard escape hatch built into all modern U.S. submarines, nuclear or diesel.

Yet the incredible irony of this situation was that when *Thresher* foundered in 1963, neither she nor any other nuclear submarine had ever even *tried* to fully blow out their main ballast tanks at "test depth." In fact, dockside "fast cruises" showed this could not be done with the deballasting equipment designed into those ships. They all, without exception, relied on getting away with a minor flooding casualty by using the enormous steam power generated by their nuclear reactors.

Toward the close of his oration, Admiral Stephan mentioned some of the outstanding oceanographers and marine scientists he had assembled on his team, and one name stands out in particular—that of Dr. Robert M. Snyder. It was Dr. Snyder, a consultant from WHOI then working (1967) in Palm Beach, Florida, who gave me his copy of the congressional hearings before the Joint Committee on Atomic Energy on the loss of *Thresher*, and whose dynamic approach fired me with the courage to start this book. But it wouldn't be an easy job, he warned. Dr. Snyder knew a great deal about the search for *Thresher*, but he didn't speculate much on the cause of her loss. His inclusion on Admiral Stephan's team had been in an advisory capacity. It had not debarred him from joining another dedicated group aboard *Atlantis II*, who, in a commendation from Vice Admiral Grenfell, were to be thanked for displaying "the highest standards of seamanship and scientific performance . . ." However, when I met Dr. Snyder the *Thresher* tragedy was already four years old and he was immersed once more in oceanographic projects that occupied all his time.

For a long while, the acronym DSSRG was on everyone's lips—everyone, that is, connected with oceanography, submarines and deep sea rescue, or drawn by the lure of survival from perilous conditions. Snatching people from the very jaws of death is an achievement that also gives the general public a vicarious thrill. The rescue of mountaineers, miners, people trapped in burning buildings, sinking ships, or lost in the desert never fails to provide people with the suspense they seek so avidly.

Yet DSSRG and its associated activities, DSSP (Deep Submergence Systems Project) and DSRV (Deep Submergence Rescue Vehicles) were little more than a delusion—a concept that began with two strikes against it and simply wasn't practical.

For a decade the Navy used up time, money, extraordinary ingenuity, and the scientific know-how of some of the best brains in the country, creating, testing and perfecting a scheme to rescue men trapped in a deepdiving, distressed nuclear submarine.

There was only one thing wrong with all this costly activity—it could not work. This is an inner-space dream. Let's look at its outer-space counterpart. It would be as futile as asking NASA to devise some means of rescuing from the moon astronauts whose lunar module had sustained irreparable damage on landing. The question would not be one of hardware, or skills, but of sheer practicality. There was and still is no way the two stranded astronauts could be rescued unless *every* condition was *exactly* right. There would have to be a second Apollo/Saturn V rocket standing on an adjacent pad, completely equipped and in an advanced state of countdown, ready to lift off. The stranded astronauts would have to be reasonable candidates for survival—not so badly injured that even if brought back their chances of recovery would be nil. They would need enough oxygen to survive at least three days—hardly likely in a wrecked lunar module and quite impossible to expect from their backpacks. And last but not least, the rescue module would need enough thrust to lift off and rendezvous with four men aboard instead of two.

The whole thing is nonsense. Pie in the sky. And that is why NASA concentrated instead on designing and building almost foolproof hardware with a computer-tested 98 per cent chance of getting the moon-walking astronauts back to their orbiting command module.

Let's return to the inner-space effort. The U. S. Navy built those fantastic nuclear-powered, steam-driven submarines that could dive to unheard-of depths, but it never bothered to give the crew some computerized backup systems against flooding emergencies. It offered them nothing like a 98 per cent chance of extricating themselves from serious trouble. FRISCO (Fast Reaction Integrated Submarine Control) apparently is not yet ready and is in any case so complex and bulky that it would leave room for little else inside the sub.

Thresher forced this problem on the Navy; it set DSSRG objectives which were absurd because they were, by definition, contradictory. "To develop a deep-sea rescue vessel, the DSRV, which could operate *below the collapse depth* [author's italics] of our fleet submarines, and which could search for and rescue surviving personnel."

Assuming the "collapse depth" (where the hull of a nuclear sub is crushed like a nutshell) to be about 2,000 feet, this is equivalent to a water pressure of 880 pounds per square inch.

As probably happened in *Thresher*, anybody caught in an airtight space where atmospheric pressure rose suddenly from 14 to 880 psi would die instantly of ruptured blood vessels. And if the water hit you first, it would be equivalent to being run over by a freight train.

About the only useful thing a DSRV could do, cruising at such depths, would be to search and locate. And perhaps gain some closer idea of the cause of the accident. The word "rescue" would therefore be hilarious but for the element of terrible tragedy involved.

And there is another thing. Taking the Atlantic Ocean alone, barely 16 per cent of its total floor is shallow enough to put even the antiquated McCann rescue chamber to any practical use. The Continental Shelf along the shores of all the continents bordering it varies greatly in width and depth, from five or perhaps 10 miles wide to between 10 and 800 feet deep. So, for 84 per cent of the Atlantic Ocean alone, a DSRV is barely necessary as a means of attempting to save life. In fact, it will so continue until engineering and metallurgical improvements enable the pressure hull of future atomic submarines to withstand "test depths" of well over 2,000 feet and "crush depths" in the neighborhood of 3,500 feet. Yet, only two years after the Navy issued its DSSRG edict, Admiral Stephan's brain trust had accomplished wonders.

It had drawn up seemingly practical plans for a DSRV, including all the associated logistics. Ignoring the absurdly contradictory nature of the Navy's demands, it had sought and obtained official approval of its hardware design and, taking matters a step further, it had found the contractors prepared to do the work and meet the specifications. Within 12 months the Navy obtained the necessary funds to start translating the Deep Submergence Systems Project plans into reality. That was in 1966. Not unexpectedly, the contractors for the first two DSRV's were Lockheed Missiles and Space Company, Sunnyvale, California, and the specifications of these vehicles merit a brief description. Except for its large propeller, protected by a wide circular band or ring stabilizer, the DSRV looks like a gargantuan version of one of those vacuum-packed aluminum tubes used for storing costly cigars. The interior, of course, is a different story. It consists of three spheres, each 7.5 feet in diameter, fabricated of tough HY-140 steel, an alloy of tremendous compression strength. The center and after-spheres accommodate rescued submariners and the third crewman. The length of the DSRV is 49.2 feet, its beam eight feet, and its displacement 35 tons. The outer hull is formed of fiberglass, but the vessel can withstand a pressure of 2,200 pounds per square inch, encountered at 5,000 feet below the surface. Silver-zinc batteries of great endurance deliver current to a powerful electric motor which propels the ship at five knots and gives it an endurance of 12 hours at three knots. In addition, four ducted thrusters (spacecraft-type) give the DSRV considerable added mobility in a small space. Carrying capacity is 24 rescuees, plus a pilot, co-pilot, and rescue sphere operator.

The original contract called for two DSRV's and the first of these was launched on January 24, 1970. The second DSRV went down the slipways on May 1, 1971. DSRV-1 was commissioned on August 6, 1971, at a cost of $41 million. DSRV-2 was placed in service on July 11, 1972, at a much reduced cost of $23 million. Following a six-week factory test, both ships underwent extensive sea trials during 1971.

Conversion work began in 1969 on the USS *Salmon* (SS-573), a *Sailfish* Class diesel submarine of 2,625 tons, to act as the parent ship. *Salmon* would be the initial test platform in a complex and farsighted undersea rescue installation. She was, however, dropped in favor of three nuclear subs then nearing completion.

Both ships were transported to San Diego, California, for rescue-system tests on the San Clemente Island Range. There were no serious faults to the plans, except of course that the chance of either of these baby submarines being used in deep-sea rescue work did not make them worth powder and shot to blow them to hell.

The initial sea trials of the two DSRV's covered only part of the total operation envisaged in case of their need. Long range, rapid action rescue requires the use of extensive shore facilities, support ships, aircraft and other related equipment, and at the time none of these was available. It was estimated, however, that the development, construction, test and support of both vehicles would reach a figure of $220 million through fiscal 1975—not exactly small potatoes.

For this reason, the concept of a six-vehicle DSRV force with two subs based at each Rescue Unit Home Port (RUHP) in San Diego, Charleston, South Carolina and New London, Connecticut, was quietly abandoned as the Navy became more acutely aware of the folly of its plans. This was expressed as "public lack of interest, changing operational concepts and funding limitations."

Let's go back to those DSRV's for a moment. They are worth a closer look, if only for the tremendous ingenuity and technical sophistication apparent in their design. Electronically, each ship is a pocket marvel. It has elaborate search and navigation radar, a closed-circuit TV system and optical devices that can determine the exact location of a disabled "large object" on the sea bed. As further backup on a search mission it also uses side-looking sonar.

Perhaps one of the most ingenious design features of the DSRV is the elaborate mating skirt under the center sphere which carries its own supply of a special sealant and can lock in over the disabled sub's escape hatch at an angle of up to 45°. The bottom ring of the transfer skirt is shock-absorbing and can withstand considerable impact without damage. The DSRV is capable of effecting a mating in a one-knot current and of withstanding impact velocities of up to two feet per second in any direction without damage.

The four ducted thrusters are designed to provide power in any of five degrees of freedom—pitch, yaw, surge, heave and sway. There is yet a sixth degree of freedom, namely roll, which is controlled by a trim and list system provided by a mercury reservoir.

The mating limitation of 45° is sensible enough (even though it is never likely to take place) because the DSSP figures that, if the distressed submarine is resting at a steeper angle, "we wouldn't give much for the survival chances of the crew. The escape compartments in a sub have the strongest bulkheads. That's a strength at least equal to the collapse depth of the pressure hull."

If any of those were to let go, we might then be looking at an implosion condition—and that would be it.

Captain William M. Nicholson, USN, a fine, modest and capable man, who was formerly head of the Ship Systems Engineering Department, was appointed project manager for the Navy's Deep Submergence Systems Project in January 1967. He took a long, hard look at the design details of the DSRV and liked what he saw, but already everything had dropped one year behind and the five-year plan (which should have made DSSP effective by 1968) was nowhere near schedule.

In October of that year, the USNS *Mizar* (T-AK 272), a specially equipped cargo ship carrying the most efficient type of deep-water cameras and bolstered by a great deal of experience in the search for *Thresher* five years earlier, located the wreckage of USS *Scorpion* (SSN-589), 400 miles southwest of the Azores, more than two miles down. Even had DSRV-1 or 2 been ready that soon, they could not have gone down to more than half the required depth; and even had they been able to reach the wreckage, could they seriously have expected to find anyone of the 99 crewmen alive—after five months?

The most that a Deep Sea *Research* (not Rescue) Vehicle could do under such conditions would be to take numerous close-up photos of the wreck. But would these photos have been any clearer—any more useful in determining the cause of *Scorpion*'s loss—than the several thousand good quality pictures obtained by the trailing deep sea underwater cameras of the *Mizar?*

Let's suppose for a moment that the Navy should be faced with *exactly* the kind of nuclear submarine casualty suited to the very limited use of a DSRV. Let's imagine this particular ship had gone down on the Continental Shelf, in just under 1,000 feet of ocean. Let's further imagine she has settled pretty much on an even keel, and that despite a flooding situation in the engine room, she is by no means a total loss. The pressure hull is undamaged, but for one reason or another the reactor is permanently scrammed, so no further steam can be generated. The EPM (Electric Propulsion Mode) cannot get her up and off because she has shipped too much water and is crippled by excessive negative buoyancy. Let's say she cannot use her main ballast tanks because one of them has been ripped open and she no longer responds to any efforts to get her trimmed.

We could go on like this for another page, but the basic facts are that this particular submarine still has the use of her communications and still has the means to scrub and revitalize her air supply. Of the crew of 100 more than 75 are alive and uninjured.

What happens then?

Well, today, with both DSRV's ready and fully tested (they are operated by COMSUBDEVGRU-1, San Diego, California), the one at the most convenient Rescue Unit Home Port would be flown by a mammoth Lockheed C5 jet cargo plane direct to the airfield closest to the port where one of three nuclear submarine mother ships might be located. It might be USS *Halibut* (SSN-587), or USS *Finback* (SSN-670) and USS *Hawkbill* (SSN-666), two of the U. S. Fleet's newest *Sturgeon*

Class submarines. Each is equipped to carry a DSRV on a special cradle, just aft of the sail. The DSRV would then be taken swiftly by road to that port and loaded on the mother sub, which would immediately steam out to the disaster scene.

However, the DSRV would never be released while on the surface or close to it. Both ships would descend to a "staging point," perhaps halfway down (500 feet), when the DSRV-1 or the DSRV-2 would be released for deep diving operations and for locating and settling on the distressed sub. In fact, it would become a shuttle. With the DSRV's mating ring secured, the transfer could be pumped dry, allowing the sub's escape hatch to be opened from within and the crewmen to clamber up into the rescue vessel, two dozen at a time.

There's little to add to this heart-stirring animated cartoon (successfully enacted with part of a simulated "distressed" sub).

Had the Navy spent $220 million on improving the metallurgy of its submarine hulls and technology so vital to the safe use of these ships, it would not have to bother much about "rescue operations." Either the distressed sub would be able to extricate itself from most situations, or those aboard would be dead long before its broken hulk settled on the ocean floor. Even a fleet of DSRV's could not have saved a single one of the 228 lives lost aboard *Thresher* and *Scorpion*.

NASA surely has demonstrated the soundness of its philosophy in designing almost foolproof hardware for use in environments where "rescue" would be nothing but a pious hope.

The U. S. Navy today, is faced with a strange paradox indeed. For two decades it had high-powered deep-diving submarines that far exceeded the performance capabilities of its rescue vessels. Today, it has rescue vessels that far exceed the performance capabilities of its submarines.

EPILOGUE

This chapter began as a preface, but after much pondering I decided to put it at the end of the book. There are, I think, some valid reasons for this, since what follows is a review of the extraordinary behind-the-scene conflicts that erupted between the Navy and the Joint Committee on Atomic Energy, Congress of the United States, on whether or not to tell the world the truth about

Thresher. Having seen what really happened to trigger the most calamitous and embarrassing episode in the history of the U. S. Navy, this is perhaps the best point at which to examine the story behind the story and to sum it up as clearly as possible—let the chips fall where they may.

When, on the morning of April 10, 1963, USS *Thresher* (SSN-593) sank in 8,400 feet of water, 220 miles east of Cape Cod, carrying with her 129 helpless human beings of whom 21 did not even belong to the ship's company, the Navy flipped its lid. It was seized with an attack of paranoia from which it has yet to recover. In truth, a decade after it occurred, the loss of *Thresher* is still a lead weight on the Navy's conscience. It is a chapter of bad decisions, shirked responsibilities, skimpy workmanship, poor quality control and stubbornly callous incompetence that can never be expurgated from the record.

The only redeeming feature of this appalling tragedy was a small band of career officers unafraid to champion the truth. Headed by Admiral Rickover, they spoke out with total honesty. But to do this, they had to stick their heads into the jaws of "The System." It was not a pleasant experience. Too many lesser men recoiled before its evil breath.

Looking back at all the buck-passing and wordy evasions that followed the *Thresher* disaster, what we are really looking at is Fear. A pervasive kind of fear that flutters silently yet with terrible menace at the elbows of commissioned officers who, otherwise, would not hesitate to risk their lives in acts of bravery, even heroism. It is a fear that can turn decent, basically honest men into fawning sycophants or nervous wrecks. It is the fear of

making a decision and the fear of not making it. The
fear of the so-called Fitness Report, which can hold up
promotion, keep a man glued to some backwater job
almost indefinitely, earn him a crushing reprimand, or
in one of many ways ruin his career. It is indeed the Fear
of "The System."

Who needs this "System"?

Early in the Navy's inquiry into the loss of *Thresher*,
Captain William D. Roseborough, Planning Officer,
Portsmouth Naval Shipyard, had unofficially spoken
about "human error" during a TV interview. If this remark had any purpose, it was ostensibly to shift the
blame from the Navy "System," which was plainly responsible for sending *Thresher* out to sea, and to place
it on the shoulders of the unfortunate crew. In fact, it
had the opposite effect and the press was quick to react
to this ill-conceived comment. Roseborough got rapped
on the knuckles by his boss, Rear Admiral Charles J.
Palmer, commander of the Yard. Palmer, who was himself hardly in an enviable position, retracted the remark.

In retrospect, however, it depends upon what Roseborough meant by "human error." If he intended to de-
flect public opinion from the flooding casualty that
almost certainly sent *Thresher* to the bottom, he was
completely wrong. But if he had in mind the possibility
that the sequence of events overwhelmed the ship's company because, *through no fault of their own,* they lacked
sufficient time *aboard Thresher,* his contention might be
worth a second look, even though it in no sense
exonerates the Navy or "The System." Statistics can be
made to tell almost any story, but the ones which defy
manipulation all seem to point in the same direction.

Here is what the record shows: of *Thresher*'s twelve regular officers, six had never been to sea with her prior to her last trip. And only two had been with the ship since her commissioning. Six officers were lieutenants junior grade, while the two men holding the most responsible jobs aboard—her commanding officer and executive officer—had three and four months respectively with that particular ship, and then only in dry dock.

Both Wes Harvey and Pat Garner were absolutely outstanding at their jobs and could draw on a vast amount of nuclear submarine experience. That much was well known. But it is conceivable that neither of them fully realized what a capricious beast *Thresher* could be, and (for reasons that have already been made painfully apparent) just how much her overhaul left to be desired.

To offset this possible handicap, they had three backup officers also with skills and experience far above average. Lieutenant Commander John S. Lyman, the Engineer Officer, and Lieutenant John Smarz, the "A" Division officer, had served under the ship's previous skipper, the exacting Commander (now Rear Admiral) Dean L. Axene. The third man in this trio was Lieutenant Commander Mike Di Nola, Main Propulsion Assistant with more than two years' experience in *Thresher*. And besides Harvey, both Garner and Di Nola were qualified for submarine command.

Still, even the world's champion driver might find two identical race cars that handled quite differently. And could he guarantee that some undiscovered mechanical flaw might not cause him to crash fatally in tomorrow's Grand Prix? Could the world's greatest pilot feel exempt from the same risk?

A survey of the 96 enlisted men who were lost with *Thresher*, however, brings into focus an even sharper picture. Some 36 (over 30 per cent) had never sailed in her but had come aboard during the nine-month overhaul. For 35 of these 36 men, *Thresher* was their first-ever submarine assignment. Five had been ordered to the ship a month or less before she went down. Of the rest, 18 crewmen had seen 26 months' service with *Thresher*; one had been with her 25 months and one exactly two years. Another 35 had been less than two years but more than one year with the ill-fated vessel; one had completed a year's service and two others showed no reporting date. Incidentally, only two enlisted men and eight chief petty officers remained from the original commissioning crew.

Unluckiest of all was Alan Dennison Sinnett (mentioned by Lieutenant Commander Ray McCoole). Sinnett, a Fire Control Technician 2nd Class, not quite 29, assigned to *Thresher*, on April 4, 1963, had only six days to live.

In terms of service continuity, this is not an impressive picture, even though *individually Thresher*'s minority of veterans was highly accomplished and had earned numerous medals. So who was to blame? Not these unfortunate men.

The fact that *Thresher*, as her Log shows, spent nearly twice as much time either moored or in dry dock, (undergoing an endless number of repairs and overhauls) as any other submarine in the history of the U.S. Navy was not a valid reason for shuffling her crew around like pawns on a chessboard. Quite the opposite, one would imagine—the more so, perhaps, because it is vital to remember that no two ships of the same type are alike. They are far too complex for that. "Human error."

therefore, if it has any meaning in this context, serves only to underscore negligence on the part of "The System."

For the record, however, the Department of the Navy wasted no time. On April 11, 1963, the day following the disaster, a court of inquiry was convened in New London, Connecticut, headquarters of the search and rescue efforts. Two admirals and four captains were involved in the initial proceedings. The preliminary hearing lasted two days, after which, on Saturday April 13, the court moved to the Portsmouth Naval Shipyard, where *Thresher* was built. "Open sessions" were held, except when the court was cleared while "classified" information was being discussed—which was too often. In spite of this, the Navy Court of Inquiry got off to a great start and made sure that the Press knew about it. One of the first three witnesses called was a Captain C. James Zurcher of the office of the Deputy Commander, Atlantic Submarine Command. Zurcher said, according to an AP report, that he had asked Commander Harvey about the condition of the ship before she left Portsmouth for her diving tests. He also said that Harvey "indicated" that he "considered" *Thresher* completely seaworthy. Was this before or after the sub's initial dockside "fast cruise," which proved such a disaster that Harvey gave orders to abort it? This vital fact never surfaced. If it had, the Press would have said so.

Following an Easter Sunday recess, the inquiry was resumed April 15 in the Administrative Building of the Yard. (It was here that in 1905 the peace treaty was signed between Russia and Japan, with President Theodore Roosevelt participating.)

The Navy's probe into the loss of *Thresher* concluded

its hearings on June 3, 1963. During a 56-day period, the court heard testimony from 120 witnesses, recorded 1,700 pages of evidence and opinion, and examined 255 exhibits, including charts, letters, drawings, photos, directives, debris and other evidence bearing on the sinking.

Since the Joint Committee on Atomic Energy is required by law to make continued studies of all problems relating to the development, use and control of atomic energy, Senator John O. Pastore, then Joint Committee Chairman, had dispatched to New London the two most qualified members of his staff. Their job was to observe the proceedings, report on them and, where appropriate, ask questions. The questions raised and the inevitable conclusions to which they pointed possibly had some bearing on the Joint Committee's decision to hold separate hearings.

At the end of its inquiry, the Department of the Navy made available to the Joint Committee a 12-volume record of the court proceedings, including "findings, opinions and recommendations." It could do no less, particularly since very little material was released to the Press. Furthermore, the Joint Committee on Atomic Energy had already agreed that "no outside investigation into the cause of the tragedy should be held until after the Department of the Navy has been given an opportunity to complete its investigation."

The Joint Committee therefore did not begin its hearings until Wednesday, June 26, 1963—three weeks after the Navy's investigation closed. By that time the Navy had picked up the ball and was running with it. In a somewhat disastrous unilateral decision, it decided to publish *none* of its own 12-volume record of the inquiry into the loss of *Thresher*, on the grounds that it contained "secret information." Instead, it fobbed off an emasculated two-and-a-half-page statement on the press and public, "summarizing" its findings. These were that the "bulk of the Court of Inquiry's recommendations stressed the need for a careful review of the design, construction and inspection of vital submarine systems."

The effrontery of this ploy did not end there.

On August 13, 1963, 10 days after the conclusion of the independent hearings by the Joint Committee for that year, the Honorable Fred Korth, then Secretary of the Navy, wrote to John T. Conway, Executive Director, Joint Committee on Atomic Energy, Congress of the United States: "After a thorough review and most careful consideration of the situation, I do not believe it is in the best interests of the Navy to undertake any declassification action at this time. *I consider the entire subject classified,* and until the Court of Inquiry Records have been reviewed and the hearing completed, *I would be loath to release portions of the hearings* [author's italics] . . ."

This was a bit too much to swallow, and when the decision was passed on to Clinton P. Anderson, Chairman of the Subcommittee on Security, he reacted strongly in a letter to Secretary Korth dated August 19, 1963. The letter stated in part:

"I must say I am astonished by the idea that the entire subject of the loss of Thresher is classified. I believe thoroughly and completely in protecting defense information and restricted data, but I do not believe you would wish to use security classification to protect the people from the truth, *nor to keep embarrassing information from the public* [author's italics]. Accordingly, I request that you reconsider your decision."

On August 29, 1963, Korth reaffirmed his conclusions of August 13, using substantially the same arguments as he had in his letter to Conway, but adding the canard, "Such release could have an extremely detrimental effect on the Navy's current endeavors to integrate qualified volunteer line officers into the nuclear submarine program."

This did not deceive Chairman Anderson. On March 16, 1964, he addressed himself to the Honorable Paul H. Nitze, who had meantime succeeded Korth as SEC-NAV, and in the last paragraph of his letter bared his teeth.

"In my view, the Navy's refusal to identify specific areas of the Thresher's transcript which are classified is based in part on a desire to withhold information which rightly belongs in the public domain. *There can be no satisfactory justification for this attitude* [author's italics].

"Accordingly, should the Navy persist in its refusal to identify those areas of the Thresher transcript which are classified, *I plan to initiate action leading to the preparation of a report on the Thresher hearings, pursuant to the duty and authority vested in the Joint Committee on Atomic Energy by sections 202 and 206 of the Atomic Energy Act of 1954* [author's italics]."

What passed between the new Secretary of the Navy and his predecessor is anyone's guess, but Anderson received from Nitze two "Dear Clint" letters dated March 25 and May 26, 1964, in which the Navy reversed itself.

"We are proceeding with the sanitization [of the Navy report]. When sanitization is completed . . . we will be pleased to cooperate with your staff and assist in any way possible."

The Navy has two favorite procedures for obfuscating an issue or suppressing the facts. One is "sanitization"; the other "classification."

Sanitization can take place even before the censor's red pencil goes to work to suppress embarrassing revelations. A simple question can be sanitized by an answer such as, "The point is very well taken, sir." Or, "This is being looked into." Or, "I am not certain that I am the person best qualified to answer that question, sir." Or even (as a last resort), "I stand corrected, sir."

Let not the reader think this is some kind of sick joke. Answers delivered in precisely that phraseology by senior Naval officers occur again and again, even in the "sanitized" version of the Joint Committee's Hearings (Atomic Energy) on the loss of *Thresher*. They are an object lesson on how to gain time and save face.

Nowhere, however, will you find Admiral Rickover giving vague, equivocal answers which leave the listener totally confused—a victim of the old shell game.

"Classification" is something else. At the whim of a crayon-happy security man indoctrinated by "The System," it can mean anything. No one questions that it involves the removal of material *inaccessible to the enemy* [author's italics] which might reveal information calculated to endanger the safety of the United States. Carried to sane limits, it is a vital function, but to assume that the Russians did not know the test and crush depths of *Thresher* and had no idea of her underwater speed is ridiculous.

Given the materials of which *Thresher* was built, her size, shape and displacement and a textbook on controlled nuclear fission; and given the ability to apply a slide rule to elementary hydrodynamics, this "classified" information already stood like a neon sign before the Kremlin.

Having collided head-on with the Joint Committee on Atomic Energy and come off second best, the Navy again played for time. On May 26, 1964, Secretary Paul Nitze wrote Anderson yet another "Dear Clint" letter suggesting that "the consolidation of the *two phases* of the Hearings into a single report will place the matter in proper perspective." Nitze threw in the conciliatory tidbit that "Mr. Conway worked closely with the Navy team engaged in this long endeavor and was most helpful."

At that moment the Joint Committee was still in session, trying to make sense out of the Navy's double-talk, and would not hold its final hearing until Wednesday, July 1, 1964. The timing was excellent. Three weeks after the end of the Hearings (July 22, 1964) Conway received from Nitze a package and a covering letter.

"This transcript has been edited for accuracy by cognizant witnesses and their correction noted in green pencil markings. The areas considered classified have been bracketed by red pencil markings . . ."

The transcript to which Nitze referred related only to July 1, 1964, the last day of the Joint Committee Hearings. It was not until January 9, 1965 that the Navy finally released a 192-page "sanitized and declassified" version of the Hearings before the Joint Committee on Atomic Energy, Congress of the United States, relating to the loss of USS *Thresher.*

By then, the long-suffering press had run out of patience. On Sunday, January 10, 1965, Luther J. Carter, a Washington *Post* staffer, wrote under the headline "Navy Held Thresher Facts 18 Months."

"The Navy refused to release the transcript of the

Thresher disaster hearings by the Joint Committee on Atomic Energy for more than 18 months—and then only after increasingly impatient urging from the Committee. When the transcript was finally made public yesterday, it was completely 'sanitized', Pentagon jargon for declassification and removal of all strategic information."

Well, that's a bit too simple.

"Last July 1 [1964]," Carter went on, "a final hearing was held and Navy witnesses gave a detailed report on corrective action taken to avoid a repetition of the disaster.

"Yesterday, a year and a half after the first testimony on the Thresher was taken by the Joint Committee, the transcripts of all the hearings were made public for the first time."

The green-covered booklet issued by the U. S. Government Printing Office, Washington, 1965, cost only 55 cents but was far less sterile than the Navy would have wished. So many questions were asked of the admirals and captains present, by the seven senators and eight representatives forming the bulk of the Joint Committee on Atomic Energy, that (as must now be abundantly clear to the reader) not all the circumlocution of the Navy brass could camouflage the dismal and tragic truth.

That booklet did not come to my notice until 1967, and by then I was under contract to my publisher to write a documentary on the *Thresher* tragedy—the worst submarine disaster in history and the greatest and most pointless sacrifice of human life. I read the booklet several times, and on each occasion uncovered some new and significant piece of information. Each discovery only increased my gratitude to Dr. Robert M. Snyder of Woods Hole Oceanographic Institution, Massachusetts, who had given me his personal copy. This highly capable scientist had been involved in the search for *Thresher* aboard *Atlantis II* and had made significant contributions toward the success of the most difficult underwater search of all time.

I was then working in West Palm Beach at the headquarters of the Navy's Undersea Test and Evaluation Center (AUTEC), and this it seemed to me was a fortunate circumstance, if only because I frequently flew over the Ranges where *Thresher* had operated.

Through Dr. Snyder, I was able to talk to Dr. Columbus O'Donnell Iselin, another outstanding Woods Hole oceanographic scientist, who came up with an interesting theory about low salinity currents, which may well have hastened *Thresher*'s doom by depriving her still further of any buoyancy.

When I arrived in Washington, August 1967, with a carefully docketed list of prospects to interview in connection with my book, I hadn't the slightest inkling of the incredible run-around the Navy was about to give me. The tragedy was then four years old and one might have thought that things had cooled down a little, but this was far from being the case. I should have realized, of course, that being a Navy *civilian* employed as a public affairs officer, I had two strikes against me from the start. And as I look back on my notes of the time, it is like reliving a nightmare compounded of frustration, bafflement and a lurking suspicion that I might be losing my mind. Yet those contacts, though mostly of the "mutual friend" variety, were impressive enough. They included a full admiral (retired), a vice admiral, a rear admiral, four captains, five commanders, a lieutenant commander, a lieutenant and a civilian chief scientist. All these men had been closely associated with the *Thresher* disaster inquiry and search, but suddenly not one of them was available.

From a host of well-trained secretaries came a barrage of platitudinous excuses that rang about as true as a cracked bell.

"On travel."

"Out of town for at least 10 days."

"In conference."

"Tied up at the moment."

"Just reassigned to the West Coast."

"Called away suddenly."

"Not available right now."

"Very sorry, sir . . ."

The transparency of these rebuffs was, of course, typical of "The System," but the effect proved devastatingly effective just the same. I finally had to concede defeat and inform my publisher there was no way of doing the job he wanted; or at least of doing it decently. The Navy had blown up all its public relations bridges. In the event, it took me the best part of six years to piece together and write the *Thresher* story—a job I should have been able to do in perhaps six months.

In the darkness of that Washington visit, there was however one faint ray of light. Alone the fifth commander, William T. Hussey, made a valiant show of responding from the Pentagon. What I wanted was a taped description of how things felt aboard a nuclear attack submarine during her sea trials. By then I had learned not to utter the name *"Thresher"* over a telephone, and when you have come all the way from Florida for an interview and are seated in a hallowed

office chair, it is more difficult for your host to throw
you out.

Commander Hussey made no attempt to evict me. His
cordiality even extended to an admission that he had
been aboard *Thresher* in the Tongue of the Ocean. He
left out, naturally, that, as a junior officer (lieutenant),
he had been one of the commissioning crew and had
served under Commander Axene as communications
officer for 11 months, ample time to become thoroughly
familiar with the ship. Years later, while taping
Thresher's Deck Log, I noticed Hussey's signature on
many Watch entries. During our interview, he made no
mention of SS-593, or her crew, but there were some
good descriptions of general procedures aboard a nuclear sub. It was only much later, in the light of acquired
knowledge, and using a little hindsight, that I was able
to identify some of this material with the lost ship. At
the time, I set aside the tape and wrote it off as another
failure. Still, my gratitude goes to Commander Hussey
for being the only one of 15 contacts who would even
give me the time of day.

Lieutenant Commander Raymond McCoole (Retd.),
who missed *Thresher*'s last dive through a miraculous
combination of last-hour circumstances, turned out to
be the one man with the honesty and courage to proffer
the help I so badly needed. But that also was in the future. At the time of my Washington visit, he really was
away in the Caribbean.

When (after his retirement) we finally met, he gave
me unstintingly of his valuable help in many areas related to *Thresher*. Without his unique store of knowledge of that particular ship, I never could have written
this book according to plan. And that plan called for

something more than a bunch of press clippings glued
end to end.

In the fall of 1972, the Navy relented a little, and I
hasten to give credit and offer thanks where these are
due. I received a photostat of the (declassified) UQC
transmissions between *Thresher* and *Skylark* during
those final, agonizing minutes before the sea tore at the
crippled submarine with a stunning force of nearly 800
pounds per square inch. I was permitted, further, to
tape *Thresher*'s Deck Log at the Washington National
Records Center, from the day of her commissioning until the end of March 1963. This windfall came from the
Judge Advocate's office.

My thanks, also, to the Flag Secretary, COMSUB-
LANT, Commander A. Riendeau, Jr., USN, for sending me a rare copy of the limited edition of *In
Memoriam*, a condensed photo biography of every man
who perished on *Thresher*. With this book came a little
note which began: "In an effort to restore your faith in
humanity (the Navy in particular) thought I'd send you
this copy with my compliments . . ." I much appreciated this gesture.

No less am I in debt to Captain Dave Purinton, Administrative Officer, Portsmouth Naval Shipyard, for his
sympathetic understanding of my problems. Captain
Purinton went to much trouble (unofficially) digging
through old files and records for some fine pictures of
Thresher's launch and commissioning. The most moving paragraph in his letter was a heartfelt agreement
about "the number of people who always seem to throw
roadblocks in the way of progress, and the small number
who are willing to help . . ."

I was beginning to feel rather unkindly about the Navy, but it has its quota of fine and decent individuals.

By the time this volume is published, more than a decade will have elapsed since the *Thresher* disaster. A new generation of career officers is taking over. The Navy's Jekyll and Hyde reaction to the loss of that magnificent submarine, SSN-593, is becoming less violent. It is certainly not my intention to reopen old wounds, the more so because many of the womenfolk of the lost crew have put the past behind them.

Perhaps worthy of note, however, is the fact that the Navy's Photographic Center took *five years* to mail my publisher a set of declassified photos I had picked out in August 1967. This was the finishing touch. It was, more than anything else, what got me going again.

One might reasonably have thought this was the end of a ridiculous bureaucratic steeplechase fraught with obstacles that belong in the dark and dismal recesses of sick minds; but it was not. The final hurdle had a deep ditch filled with murky water hidden on its far side. The last of my dealings with "The System" stretched its credibility gap far beyond the breaking point. For this reason, I cannot allow to go unrecorded the mealy-mouthed and spineless attitude of certain individuals in the Naval Ordnance Laboratory. It has been an open secret for many years that *Thresher*, during her underwater shock tests at Key West in 1962, steered too close to a detonation as the result of a navigational error. Why or how this error occurred was not the purpose of my inquiry. It has been demonstrated beyond doubt that the extremely severe jolting *Thresher* received as a result had nothing whatever to do with her ultimate loss.

However, since NOL was responsible for the organization and evaluation of *Thresher*'s underwater shock tests, they were the logical people from whom to find out how such tests were conceived and how they operated—using, of course, "unclassified" explanations.

At long last (after three telephone referrals) it looked as though I was going to make some real headway. By chance, the man to whom I spoke was a civilian scientist who had actually been aboard *Thresher* during her shock tests. Once I had identified myself, this individual was affable, lucid and perfectly willing to talk (within the framework, of course, of what he could and could not tell me). His explanation made sense and his recollection of the time and place of the incident coincided with my own records, taken from *Thresher*'s Deck Log.

Because of his apparent willingness to help (and not through any obligation) I promised to send this man a draft of what I proposed to say about the incident that subjected *Thresher* to a shock test about 20 per cent more severe than was intended. I kept my promise, scrupulously omitting what he had asked me not to mention, thanking him for his valuable assistance and in fact leaving the final editing to him.

After some delay I got back a registered letter (return receipt requested), expressing blind panic at the most innocent generalities, denying all that he had told me, and insisting that he not be mentioned by name. It could be inferred from this letter that I had invented our entire telephone conversation—except that it happened to be monitored from my end.

Surely, this must rank as an outstanding example of

the moral cowardice with which "The System" can taint
people working for it.

In *Geo Marine Technology* of February 1965, there
appeared an unsigned article titled "In the Wake of 593-
Boat," which began with a quotation from William
Shakespeare. It is particularly apposite to the *Thresher*
tragedy.

"In persons grafted with a serious trust, negligence
is a crime."

The article went on, "Secretary of the Navy [the new
one] Paul H. Nitze, was recently quoted as saying that
'the men of the Thresher did not die in vain.' Such un-
bounded optimism is not rare among men in high office.
Much rarer is the devotion to cause, in spite of the System, in spite of expediency, displayed by [Admiral]
Hyman Rickover. He may be hated in the pipe shops of
Portsmouth and other yards, and he may be hated in
the inner sanctum of BuShips, but men of his caliber
can only be held in the highest regard by friends and
relatives of the Navy men who go down into the sea."

Sooner or later, the real story had to be told of "the
men of the Thresher [who] did not die in vain."

As to the truth of that statement, let the reader be
the judge. There will be the usual quota of nit-pickers
and "experts," of course, ready to throw more dust in
the wind by making a federal case out of some mere
technicality. But there's not much they can do with the
main issue.

J.B.

INDEX